English Unlimited

A2 Elementary
Coursebook with e-Portfolio

Alex Tilbury, Theresa Clementson, Leslie Anne Hendra & David Rea
Course consultant: Adrian Doff

CAMBRIDGE
UNIVERSITY PRESS

Acknowledgements

The authors would like to thank all the team at Cambridge University Press for their ideas, support and commitment to *English Unlimited*, in particular their editors Karen Momber and Keith Sands, and David Lawton for his work on the cover and page design. They'd also like to thank Adrian Doff for his consistently encouraging and remarkably detailed feedback; and Dave Willis, Jane Willis, Alison Sharpe and Sue Ullstein for their ideas and inspiration in the early days of this project.

Thanks are also due to Michael Stuart Clark, Ralph Clementson, Dagmara Gumkowska, Monica Koorichh, Margot Richardson and Sławomir Smolorz for particular ideas and contributions.

Alex Tilbury would like to dedicate his work on *English Unlimited* to Geoffrey William Tilbury, Carol Tilbury and Sławek Smolorz, with love and thanks.

David Rea would like to thank the students, teachers, trainers and staff at IH Kraków, IH Heliopolis, IH Buenos Aires, IH Paris and IH London for all the support, development and fun over the years. He'd also like to thank Emma McLachlan: the most beautiful woman in the world.

Leslie Anne Hendra would like to thank Michael Clark for his patience, support and humour. Thanks also to the teachers and staff at International House London for being such great colleagues and sharing their knowledge, time and energy so generously while I was teaching there.

Theresa Clementson would like to thank Anthony, Sam and Megan for their ideas, support and unwavering confidence, and Cristina Rimini for her help and advice on all matters TEFL over the years.

The authors and publishers would like to thank the following teachers for invaluable feedback they provided when reviewing draft material:
Howard Smith, Rosie Ganne, Chris Cavey, Stephanie Dimond-Bayir (UK); Sarah Moss, Isidro Almenadrez (Spain); Maggie Baigent, Chris Rose, Kathryn Britton (Italy); Justyna Kubica (Poland); Tim Marchand (Japan); Wayne Trotman (Turkey); Colin Mackenzie (France); Kirsteen Donaghy (Malaysia); Steve Broadbent (Saudi Arabia); Marilisa Shimazumi (Brazil); Jason Ham (Korea); Catherine Morley (Mexico); Helen Paul (Germany); Olga Rojas (Colombia); and the various members of the Cambridge Adult Courses Advisory Panel.

We would also like to thank the following teachers and institutions for piloting early versions of the material:
Allan Dalchar at The Language Company, Switzerland; Vicente Sanchis Caparros at the EOI Valencia, Spain; Philip Bashford at Anglo-continental, Bournemouth, UK; Alfonso Garcia Balan at the EOI Mieres, Spain; Fabio Ordonez at UJTL, Bogota, Colombia; Chelly Davidson at International House, Bath, UK; Sherrill Glasser at MPI Bell Centre of English, Macau, China; Marta Staniszewska at Multischool, Warsaw, Poland; Jan P Isaksen, Belinda Fourie, Frida Abrev, and Brenda Estefania Rocha Osornio at Stratford Institute, Leon, Mexico; Violeta Hernandez Flores at FES Iztacala UNAM, Mexico; Ana Cecilie L.M. Smith and Wagner Barbara Bastos at Curso Oxford, Rio de Janiero, Brazil; Tim Marchand at Smith's School of English, Nagaokakyo, Japan; Rebecca Blakey at the British School of Trieste, Italy; and Camila, Thiago and Ana Carolina at Cultura Inglesa in Sao Paolo, Brazil.

We are also grateful to the following contributors:
Text design and page make-up by Stephanie White at Kamae Design.
Picture research: Hilary Luckcock
Photography: Gareth Boden
Audio recordings: John Green at Audio Workshop and id-Audio, London

The authors and publishers would like to thank all of those who took part in the authentic recording sessions, especially:
Amina Al-Yassin, Andrew Reid, Angharad Monnier, Anna Barnard, Anri Iwasaki, Astrid Gonzales-Rabade, Chie Obata, Claudia Payer, Dorien van der Poll, Greg Sibley, Khalid Gafar, Onyinye Nwulu, Paula Porroni, Ruth Cox and Seung-wan Yang.

The authors and publishers acknowledge the following sources of copyright material and are grateful for the permissions granted. While every effort has been made, it has not always been possible to identify the sources of all the material used, or to trace all copyright holders. If any omissions are brought to our notice, we will be happy to include the appropriate acknowledgements on reprinting.
Charlie Hicks for the adapted text on p. 52 'Weird fruit and veg', from 'Yes we have no pitahayas', The Guardian 3 May 2006. Reproduced by permission of Charlie Hicks; The Independent for the adapted text on p. 67 and p. 126 from 'How we first met, Ed Smith & Vikram Seth', by Fiona McClymont, The Independent 23 May 2004. Copyright © Independent News & Media Limited; Forward Ltd for the adapted text on p. 76 'One-Wheeled Wonder' from the AA Magazine February 2004. Reproduced by permission of Forward Ltd; Telegraph Media Group Limited for the recording script on p.159, adapted from 'Barry Cox - shelf stacker to Chinese Crooner', The Telegraph 6 December 2007. Copyright © Telegraph Media Group Limited; Barry Cox for further biographical information in the recording script on p.159. Reproduced by kind permission of Barry Cox, www.barry-cox.com.

The publishers are grateful to the following for permission to reproduce copyright photographs and material:

Key: l = left, c = centre, r = right, t = top, b = bottom

Alamy Images/©Westend61 for p7(cr), /©Elvele Images Ltd for p 7(bl), /©Ron Chapple Stock for p 14(cl), /©Bon Appetit for p18(C), /©Amana Images for p18(D), /©David R Frazier Photolibrary Inc for p18(bl), /©Jeff Morgan Education for p 18(bc), /©Blend Images for p20(bl), /©Oliver Knight for pp20(br), /©Vehbi Koca for 22(tl), /©Itani for p26(tl), /©BlueMoon Stock for p27(b), /©D Hurst for p34(bl), /©JupiterImages/Polka Dot for 38(tc), /©David R Frazier Photolibrary Inc for p38(br), /©Niall McDiarmid for p39(F), /© Yadid Levy for p42(b), /©Matteo Del Grosso for p42(c), /©Juncal for p42(tl), /©Charles Sturge for p42(br), /©Inmagine for p43, /©Blend Images for p51(b), /©Bon Appetit for p52(A), /©Food Features for p52(B), /©Oleksiy Maksymenko for p52(D), /©Arco Images GmbH for p52(G), /©Radius Images for p54(inset), /©fstop2 for p59(bl), /©Randolph Images for p59(cl), /©Laurence Torao Konishi for p62(tr), /©Blend Images for p62(cl), /©David R Frazier Photolibrary Inc for p66, /©Dave Penman for p70(b), /©BlueMoon Stock for p73, /©Radius Images for p74(t), /©Anglia Images for p78(b), /©Ben Ramos for p79(t), /©Radius Images for p80(l), /©Radius Images for p80(r), /©blickwinkel for p92(A), /©ArcoImages GmbH for p92(B), /©Eureka for p92(D), /©David Cattanach for p92(E), /©JupiterImages/Thinkstock for p99, /©Rubberball for p106(tl), /©JupiterImages/Bananastock for p106(tr), /©Stephen Frink Collection of p107(l), /©Jacques Jangoux for p108(tl), /©ImageState for p109, /©Pictorial Press Ltd for p123, /©Steve Skjold for p125; Art Directrs/©Juliet Highet for p126(cr); Aviation-images.com for p54; Bridgeman Art Library/©Private Collection for p127; Chatswood Chase, Sydney for p50; Corbis/©Helen King for p7(tc), /©image100 for p27(t), /©Roulier/Turiot/photocuisine for p53C, /©Pierre Vauthey/Corbis Sygma for p62(tl), /©Helen King for p64, /©Martin Harvey for p68(br), /©Jim Criagmyle for p77, /©Gianni Dagli Orti for p87(r), /©Martin Meyer/Zefa for p104(tl), /©Dave G Houser for p108(tc), /©A Muriot/Photocuisine for p111(c); Eversole Research Collection for p108(c); Getty Images for pp 38(tll), 111(b); Getty Images/©Sean Justice for p12(tc), /©Steve Niedorf Photography for p12(tr), /©Larry Bray for p13, /©Eric McNatt for p20(t), /©Hulton Archive for p25, /©Photonica for p26(tr), /©Javier Pierini for p26(bl), /©Asia Images for p26(br), /©AFP for p38(tr), /©Yu Mizuno/ailead for p40, /©Jason Hawkes for p46, /©Michael Edwards for p52(tr), /©PhotoDisc for p53(D), /©Mark A Leman for p59(t), /©Mike Hewitt for p67(t), /©Roger Viollet for p68(t), /©Popperfoto for p87(l), /©Fresh meat Media LLC for p88, /©DK for p101, /©Walter Hodges for p106(b), /©AFP for p111(t), /©Marc Romanelli for p112(c), /©AFP for p116(t), /©Bertrand Gardel for p116(b), /©Hulton Archive for p122, /©Hulton Archive for p126(l), /©Koki Iino for p126(r); Hak-Ju Kim, Gangneung City Hall for p28(tll); istockphoto/©Robyn Mackenzie for p69, /©Brad Killer for p102(bl), /©Oleg Brikhodko for p102(br), /©Duard van der Westhuizen for p115; Leslie Hendra for p7(tr); Mary Evans Picture Library for pp68(bl, 126(cltt); Masterfile/©Steve Prezant for p29; Motorola Collective for p34(tr); NASA Johnson Space Center for p35(t); PA Photos/©Bikas DAS/AP for p67(b); Photolibrary/©PhotoDisc for p7(tl), /©Botanica for p8(tl), /©PhotoDisc for p8(b), /©PhotoDisc for p12(tll), /©.IBID for p14(tl), /©Nonstock for p14(b), /©Sprint for p53(E), /©PhotoDisc for p72, /©Index Stock Imagery for p110(tl), /©PhotoDisc for p112(r), /©PhotoDisc for p118(B), /©Oxford Scientific (OSF) for p118(D); Photostage for p62(tc); Punchstock/©Dex Image for p7(br), /©Digital Vision for p8(tr), /©Digital Vision for p9, /©Blend Images for p14(cr), /©Valueline for p18(A), /©Digital Vision for p18(B), /©Valueline for p18(c), /©Digital Vision for p18(br), /©Stockbyte for p21, /©DAJ for p22(tc), /©DAJ for p22(lb), /©Glowimages for p22(r), /©Photographers Choice for p28(tr), /©Valueline for p28(bl), /©Image Source for p30(tr), /©Digital Vision for p48(t), /©Digital Vision for p51(t), /©Brand X Pictures for p52(E), /©Polka Dot for p57(r), /©Dex Image for p61(r), /©Photosindia for p74(b), /©Digital Vision for p79(b), /©Digital Vision for p82(t), /©for p96(t), /©Blend Images for p96(b), /©Digital Vision for p102(t), /©Photographers Choice for p108(tr), /©Blend Images for p112(l); PYMCA/©Paul Hartnett for p126(clb); Rex Features for p52(F); Rex Features/©Goffredo for p28(br), /©Masatoshi Okauchi for p34(tcl), /©SIPA Press for p52(C), /©Alisdair Macdonald for p76; Ronald Grant Archive/©Les Films Cisse for p82(cr), /©Sogecine for p82(bl); Ruth Cox for p31(l); Science Museum for p34(cl); Seth Lazar for p75(tl); Shutterstock/©Ramzi Hachicho for p31(r), /©okx for p34(tcr), /©Simone van den Berg for p39, /© jocicalek for p39(e), /©PhotoShutter for p48(b), /©Sasha Davas for p52(H); /©Gregory Gerber for p53(A), /©Matka Wariatka for p53(B), /©Monkey Business Images for p61(tll), /©Zsolt Nyulaszi for p61(bl), /©Salamanderman for p75(tr), /© Leigh Prather for p86(b), /©Konstantin Kikvidze for p92(C), /©Philip Date for p92(F), /©Monkey Business Images for p104(tr), /©Sculpies for p107(r); istockphoto /© Myron Unrau for p118(a), /© Cory Johnson for p118(c).

The following photographs were taken on commission by Gareth Boden for CUP:
10(tl,tr,b), 12(b,l), 16, 30(cr), 32(t,b), 56(tl,bl,tr), 60(l,r), 86, 104(b), 108(b), 110(tr,bl), 114.

We are grateful to the following for their help with the commissioned photography:
Alison & Chris Price, Claire Butler, Frank Lee Leisure Centre, Addenbrooke's Hospital, Cambridge, Vicky & Philip Green.

Illustrations by Derek Bacon, Kathy Baxendale, Thomas Croft, Mark Duffin, Kamae Design, Julian Mosedale, Nigel Sanderson, Sean Sims and Dan Taylor.

Contents

How to use this coursebook

Every unit of this book is divided into sections, with clear, practical **goals** for learning.

The first four pages of the unit help you build your language skills and knowledge. These pages include speaking, listening, reading, writing, grammar, vocabulary and pronunciation activities. They are followed by a **Target activity** which will help you put together what you have learned.

The **Explore** section of the unit begins with a **Keyword**, which looks at one of the most common and useful words in English. It also includes either an **Across cultures** or an **Independent learning** section, and then an **Explore speaking** or **Explore writing** task. The Explore section gives you extra language and skills work, all aiming to help you become a better communicator in English and a more effective learner.

The **Look again** section takes another look at the target language for the unit, helping you to review and extend your learning.
Sometimes you will also find this recycling symbol with the goals, to show when a particular goal is not new but is recycling language that you have met before.

This symbol shows you when you can hear and practise the correct pronunciation of key language, using the audio CD.

The **e-Portfolio** DVD-ROM contains useful reference material for all the units, as well as self-assessment to help you test your own learning, and Wordcards to help you test your vocabulary learning.

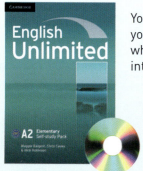

You can do more practice by yourself using the **Self-study Pack**, which includes a workbook and interactive DVD-ROM.

The DVD-ROM contains video and over 300 interactive activities.

About you

Intro goals
- ◎ introduce yourself
- ◎ ask for and give personal information
- ◎ fill in a form
- ◎ say what you can do

Hi, my name's Anna

Hi, my name's Anna. I'm from the United States, from San Francisco, and I speak French and Arabic.

Hello, I'm Astrid. I'm from Mexico. I speak Spanish, English, French and a little German.

Hello, my name's Andrew and I'm from Wales and I can speak some French, some Japanese and some Hungarian.

Hi, my name is Claudia. I'm from Austria. My home town is Graz. It's quite small. I speak German of course, a bit of French, Russian and English.

My name is Sameh and I am from Egypt. My home town is Cairo and I speak Arabic and English.

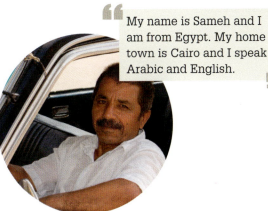

Hi, my name is Anri. I'm from Japan. I speak English and Japanese.

VOCABULARY

Countries and languages

In Switzerland, they speak French and German.

1 a 🔴 **1.1** Listen to the introductions. Number them in the order you hear them.

b Find and underline:
1 six countries. *The United States, ...*
2 eight languages. *French, ...*

c 🔴 **1.2** Listen to check. Then repeat the words. ℗

d Think of five more countries. What languages do people speak there?

VOCABULARY

Introducing yourself

Hello, I'm Martin.

Hi, I'm Eba. I'm from ...

2 a Write sentences to introduce yourself.

I'm ... / My name's ...   I speak ... and ...
I'm from ...   I speak some ...
My home town is ...   I speak a little / a bit of ...

b Talk in groups. Introduce yourselves.

What's your email address?

LISTENING

1 **a** 🔊 **1.3** Listen to Agata's phone call about a yoga course. Complete the form.

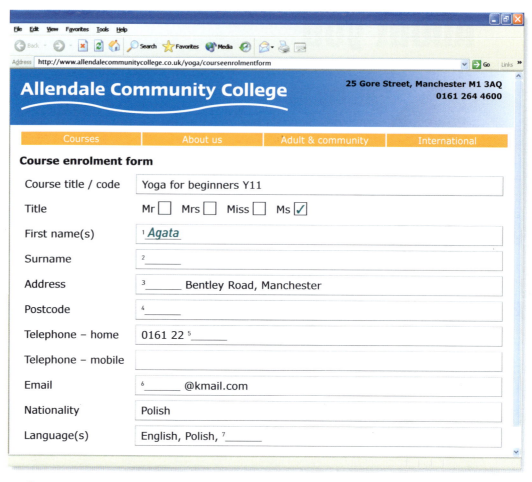

Allendale Community College

25 Gore Street, Manchester M1 3AQ
0161 264 4600

Courses	About us	Adult & community	International

Course enrolment form

Course title / code	Yoga for beginners Y11
Title	Mr ☐ Mrs ☐ Miss ☐ Ms ☑
First name(s)	¹ *Agata*
Surname	² _____
Address	³ _____ Bentley Road, Manchester
Postcode	⁴ _____
Telephone – home	0161 22 ⁵ _____
Telephone – mobile	
Email	⁶ _____ @kmail.com
Nationality	Polish
Language(s)	English, Polish, ⁷ _____

b Look at the script on p148 to check.

VOCABULARY

Letters, numbers, addresses

2 How do you say these letters? Test each other.

What's this? H

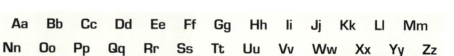

Aa Bb Cc Dd Ee Ff Gg Hh Ii Jj Kk Ll Mm

Nn Oo Pp Qq Rr Ss Tt Uu Vv Ww Xx Yy Zz

3 **a** How do you say:

1 these addresses? 25 Gore Street   113 Station Road   84 First Avenue
2 these postcodes? M1 3AQ   T5S 3X2   CA 90501
3 these phone numbers? 0161 264 4600   780 452 1111   022 258 6491

b 🔊 **1.4** Listen to check. Practise saying them. ℗

4 **a** How do you say these email and website addresses?

1 www.bbc.co.uk   2 robsilva@airnet.br   3 msuzuki@spaceblue.jp
4 sport.indiatimes.com   5 www.cambridge.org

b 🔊 **1.5** Listen to check. Can you guess the countries from the addresses?

5 **a** Think of people and places in your life. Write:

• a name   • a phone number   • an address
• an email address   • a website address

Paul Arends.
P-A-U- ...

b Work in A/B pairs. A, say the names, numbers and addresses in 5a.
B, write them down. Then change.

c Check together. Are they correct?

VOCABULARY
Personal information

subject	possessive adjective
I	my
you	your
he	his
she	her
it	its
we	our
they	their

Grammar reference and practice, p131

SPEAKING

> What's your surname?

> It's …

6 **a** Match Tom's questions with Agata's answers.

1	What's your name?	a	152 Bentley Road, Manchester.
2	How do you spell that?	b	English, Polish and a bit of German.
3	What's your address?	c	Poland.
4	What's your phone number?	d	It's K-A-R-O-L-A-K.
5	Do you have an email address?	e	It's Agata Karolak.
6	Where are you from?	f	Yes, it's ak97@kmail.com.
7	What languages do you speak?	g	My home number? It's 0161 228 3434.

b Cover the questions and look at the answers. Say the questions.

7 Look at the possessive adjectives in the table. Complete the sentences with the words in brackets.

1 How do *you* spell *your* surname? (you, your)
2 "What's _____ email address?" "Sorry, _____ aren't on the internet." (they, their)
3 "Where's _____ from?" "He's English but _____ father's from the USA." (he, his)
4 "What's _____ name?" "Karen. _____ 's Jon's sister." (she, her)

8 **a** Look at the form on p122. Ask questions in pairs and complete the form for your partner.

b Check together. Are the forms correct?

Can you …?

GRAMMAR
can for ability

> Can you speak two languages?

> No, I can't.

> Yes, I can. I can speak Arabic and French.

Grammar reference and practice, p131

1 **a** What can you remember about Agata and Tom? Circle the correct word.

1 Tom **can / can't** spell Agata's surname.
2 Agata **can / can't** remember her mobile number.
3 She **can / can't** remember her email address.
4 She **can / can't** speak three languages.

b 🎧 **1.6** Listen to check.

2 **a** Ask and answer the questions.

1 **Can you** speak two languages?
2 **Can you** ask for someone's phone number in English?
3 **Can you** say 'hello' in five languages?
4 **Can you** spell your teacher's name?
5 **Can you** remember the names of five people in the class?
6 **Can you** count from 1 to 100 in English?
7 **Can you** understand sign language?
8 **Can you** read music?

b Now complete the self-assessment.

Self-assessment

Can you do these things in English? Circle a number on each line. 1 = I can't do this, 5 = I can do this well.

◎ introduce yourself	1	2	3	4	5
◎ ask for and give personal information	1	2	3	4	5
◎ fill in a form	1	2	3	4	5
◎ say what you can do	1	2	3	4	5

1

People in your life

Nice to meet you

Maria Teresa (Maite) Rob Sally

Krishnan Isobel James

VOCABULARY

People you know

1 a Look at the photos of Rob's birthday party. Guess who the people are.

father	husband	son	brother	boyfriend	teacher	boss	friend
mother	wife	daughter	sister	girlfriend	student	colleague	

1 Sally is Rob's *girlfriend* .
2 Maria Teresa is his _____ .
3 Krishnan is his _____ .
4 Isobel and James are his _____ and _____ .

b 🎧 **1.7** Listen to two conversations and check your ideas.

PRONUNCIATION

Syllables

2 a Which words in 1a have one syllable (*wife*)? Which have two syllables (*bro-ther*)?

b 🎧 **1.8** Listen to check. ❷ Practise saying the words.

SPEAKING

3 Complete the examples in the box.

Grammar reference and practice, p132

Possessive 's (singular)
1 Sally is **Rob's** girlfriend.
2 Rob is James and _____ son.
3 Rob is _____ student.
4 James is _____ husband.

Isobel is Rob's mother.

And James is her husband.

4 Look at the pictures. What can you remember about the people at Rob's party?

5 **a** Complete the conversation with these expressions.

> ~~Nice to meet you~~   Are you   I'm   please call me   this is   what's your name again

JAMES	Hello, I'm James.
MAITE	Hi, I'm Maria Teresa.
JAMES	¹ *Nice to meet you* . And ²_____ Isobel, my wife.
ISOBEL	Sorry, ³_____ ?
MAITE	It's Maria Teresa. But ⁴_____ Maite.
ISOBEL	Hello, Maite. ⁵_____ one of Rob's colleagues?
MAITE	No, I'm not. ⁶_____ his Spanish teacher. And you?
JAMES	Oh, we're Rob's parents.

b 🔊 **1.9** Listen to check. 🅟 Practise the conversation in groups of three.

6 **a** Work in pairs. You're at a party where you don't know anyone else. Decide your relationship. Are you colleagues, friends or family?

b Introduce yourself and your partner to other pairs.

c Can you remember the names of everyone at the party? Can you remember their relationships?

> Hi, I'm Mario and this is …

> That's Mario and that's Lucia. She's Mario's boss.

Is she your sister?

Grammar reference and practice, p132

GRAMMAR

be present: am, is, are

1 Complete the positive ➕ and negative ➖ sentences with 'm, 're, 's, 'm not, aren't, isn't. 🔊 **1.10** Listen to check. 🅟

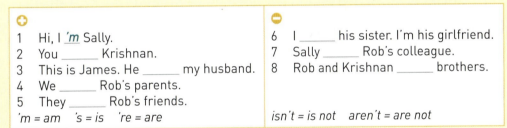

➕
1 Hi, I *'m* Sally.
2 You _____ Krishnan.
3 This is James. He _____ my husband.
4 We _____ Rob's parents.
5 They _____ Rob's friends.
'm = am   's = is   're = are

➖
6 I _____ his sister. I'm his girlfriend.
7 Sally _____ Rob's colleague.
8 Rob and Krishnan _____ brothers.

isn't = is not   aren't = are not

2 Complete the questions ❓ with Are and Is. 🔊 **1.11** Listen to check. 🅟

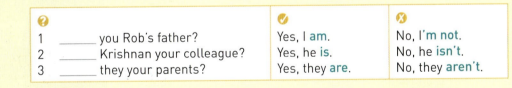

❓	✔️	✖️
1 _____ you Rob's father?	Yes, I am.	No, I'm not.
2 _____ Krishnan your colleague?	Yes, he is.	No, he isn't.
3 _____ they your parents?	Yes, they are.	No, they aren't.

3 **a** Write your name and the names of five people you know. Put a line between the people who know each other.

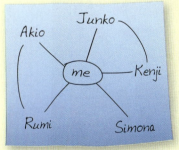

b Work in pairs. Look at your partner's names and write five questions about the people with is and are.

Is Junko your sister? Are you Simona's friend? Are Akio and Rumi colleagues?

SPEAKING

4 Ask and answer questions.

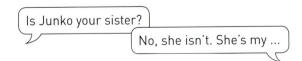

> Is Junko your sister?

> No, she isn't. She's my …

What was your first job?

A

B

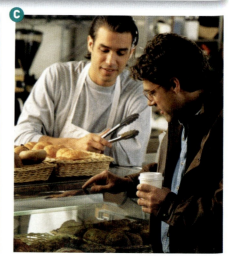
C

READING

1 Match pictures A–D with these jobs.

a journalist ☑D an office manager ☐ a shop assistant ☐ a cook ☐

2 a These are all jobs from Rob's life. Which job do you think was his first job? Which was his best? Which was his worst?

b Read the newspaper interview with Rob. Check your answers to 2a.

LIFE'S WORK

Business journalist Rob Lewis talks about his jobs: the first, the best and the worst.

What was your first job?
When I was fifteen, I was a shop assistant in a bakery at the weekend. I was at work by 6.00 am every Saturday and Sunday. That was really difficult. I'm not an early morning person!

What was your best job?
My job now. I'm a journalist. It's well paid and it's different every day. I'm often on planes or trains and in hotels and offices around the world and I meet lots of interesting people. It's a great job, really.

What was your worst job?
When I was eighteen, I was a cook in a fast food restaurant for a few months. The managers weren't very nice and the job was boring and badly paid. It was very hot in there, too. Terrible!

Is a 'job for life' a good thing?
Not for me. After university, I was a marketing assistant for four years. It was okay but it wasn't very interesting. Then I was an office manager. That was good, but it was always the same. I think change is good for you.

D

3 Read the interview again. Put Rob's jobs in the correct order, from the past to now.

a He was an office manager. ☐
b He was a shop assistant. ☑1
c He's a journalist. ☐
d He was a cook. ☐
e He was a marketing assistant. ☐

VOCABULARY

Talking about jobs

4 a Look at the expressions for talking about jobs. Match the opposites.

1	easy		a	terrible
2	interesting		b	badly paid
3	well paid		c	difficult
4	different every day		d	boring
5	great		e	the same every day

b 🔘 **1.12** Listen to check. ℗

> A journalist.
>
> Well, it's well paid, it's interesting ...

5 What do you think about Rob's jobs?

6 Look at more jobs on p145 in pairs. Choose five and say what you think about them.

When I was fifteen ...

GRAMMAR

be past: *was, were*

1 a Complete the table with was, were, wasn't, weren't.

➕	➖	
When **I was** fifteen, **I was** a shop assistant. **You were** in the office. **He** [1]_____ an office manager. **We were** at the party. **They** [2]_____ at home.	**I wasn't** there. **She** [3]_____ at the party. **They** [4]_____ in the office. *n't = not* *wasn't = was not weren't = were not*	
❓	✅	❌
[5]_____ it interesting? [7]_____ they at the party?	Yes, it [6]_____. Yes, **they were**.	No, **it wasn't**. No, **they** [8]_____.

b 🔘 **1.13** Listen to check. ℗

2 a Sally talks about her first job. Complete the gaps with was, were, wasn't and weren't.

> **"** When I [1]*was* at university in 2007, I [2]_____ an assistant in a clothes shop. The shop [3]_____ near the university so a lot of our customers [4]_____ students. One of the other assistants [5]_____ a student too, but the others [6]_____. The job was OK, but it [7]_____ well paid. It was a good first job, but it [8]_____ a job for life for me. **"**

Grammar reference and practice, p133

b 🔘 **1.14** Listen to check.

SPEAKING

> What was your first job?
>
> I was a shop assistant.
>
> Was it difficult?

3 a Think about your jobs or the jobs of someone you know well. What was the:

- first job?
- best job?
- worst job?

b Ask and answer questions about the jobs.

c Is a 'job for life' a good thing?

Target activity

Talk about someone you know well

1.3 goals
- say who people are ♻
- talk about present and past jobs ♻
- say how you know people

TASK LISTENING

Michel and Donna talk about people they know well.

1 a 🔊 **1.15** Listen to Michel talk about Roberto. How do they know each other?

b Now listen to Donna talk about Adam. How do they know each other?

2 a Complete the profiles with these words.

~~best friends at school~~ Canadian teacher Brazilian good friends married media colleagues television

Name: Roberto
Nationality: ¹_____
Age: about 55
How you know the person: We were ²_____ .
Relationship now: ³_____
Past occupation: director of a shipping company
Present occupation: mathematics ⁴_____

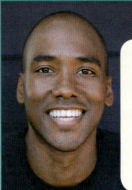

Name: Adam
Nationality: ⁵_____
Age: 26
How you know the person: We were ⁶ *best friends at school* .
Relationship now: ⁷_____
Past occupation: ⁸_____ student
Present occupation: ⁹_____ presenter

b 🔊 **1.15** Listen again to check.

TASK VOCABULARY

How you know people

3 a Replace the highlighted words in 1–5 with these words to make new sentences.

~~classmates~~ neighbours office teacher university

1 We were **friends** at school. *We were classmates at school.*
2 We were at **college** together.
3 We were in the same **class**.
4 We were **colleagues** in Melbourne.
5 She was my **boss**.

b 🔊 **1.16** Listen to check. ⓟ

TASK

OK, this is about my colleague, Krishnan ...

4 a Prepare to talk about a person you know well. Think about what to say:

the person: name, nationality, age
past: how you know him or her, past occupations
present: occupation now, relationship now

b Tell each other about the people.

Keyword *OK*

1 a Match the conversations to pictures A–D.

1 A Can I use your mobile phone?
   B **OK**. Here it is.

2 A I'm sorry I'm late.
   B That's **OK**. Take a seat.

3 A My name's Lesley – with a 'y'.
   B L-E-S-L-E-Y. **OK**.

4 A Hi. How are you?
   B I'm **OK**, thanks. And you?

b What does **OK** mean in each conversation?

OK = I understand   OK = all right / good
OK = no problem   OK = yes, you can

2 a Practise the conversations in pairs.

b Test each other. Take turns to start the conversations 1–4 and remember the responses.

3 a Work in pairs. Think of answers to 1–6 using **OK**.

1 How was your weekend?
2 Can I use your computer?
3 How's Michael?
4 Sorry, I can't remember your name.
5 My address is 143, not 134!
6 Can I open the window, please?

b Compare your ideas with another pair. Then practise 1–6 and your answers.

> How was your weekend?
>> It was OK, thanks. What about you?

Across cultures Greetings

1 Match the words and expressions with the pictures.

> bow   kiss   exchange cards   hug   shake hands   say hello / hi

2 a 🔊 **1.17** Seung-wan talks about how people greet each other in South Korea. What does he say?

Two male friends usually ...
Two female friends usually ...
Male and female friends usually ...

b 🔊 **1.18** Paul talks about greetings in England. How does he say they're different?

> At a party, friends usually hug.

> Colleagues at work usually say hello.

3 What do you do when you meet people? What do people usually do in your country? Talk about:

- two friends at a party
- two colleagues at work
- two strangers at a friend's home
- a young and an old person at a friend's home
- two business people meeting

4 Do you know anything about greetings in other cultures?

> In Japan, I think friends usually ...

1 EXPLORE Speaking

Goals
- ask people to repeat
- ask questions to check information

1 a Listen to Maite and Krishnan talking at Rob's party. Circle the things they *don't* understand at first.

1 Maite doesn't understand Krishnan's (name) / nationality / job.
2 Krishnan doesn't understand Maite's name / nationality / job.

b Read the script to check.

2 Look at the questions in the script. Which questions ask someone to repeat? Which questions check information?

3 a Complete the questions.

1 **A** I'm at the Ellersley House Hotel.
   B Sorry, which **hotel**?
2 **A** OK, page one hundred and three, please.
   B Sorry, which _____?
3 **A** He's on the 9.47 train.
   B Sorry, which _____?
4 **A** Look at exercise 3b.
   B Sorry, which _____?
5 **A** We're in room 382.
   B Sorry, which _____?

b Test each other in pairs.

> I'm at the Ellersley House Hotel.

> Sorry, which hotel?

> The Ellersley House Hotel.

4 Match 1–5 with a–e.

1 Agata's on the phone.
2 The bus is at 10.53.
3 Kevin's in Uppsala.
4 Your appointment's on Friday, March 17.
5 That's $45.23, please.

a Sorry, what time?
b Sorry, how much?
c Sorry, when?
d Sorry, where?
e Sorry, who?

5 a In pairs, complete the conversations with expressions from 2, 3 and 4.

1
A Your appointment's on May 21st at 3 pm.
B Sorry, ¹ **what time**?
A 3 pm, with Doctor Fenman.
B Sorry, ² _____?
A Doctor Fenman.

2
A My brother's in Uppsala.
B Sorry, ³ _____?
A Uppsala.
B Oh, OK. ⁴ _____ _____ in Scandinavia?
A Yes, it's in Sweden.

b Practise the conversations.

MAITE	Hello, I'm Maria Teresa.
KRISHNAN	Hi, nice to meet you. I'm Krishnan.
MAITE	Sorry, can you say that again?
KRISHNAN	Krishnan.
MAITE	Krishnan?
KRISHNAN	Yes, that's right. And what's your name again? Maria …?
MAITE	Maria Teresa, but you can call me Maite. It's short for Maria Teresa.
KRISHNAN	Maite, OK. So, what do you do?
MAITE	I'm a Spanish teacher here in the summer … but in Spain, I'm a historical linguist.
KRISHNAN	Sorry, what's that again?
MAITE	A historical linguist.
KRISHNAN	Oh, right. Is that about the history of language?
MAITE	Yes, that's right. And what do you do?

6 a Write five sentences with a name, place or number in them. For example:

- your favourite café, park or hotel
- the price of something
- where a friend is now

My new shoes were $45.95.

b Work in pairs. A, say your sentences. B, ask questions to check the information.

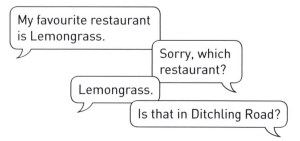

> My favourite restaurant is Lemongrass.

> Sorry, which restaurant?

> Lemongrass.

> Is that in Ditchling Road?

Then change roles.

Review

GRAMMAR *be* past and present

1 a Complete the profile of Alvaro with the correct form of *be*, past or present.

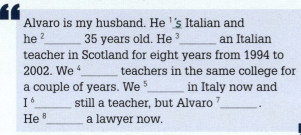

Alvaro is my husband. He ¹'s Italian and he ² _____ 35 years old. He ³ _____ an Italian teacher in Scotland for eight years from 1994 to 2002. We ⁴ _____ teachers in the same college for a couple of years. We ⁵ _____ in Italy now and I ⁶ _____ still a teacher, but Alvaro ⁷ _____. He ⁸ _____ a lawyer now.

b Write a short profile like this about someone you know well.

c Look at another student's profile. Ask questions to find out more.

> Were you at university together?
>
> No, we were in the same office.

VOCABULARY People and jobs

2 a Which of these words are about family (F)? Which are about work (W)?

colleague *W*   architect   brother   lawyer
sister   boss   wife   office manager   husband
teacher   father   son   marketing assistant
mother   accountant   daughter

b Say what you remember about students in the class.

> I think José Carlos is a builder. He's a husband, I think, and a father.

CAN YOU REMEMBER? Intro – Questions

3 a Complete the questions from the Intro unit.

1 *What*'s your name?
2 _____ are you from?
3 _____ languages do you speak?
4 _____ do you spell your surname?
5 _____'s your email address?

b In pairs, think of four more questions to ask a person in your class.

c Ask and answer all your questions.

> What languages do you speak?
>
> Turkish, and a bit of English.

Extension

SPELLING AND SOUNDS Vowels and consonants

4 a Look at the letters of the alphabet. Which are vowels? Which are consonants?

a e i o u   b c d f g h j k l m n p q r s t v w x y z

b Complete the words from this unit with vowels.

1   *uni*versi*ty*
2   sh_p   _ss_st_nt
3   g_rlfr__nd
4   d__ght_r
5   n__ghb__rs
6   j__rn_l_st

c 🔊 **1.20** Listen to check.

d Find six more words from Unit 1. Write a test like 4b for a partner.

e In pairs, do each other's tests.

NOTICE *really, very, not very*

5 a Look at the sentences from the interview with Rob Lewis. Can you remember the three jobs?

❶ I was at work by 6.00 am every Saturday and Sunday. That was really difficult.

❷ The job was boring and badly paid. It was very hot in there, too.

❸ It was okay but it wasn't very interesting.

b Look at the interview on p12 to check.

c Choose three jobs on p145. Write three sentences about each job with really, very and not very.

It's very …
It isn't very …
It's really …

d Listen to each other's sentences. Can you guess the jobs?

Self-assessment

Can you do these things in English? Circle a number on each line. 1 = I can't do this, 5 = I can do this well.

introduce people	1	2	3	4	5
say who people are	1	2	3	4	5
talk about present and past jobs	1	2	3	4	5
say how you know people	1	2	3	4	5
ask people to repeat	1	2	3	4	5
ask questions to check information	1	2	3	4	5

- For Wordcards, reference and saving your work → e-Portfolio
- For more practice → Self-study Pack, Unit 1

2.1 goals
- make and respond to requests
- make and respond to offers

Away from home

I miss my friends

LISTENING

1 a Find these things in pictures A–D.

sun   snow   rabbits   food

b Read the quotes. Can you guess who misses each thing? Complete the sentences.

A    **B**    **C**    **D**

> I'm from Canada but I live and work in Japan. When I'm in Japan, away from home, I really miss the _____ in winter and my brother, Scott.
> *Carly, from Canada*

> When I'm away from home, I really miss my mother and my sister. I also miss the _____. Sudanese food is really nice.
> *Khalid, from Sudan*

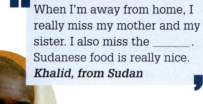

> When I'm not at home, I really miss the _____, I miss my friends, and especially I miss my dog.
> *Paula, from Argentina*

> When I'm away from home, I really miss my family, my _____ and the food.
> *Angharad, from Switzerland*

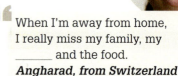

c 🔊 1.21 Listen to check.

2 What do you miss when you're away from home?

> When I'm away from home, I really miss the seafood.

3 Read the email. Where's Carly? Where's Scott?

Hi Carly,
My flight arrives at Tokyo Narita airport at 9am on Friday.
Would you like anything from Canada? Phone me!
Scott

4 a 🔊 1.22 Listen to Carly and Scott on the phone. Tick (✓) the things they talk about.

newspapers ✓   magazines ☐   a camera ☐   boots ☐
a winter coat ☐   two books ☐   a rucksack ☐

b 🔊 1.22 Listen again. What's Scott happy to bring? What's he not happy to bring?

c Read the script on p149 to check.

Would you like …?

VOCABULARY

Offers and requests

1 Make short conversations from the offers, requests and answers. Which answers can you use with offers? Which answers can you use with requests?

Offers

Would you like	some magazines? anything from home?

Requests

Can I Could I	use your old rucksack?
Can you Could you	bring my winter coat?

Answers
OK.
All right.
No, sorry.
No, thanks.
Yes, of course.
Yes, please.
No problem.
No, I'm afraid not.

Can I use your dictionary?

Yes, of course.

Thanks.

2 Make more offers and requests.

Offers
• some books • a newspaper • something to eat • a drink
Requests
• use your dictionary • have your email address • spell your name • open the window

GRAMMAR

a, an, some

3 a Write a, an or some.

1   *a* cup of coffee

2   *some* books

3   _____ glass of apple juice

4   _____ apple

_____ magazines

6   _____ sandwich

7   _____ newspaper

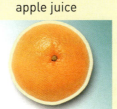

8   _____ orange

9   _____ oranges

10 _____ clothes

b 🔊 **1.23** Listen to check. Complete the rules in the box.

a, an and *some*
_____ a _____ or _____ an _____ = 1. _____ = 2, 3, 4, … Use _____ before a vowel (a, e, i, o, u). Use _____ before a consonant (b, c, d, …).

Grammar reference and practice, p133

PRONUNCIATION

Word stress 1

4 a Look at the words in 3a. Which words have two syllables (coff-ee)? Which have three syllables (news-pa-per)? Where's the stress in each word?

coff-ee, news-pa-per, …

b 🔊 **1.24** Listen to check. Practise saying the words.

SPEAKING

5 a Work in A/B pairs. Read the situations below.

1 You're friends. A, you live abroad. B, you live here. You visit A next week. B, ask A what he / she wants from here. A, tell B what you want.

2 You're colleagues. It's lunchtime. A, you go to a shop to get lunch. Ask B what he / she wants from the shop. B, tell A what you want from the shop.

b Have conversations in the two situations.

2.2 goals
- say what your interests are
- say what you want to do

Sofasurfing

1 When you travel, do you stay in hotels? with friends? on campsites? somewhere else?

2 Read the introduction to the website Sofasurfing.com. Is it for people who:

1 want to travel / stay at home?
2 have / don't have a lot of money?
3 want to stay with old friends / make new friends?

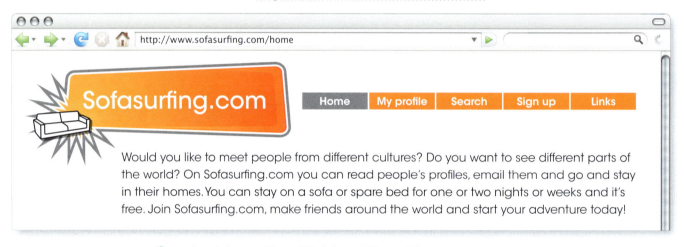

http://www.sofasurfing.com/home

Sofasurfing.com

Home | My profile | Search | Sign up | Links

Would you like to meet people from different cultures? Do you want to see different parts of the world? On Sofasurfing.com you can read people's profiles, email them and go and stay in their homes. You can stay on a sofa or spare bed for one or two nights or weeks and it's free. Join Sofasurfing.com, make friends around the world and start your adventure today!

3 a Read the profiles of Melek and Fiona. What do they have in common? Think about work, languages, interests and travel plans.

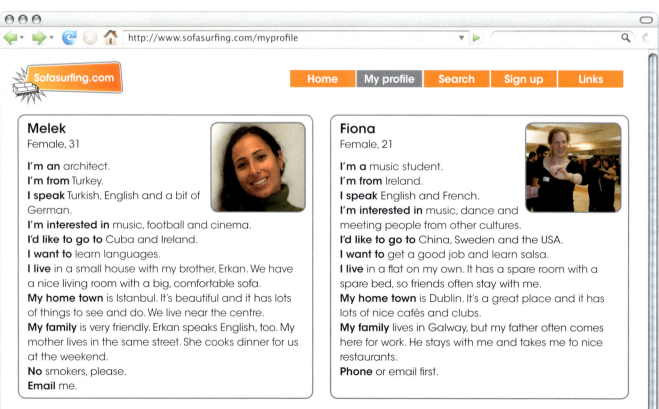

http://www.sofasurfing.com/myprofile

Sofasurfing.com

Home | My profile | Search | Sign up | Links

Melek
Female, 31

I'm an architect.
I'm from Turkey.
I speak Turkish, English and a bit of German.
I'm interested in music, football and cinema.
I'd like to go to Cuba and Ireland.
I want to learn languages.
I live in a small house with my brother, Erkan. We have a nice living room with a big, comfortable sofa.
My home town is Istanbul. It's beautiful and it has lots of things to see and do. We live near the centre.
My family is very friendly. Erkan speaks English, too. My mother lives in the same street. She cooks dinner for us at the weekend.
No smokers, please.
Email me.

Fiona
Female, 21

I'm a music student.
I'm from Ireland.
I speak English and French.
I'm interested in music, dance and meeting people from other cultures.
I'd like to go to China, Sweden and the USA.
I want to get a good job and learn salsa.
I live in a flat on my own. It has a spare room with a spare bed, so friends often stay with me.
My home town is Dublin. It's a great place and it has lots of nice cafés and clubs.
My family lives in Galway, but my father often comes here for work. He stays with me and takes me to nice restaurants.
Phone or email first.

b Compare your ideas with a partner.

GRAMMAR

Present simple:
positive
sentences

4 a Complete the sentences in the table with these verbs.

~~speak~~ ~~speaks~~ stay stays have has live lives

I, you, we, they	he, she, it
1 I *speak* English and French.	2 Erkan *speaks* English, too.
3 I _____ in a small house.	4 My mother _____ in the same street.
5 We _____ a nice living room.	6 It _____ lots of nice cafés and clubs.
7 Friends often _____ with me.	8 He _____ with me.

b 🔴 **1.25** Listen to check. **P**

5 Read Fiona's reply to an email from Melek. Complete the email with the verbs in brackets.

○ ○ ○

🚫 ◀ ◀◀ ▶ 🖨
Delete Reply Reply All Forward Print

Hi Melek

Thanks for your email. Here are the answers to your questions. Yes, Dublin ¹*has* (have) great museums and parks –
a lot of tourists ²_____ (visit) the National Museum of Ireland on Kildare Street. The city also ³_____ (have) lots of good
musicians and bands. Visitors really ⁴_____ (enjoy) the music here. My spare room's small, but friends often
⁵_____ (stay) with me and they ⁶_____ (like) it.
You say you want to go out of Dublin and see more of Ireland. Well, my sister Kathy ⁷_____ (live) and ⁸_____ (work) in
Kildare, a city near Dublin. She ⁹_____ (say) you can stay with her for a few days.
Anyway, see you soon,
Fiona

6 a Write five sentences about you and your family, three true and two false.
Use have, live, speak and stay.

I live in a big house with my parents. My sister lives with her husband.

Grammar reference
and practice, p134

b Listen to each other's sentences. Guess which are false.

I'm interested in ...

VOCABULARY

Interests and
wants

1 a What can you remember about Melek and Fiona? Cover their profiles and make sentences.

Melek Fiona	is interested in	music	cinema	dance	football	
	would like to go to	Cuba	China	Sweden	Ireland	the USA
	wants to	learn salsa	get a good job	learn languages		

b Look at the profiles again to check.

WRITING

2 a Think about:

1 things you are interested in.
2 things you want to do / would like to do.

b Write a profile like Melek's or Fiona's for the *Sofasurfing* website.

3 a Read other students' profiles. Choose two people to talk about.

b Tell a partner about the two people.

Magda and Kuba are interested in languages and Kuba's also interested in ... .

Take care of a guest

2.3 goals

- make and respond to requests ♻
- make and respond to offers ♻
- say what your interests are ♻
- say what you want to do ♻

TASK READING AND LISTENING

Erkan

Akira

Koji

1 **Read the email and answer the questions.**

1 Where do Erkan, Akira and Koji live?
2 How do Erkan and Akira know each other? What about Koji and Akira?

http://www.webmail.com/inbox

Create message
Inbox (4 new)
My folders
Contacts
Search messages
Search contacts
Settings
Help

reply | reply to all | forward | delete | print | print as fax | save to pc | mark as unread | done | Move to folder...

From: Akira
Subject: Hello

Hi Erkan
Hope you're OK. I'm fine but I miss Istanbul and everyone in the office. Tokyo is hot and the new job is hard work, but it's interesting. One of my colleagues, Koji, is going to Istanbul next month. He doesn't know anyone. Could you meet him and show him the city one day? He's very nice!
Akira

2 **1.26** Koji arrives at Erkan's home in Istanbul. Listen and tick (✓) the things Erkan asks him about.

his family ☐   a drink ☐   food ☐   things to do ☐   sports ☐   places to go ☐

TASK VOCABULARY

Taking care of a guest

3 **a** Match the questions and answers.

1 **Would you like** something to drink?
2 **Do you want** something to eat?
3 **Are you interested in** seeing some sights?
4 And **would you like to** take a boat trip on the Bosphorus?
5 **What else would you like to** do?

a Yes, I am. I'm really interested in architecture.
b No, I'm fine, thank you. The hotel food is very good.
c Well, I'd like to eat some real Turkish food later.
d Oh yeah, please. I like boat trips.
e Er, just a glass of water, please.

b **1.27** Listen to check. ℗

TASK

4 **a** You have a guest in your home. Think about how to:

1 offer your guest something to eat and drink.
2 find out what your guest is interested in.
3 find out what your guest would like to do and see.

b In pairs, take turns to be the guest. Have two conversations.

Keyword *in*

1 a Add these highlighted expressions with **in** to the table.

> 1 I'm from Canada but I live and work **in Japan**. Unit 2
> 2 I live **in a small house** with my brother, Erkan. Unit 2
> 3 My mother lives **in the same street**. Unit 2
> 4 We were neighbours **in Melbourne**. Unit 1
> 5 We were **in the same office**. Unit 1
> 6 When I was at university **in 2007** ... Unit 1
> 7 Can you do these things **in English**? Intro unit

in Istanbul

in the morning

Places	Times	Languages
in Istanbul	in the morning	in Japanese

b Add these expressions to the table.

in winter   in the afternoon   in German   in Germany   in March   in the evening

2 a Add **in** to these sentences.

in

1 My birthday is ∧ October.
2 I work a small shop.
3 I was Athens in the summer of 2009.
4 People often visit my country the winter.

5 I live a flat with my wife and children.
6 My friend and I were in Spain together 1989.
7 I can say 'I love you' Korean.
8 I work the morning.

b Change the sentences so they're true for you.

My birthday is in ~~October~~ *March*.

c Compare your sentences.

Independent learning Finding information

1 Do the quiz in groups.

Your coursebook
Where in this book can you find:

1 a plan of the book? *pages 3 to 5*
2 listening scripts? *pages ___ to ___*
3 a chart of English sounds? *page ___*
4 grammar reference and practice? *pages ___ to ___*
5 a list of irregular verbs? *page ___*
6 vocabulary reference? *pages ___ to ___*

2 a Look at words 1–5. They describe different kinds of word. Find two more *pronouns, verbs, prepositions, nouns* and *adjectives* in the paragraph from Fiona's profile.

b Check your answers in a dictionary or with your teacher.

1 pronoun **2** verb **3** preposition **4** noun **5** adjective

> **I live in** a **flat** on my own, in Dublin. It's a **great** place and it has lots of nice cafés and clubs. My family lives in Galway, but my father often comes here for work. He stays with me and takes me to nice restaurants.

> **great** /greɪt/ *adj*
> **1** very good: *We had a great time.*
> **2** important or famous: *a great actor*
> **3** large: *a great crowd of people*

2 EXPLORE Writing

1 Read the emails and (circle) the correct answer.

1 Ju-Yung is in Istanbul / Korea / (Lebanon).
2 He wants to stay with Erkan in Turkey / return to Korea / meet Erkan in Lebanon.
3 He offers Erkan information about museums / a gift from Lebanon / some food.

Goal

◉ write a letter or email requesting something

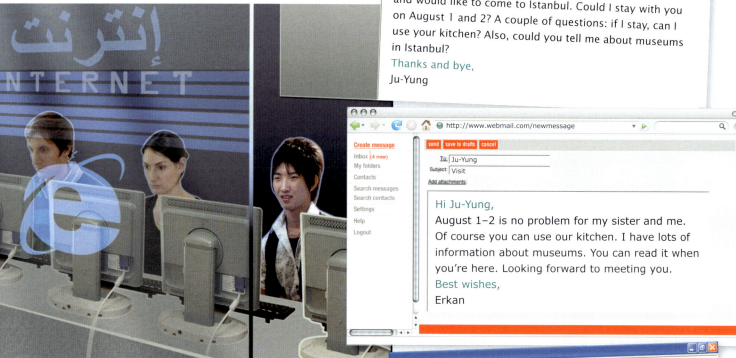

> Dear Erkan,
>
> My name's Kim Ju-Yung and I'm from Korea. You can check my profile on Sofasurfing.com. I'm in Lebanon now and would like to come to Istanbul. Could I stay with you on August 1 and 2? A couple of questions: if I stay, can I use your kitchen? Also, could you tell me about museums in Istanbul?
>
> Thanks and bye,
> Ju-Yung

> http://www.webmail.com/newmessage
>
> send save to drafts cancel
> To: Ju-Yung
> Subject: Visit
> Add attachments:
>
> Hi Ju-Yung,
> August 1–2 is no problem for my sister and me. Of course you can use our kitchen. I have lots of information about museums. You can read it when you're here. Looking forward to meeting you.
> Best wishes,
> Erkan

> Hi again,
> Thanks very much, Erkan. Would you like something from Lebanon?
> See you soon.
> Ju-Yung

2 Look at the highlighted expressions in the emails. Which are greetings? Which are goodbyes?

3 Add these words to 1, 2 or 3.

> telephone   on Saturday   on 31 July   shower
> restaurants   next Thursday   computer
> tomorrow   concerts   washing machine
> sports events

1 Could I stay with you _on August 1 and 2_ / _____ / _____ / _____ / _____ ?
2 Can I use your _kitchen_ / _telephone_ / _____ / _____ / _____ ?
3 Could you tell me about _museums_ / _____ / _____ / _____ in your city?

4 a *Capital letters*. Complete the rules with words from the emails.

> Use capital letters (A, B, C) with:
> • countries and cities: _Korea_, _Lebanon_, _____
> • people's names: _Erkan_ , _____
> • nationalities and languages: _Korean_, _English_
> • words at the start of sentences: _My_
> • I: _Could I ...?_
> • days and months: _Monday_, _____
> • public holidays: _Eid-al-Fitr_ , _May Day_

b Cover the emails and 4a. Add capital letters to these sentences.

1 my name's kim ju-yung and i'm from korea.
2 i'm in lebanon now and would like to come to istanbul.
3 could i stay with you on august 1 and 2?
4 thanks very much, erkan.
5 would you like something from lebanon?
6 see you soon.

c Read the emails again to check.

5 You decide to use Sofasurfing.com to find a place to stay in another country. Write an email to your host.

1 Give information about yourself.
2 Ask two or three questions.
3 Check your email. Are the capital letters correct?

6 a Read another student's email and write a reply.

b Read the reply to your email. Did the host answer all your questions?

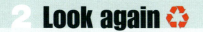
Review

1 a Match 1–7 with a–g to make seven sentences.

1 I live
2 I have
3 Miki lives
4 I work
5 Miki and I speak
6 I want
7 Miki wants

a Japanese and English.
b with our mum and dad in Osaka. She stays with me at the weekend.
c to travel to Europe.
d to live with me in Tokyo.
e in a flat in the centre of Tokyo, Japan.
f a sister. Her name is Miki.
g for the Sony Corporation. I'm a marketing assistant.

b Write sentences about you and a family member or a friend. Use the verbs from 1–7.

2 a Write offers or requests for the situations.

1 You're a guest in someone's home. Ask for a drink. *Can I have a glass of water?*
2 You have guests in your home. Offer them something to eat.
3 You want to know a word in English. Ask for a dictionary.
4 Your guests want to go for a walk but they don't know your home town. Offer them a map.

b Take turns to make your offers and requests, and reply.

3 a Complete the quiz questions with *is, are, was, were*.

b Do the quiz. Then check your answers on p122.

1 When *was* the first football World Cup?
   a 1924   b 1930   c 1954

2 What _____ the capital of Poland?
   a Krakow   b Wroclaw   c Warsaw

3 How long _____ the First World War?
   a 4 years   b 8 years   c 100 years

4 What _____ the official languages of Canada?
   a English and Spanish   b English and French
   c English, French and Spanish

5 Where _____ the first Olympic Games?
   a in Italy   b in Greece   c in Turkey

Extension

4 a ⬤ **1.28** Listen to these words from units 0, 1 and 2. Can you hear the two highlighted consonants? Say the words.

travel   swim   student   help   speak

b Underline the two consonants that are together. Say the words.

want   Sweden   lots   please
host   Spain   great   guest

c ⬤ **1.29** Listen and check on p149.

d ⬤ **1.30** Spellcheck. Close your book. Listen to ten words and write them down.

e Check your spelling.

5 a Do you know the opposites of these adjectives?

A	B
short – *long*	uncomfortable – *c* ____
light – *h* ____	ugly – *b* ____
empty – *f* ____	unfriendly – *f* ____
new – *o* ____	different – the *s* ____

b Check your answers to A in Scott and Carly's conversation on p149, ⬤ **1.22**. Check your answers to B in Melek's profile on p20.

c Test each other in pairs.

Self-assessment

Can you do these things in English? Circle a number on each line. 1 = I can't do this, 5 = I can do this well.

◎ make and respond to requests	1	2	3	4	5
◎ make and respond to offers	1	2	3	4	5
◎ say what your interests are	1	2	3	4	5
◎ say what you want to do	1	2	3	4	5
◎ write a letter or email requesting something	1	2	3	4	5

• For Wordcards, reference and saving your work → e-Portfolio
• For more practice → Self-study Pack, Unit 2

Your time

3.1 goals
◎ say what you do in your free time
◎ say what you like and dislike

Happiness

READING

1 Read the web postings about happiness. Which ones match pictures A–D?

A

B

Happiness is ...

Thank you for your comments. Here are some of the best.

[1] What's happiness? Talking to my husband and watching something good on TV with him. We don't go out a lot but we're happy. *Berthe, 88, France*

[2] Happiness is going fishing on a boat with my friends and a very cold drink. And catching fish, of course. *Juan Carlos, 43, Brazil*

[3] My work. I'm a photographer and I love taking photos. It's not very well paid, but money doesn't make you happy. *Chin-Mae, 28, Korea*

[4] Happiness is playing the drums really loud, but my dad doesn't like it! *Jason, 15, USA*

[5] My friends … talking to them over a coffee, listening to jazz, going to parties together. And my cat. She doesn't like my boyfriend, but she loves me! *Andrea, 32, Australia*

[6] Seeing my grandchildren – that's happiness. I love them so much. I also enjoy reading a good book, but I don't read newspapers. I don't like bad news. *Jakub, 67, Poland*

[7] I like learning new things and meeting new people, so I do a different course every year. This year it's dancing the tango. *Chiara, 38, Italy*

[8] Chocolate! I love it! *Sally, 21, UK*

C

D

Pronouns	
subject	object
I	*me*
you	you
he	
she	her
it	
we	us
they	

Grammar reference and practice, p135

2 Read again and <u>underline</u> three things you like. Then compare in groups.

3 Complete the Pronouns table with the highlighted words in the web postings.

4 a Complete the expressions with words from the postings.

talking to *my husband*	going to _____
watching something good on _____	seeing my _____
going _____	reading a good _____
taking _____	learning new _____
playing _____	meeting new _____
listening to _____	dancing _____

b 🔲 **1.31** Listen to check. **P**

> Playing?
>> Playing the drums, playing football …

5 a Use these words to make five more expressions with the words in 4a.

football   languages   newspaper   the cinema   the radio

b Test each other in pairs. Say a verb and remember the expressions.

6 a What is happiness for you? Use the highlighted words and write six sentences. Give them to your teacher.

Happiness is playing football in the park with my friends.
I like / **enjoy** taking photos of people.
I love dancing the tango.

b Listen to other students' sentences. Can you guess whose sentences they are?

I don't like bad news

1 a Complete the sentences in the table.

~~don't like~~   ~~doesn't like~~   don't go   doesn't like   doesn't make   don't read   don't watch

I / you / we / they	he / she / it
1 I *don't like* bad news.	5 My dad *doesn't like* my music.
2 You _____ newspapers.	6 She _____ my boyfriend.
3 We _____ out a lot.	7 Money _____ you happy.
4 They _____ TV.	

b 🔲 **1.32** Listen to check. **P**

2 a Circle the correct word.

1   My daughter don't / doesn't like chocolate.
2   My mobile phone don't / doesn't take photos.
3   I don't / doesn't watch TV in the morning.
4   My husband don't / doesn't speak English.
5   My friends and I don't / doesn't usually go out on work days.
6   My home town don't / doesn't have a cinema.

b Write five sentences about yourself and people you know with **don't** and **doesn't**.

My friend Carla doesn't have a computer.

Moira

Sam

3 a 🔲 **1.33** Listen to Moira and Sam talk about free time. Tick (✓) the things they do.

Moira	reads books and newspapers ✓ reads magazines watches TV cooks goes to restaurants
Sam	goes for walks goes jogging drives to the sea plays tennis goes to a gym goes shopping at weekends

b Read the script on p149 to check.

4 a Think about things you do and things you don't do in your free time.

b Talk to other people. Find out who does similar things to you.

Do you like New Year?

3.2 goals
◉ say what you do in your free time ♻
◉ talk about habits and customs

LISTENING

> We celebrate Diwali, the Hindu New Year. It's usually in October or November.

1 When do you celebrate New Year? Do you like it? Why? / Why not?

2 ▸ 1.34 Listen to Min from Korea and Paul from the UK talk about New Year. Do they like it?

Min

Paul

3 a Circle the correct words from the conversations.

Min
1 I usually go to my parents' / brother's house.
2 We all play family games / football.
3 We eat fish / soup with rice cakes.
Paul
4 I stay at home and play computer games / read.
5 I usually stay up late / go to bed early.
6 My wife loves / doesn't like parties.

b ▸ 1.34 Listen again to check.

Possessive 's and s'

singular
my brother's house
plural
my parents' house

Grammar reference and practice, p132

VOCABULARY

Adverbs of frequency

4 Read how often Min and Paul do things. Complete 1–3 with the highlighted words.

My family and I sometimes go to the sea.
In the afternoon or evening, we always see friends.
My brother and his family often come too.
She usually goes out with friends from work.

| HOW OFTEN? | never 0% | 1 _____ | 2 _____ | 3 _____ | 4 *always* 100% |

PRONUNCIATION
Word stress 2

5 **a** How many syllables are in these words? Where's the stress? Put them in the table.

~~always~~   enjoy   usually   afternoon
sometimes   important   never   traditional   often

¹ ●●	² ●●	³ ●●●	⁴ ●●●	⁵ ●●●	⁶ ●●●●
always					

b 🔘 **1.35** Listen to check. ⓟ Practise saying the words with the correct stress.

SPEAKING

6 **a** What do you usually do for New Year? Think about:

• food and drink   • people   • activities

b Tell each other what you do.

In the morning, I usually go ...   I sometimes see ...   We always eat ...

What do you usually do?

GRAMMAR
Present simple:
questions

1 **a** Complete the questions and answers in the table with do, don't, does, doesn't.

I, you, we, they	He, she, it
1 _Do_ the children do anything special?	5 _Does_ she stay at home with you?
2 Yes, they _____ . / No, they _____ .	6 Yes, she _____ . / No, she _____ .
3 What _____ you usually do?	7 What _____ your wife do?
4 What _____ we eat?	8 What _____ _Seollal_ mean?

b 🔘 **1.36** Listen to check. ⓟ

2 **a** Put the words in order to make questions.

1 birthdays / Do / like / you ? _Do you like birthdays?_
2 do / What / in / you / do / the morning ?
3 Do / work / you / to / go ?
4 of food / eat / do / you / What kind ?
5 see / you / friends / Do ?
6 go out / Do / at night / you ?
7 your husband / like / birthdays / Does ?
8 family / does / do / your / What ?

Grammar reference and practice, p134

b 🔘 **1.37** Listen to check. ⓟ

SPEAKING

3 **a** Choose a day or time that you enjoy, for example:

• your birthday   • your name day   • your wedding anniversary
• holidays   • weekends

Think about your answers to the questions in 2a.

b In pairs, ask each other about your days or times. Use questions from 2a and your own questions to find out more.

What do you do for your anniversary?   Well, we usually go out for a meal.

4 Change pairs and tell each other about your first partner.

For her anniversary, Marta usually goes out for a meal with her husband.

Invite someone out

3.3 goals
◎ say what you like and dislike ♻
◎ make and respond to invitations

TASK LISTENING

1 Do you often invite people to your home?
Do you invite people to go out? Who do you invite?
Where do you go?

> I sometimes invite friends to cafés.

2 🔴 **1.38** Listen to Rocio and Léon inviting friends out.

1 Where do they invite them?
2 Can the friends go?

Rocio and Blake

TASK VOCABULARY

Invitations

3 a Complete the sentences with these words.

> ~~free~~   like   Yes   want   Are   sorry

checking
1 Are you _free_ on Saturday evening?
2 _____ you interested in football, Roberto?
inviting
3 Do you _____ to come to my place for dinner?
4 Would you _____ to come with me?
answering
5 _____, please. That sounds great.
6 Oh no, I'm _____. I can't.

b 🔴 **1.38** Listen again to check.

Léon and Roberto

TASK

4 a Think of three things you'd like to invite a friend to. For example:

- a meal at your home
- a sports event
- a concert
- a café or restaurant
- a party
- a picnic

b Decide the date and time of each thing and other details. For example:

a meal: what kind of food? how many people?
a sports event: what sport? which teams?
a concert: who? where?
a café or restaurant: what restaurant? what kind of food?
a party: where? what for?
a picnic: where? what do you need to bring?

> Hi, Siu Tong. Are you free on Sunday?

5 Invite different people to your three places. Find someone to go to each place.

Keyword *go*

1 a Complete sentences 1–6 with the words on the right.

1 We don't go out a lot but we're _____. Unit 3
2 Happiness is going fishing on a _____ with my friends. Unit 3
3 I guess I go to _____ at one or two. Unit 3
4 She usually goes out with friends from _____. Unit 3
5 We usually go for a _____. Unit 3
6 I'd like to go to Cuba and _____. Unit 2

> Ireland   bed   meal
> boat   work   happy

b Look at the highlighted expressions in the sentences. Then add these words to the table.

~~concerts~~ drink colleagues family parties shopping walk skiing Japan

go to	concerts
go for a	
go out with	
go + *-ing*	

c Cover the table. Test each other in pairs. How many expressions can you remember with:

1 go to …   2 go for a …   3 go out …   4 go + *-ing* ?

2 a Match the questions and answers.

1 **How often do you go** for a walk?
2 **Do you ever go** to restaurants?
3 **Would you like to go** to Cuba?
4 **Where do you go** shopping?
5 **Do you like going** out with colleagues?

a Yes. We always go for a drink on Friday evenings.
b Yes, I'd love to!
c Sometimes, but I like cooking at home.
d Not very often. I don't have time.
e I go to the supermarket in the town centre.

b Write questions for a partner. Use the highlighted expressions in 2a.

c Ask and answer your questions. Try to find out more information.

Across cultures Conversation 'dos and don'ts'

1 Match the pictures A–H with these topics.

age religion money work politics health home family

2 a 🔊 **1.39** Listen to Ruth from the UK. Which topics from 1 does she say are OK to talk about with people you don't know very well? Which topics are not OK?

b 🔊 **1.40** Now listen to Amina from Lebanon. What does she say about the topics?

Ruth

Amina

3 Think about which topics are OK to talk about with people you don't know very well.

I usually / don't usually talk about …   It's not OK / not polite to discuss …
It's OK / polite to talk about …   People don't usually like talking about …

4 Discuss your ideas with other students. What about in other countries you know?

> I don't usually talk about money with people I don't know well, but it's OK to talk about family …

1 Look at the pictures. Who's calling? Who's taking a message?

2 **a** 🔴 **1.41** Listen to Rocio and Paul's conversation. Complete Paul's note.

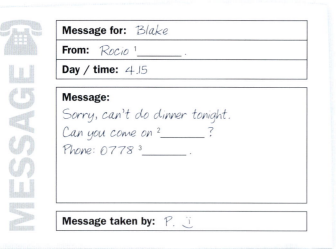

MESSAGE

Message for:	*Blake*
From:	*Rocio* ¹_____ .
Day / time:	*4.15*

Message:
Sorry, can't do dinner tonight.
Can you come on ²_____ ?
Phone: 0778 ³_____ .

Message taken by: *P. J.*

b Read the conversation to check.

3 **a** Look at the highlighted expressions in the conversation. Which can you use:

  1 when you want to talk to someone?
  2 when the person isn't there?
  3 when you offer to take a message?
  4 when someone speaks too fast?
  5 when you want someone to repeat?
  6 to say you understand? (x3)

b 🔴 **1.42** Listen to check. 🅟

4 **a** Complete the conversations.

1
SIMON   _____ _____ speak to Sara, please?
JULIA   Sorry. _____ isn't _____ . She's in France.
SIMON   I _____ .

2
MIKI   My name's Miki Nakamura.
JOANNE   Sorry, _____ you _____ that again, please?
MIKI   Miki Nakamura. N-A-K-A-M-U-R-A.
JOANNE   OK, thanks.

3
IAN   My address is 3b, 3064 Tenth Avenue.
DEBRA   Sorry, _____ you _____ down, please?
IAN   Oh, sorry ... 3b, 3064 Tenth Avenue.
DEBRA   Right, thanks.

b Practise the conversations in pairs.

c Look at 4a and change the names, places and addresses. Then have new conversations in pairs.

Goals
◎ take a phone message
◎ ask people to repeat and speak more slowly
◎ show you understand

Rocio

Paul

PAUL	Hello?
ROCIO	Hello, it's Rocio. Can I talk to Blake, please?
PAUL	Sorry, he isn't here at the moment.
ROCIO	Oh, I see.
PAUL	Can I take a message?
ROCIO	Oh, yes please. It's Rocio Gilberto, and ...
PAUL	Sorry, can you say that again?
ROCIO	Rocio Gilberto. G-I-L-B-E-R-T-O.
PAUL	G-I-L-B-E-R-T-O. OK. And what's the message?
ROCIO	Just to say I'm sorry but I'm really busy at work and I can't do dinner tonight.
PAUL	Right.
ROCIO	And can he come on Friday?
PAUL	OK, er, does Blake have your phone number?
ROCIO	I'm not sure. It's 0778 944 6532.
PAUL	Sorry, can you slow down a bit, please?
ROCIO	Sorry, it's 0778 944 6532.
PAUL	Three, two. OK.
ROCIO	Well, thanks a lot. Bye.
PAUL	Bye.

5 **a** Work in A/B pairs. A, use these role cards. B, use the cards on p123. Have two new conversations.

CONVERSATION 1
Your name: John (or Joanne) Tredennick
Your phone number: 614 573 1246
You want to talk to Paula.
Your message: meet at Gino's Café at 7.00 on Saturday

CONVERSATION 2
Student B wants to talk to Léon but he isn't at home. Take a message.

b Check each other's messages. Is all the information correct?

3 Look again ♻

Review

GRAMMAR Present simple

1 a Add *do*, *does*, *don't* or *doesn't* to the questions and answers.

    1 **A** How many days a week *do* you work?

        B Three days. I *don't* work on Thursday or Friday.

    2 **A** You enjoy your job?

        B Well, usually, but I like it at the moment.

    3 **A** What time the supermarket shut?

        B Sorry, I remember. At six, I think.

    4 **A** You go to the gym at the weekend?

        B On Saturdays, yes, but it open on Sundays.

    5 **A** Where you go out to eat?

        B We often go out. My husband loves cooking.

    6 **A** You go out on Friday nights?

        B No, never. I like going into town at night.

b Ask each other the questions. Answer with your own ideas.

VOCABULARY Activities

2 a Make a list of all the activities you remember with *-ing*.

playing football, dancing, ...

b Take turns to mime an activity. Watch and guess the activity.

c In pairs, ask and answer questions about the activities.

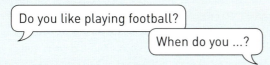

> Do you like playing football?
>
> When do you ...?

CAN YOU REMEMBER? Unit 2 – Offers and requests

3 a Match 1–6 with a–f to make questions.

  1 Can you open   a that dictionary?
  2 Would you like to go   b the window?
  3 Could you get me a   c workbook, please?
  4 Can I use   d your surname?
  5 Could you spell   e something to eat?
  6 Would you like   f for a coffee?

b Ask and answer the questions.

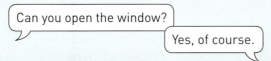

> Can you open the window?
>
> Yes, of course.

Extension

SPELLING AND SOUNDS *ch*, *tch* and *sh*

4 a 🔊 **1.43** Read and listen. Notice how we say *ch*, *tch* and *sh*.

/tʃ/	/ʃ/
ea**ch** wat**ch**ing	**sh**e fi**sh**ing

b Complete words from this unit with *sh*, *ch* or *tch*.

  1 __eck   5 Mar__
  2 whi__   6 __opping
  3 __ildren   7 __ocolate
  4 relation__ips 8 ma___

c 🔊 **1.44** Spellcheck. Close your book. Listen to eight words and write them down.

d Check your spelling on p150.

NOTICE Time expressions

5 a Complete the sentences from conversations in unit 3 with *at*, *on* and *in*.

  1 ... and *at* the weekend, my friends come to my flat ...

  2 _____ **Friday evening**, I go shopping for food.

  3 We have two New Years, one _____ **January 1st** ...

  4 ... and Seollal, _____ **January** or February.

  5 I guess I go to bed _____ **one** or two.

b Read scripts 🔊 **1.33** and 🔊 **1.34** on p149–150 to check. Then add the expressions in 5a to the table.

at	on	in
at night *at the weekend*	on Monday	in 2008

c Tell each other what you usually do at different times. Use expressions from the table.

Self-assessment

Can you do these things in English? Circle a number on each line. 1 = I can't do this, 5 = I can do this well.

⊚ say what you do in your free time	1	2	3	4	5
⊚ say what you like and dislike	1	2	3	4	5
⊚ talk about habits and customs	1	2	3	4	5
⊚ make and respond to invitations	1	2	3	4	5
⊚ take a phone message	1	2	3	4	5
⊚ ask people to repeat and speak more slowly	1	2	3	4	5
⊚ show you understand	1	2	3	4	5

- For Wordcards, reference and saving your work → e-Portfolio
- For more practice → Self-study Pack, Unit 3

4

4.1 goals
◎ talk about past events
◎ talk about first times

Changes

Technology firts

1   Talk about the questions.

1   Do you have a mobile? What do you use it for?
2   Do you use a laptop? How big is it? What do you use it for?
3   Do you have a personal music player? Where do you use it?

2   a   Look at the pictures. Do you think these sentences are true or false?

1   Mobiles, laptops and personal music players were inventions of the 1970s.
2   They were all very expensive.

b   Read the article to check.

Three small things that changed the world

The first mobile phone
Martin Cooper, who worked for Motorola in the USA, made the first mobile phone in 1973. On April 3, he went for a walk in New York and used the new phone to call another communications company, AT&T. This was the first mobile phone call. Ten years later, in 1983, people could buy the mobile in shops – the DynaTAC 8000X. It was more than 30cm long and it cost $3,995.

The first laptop
The first real laptop was the GRID Compass. A British man, William Moggridge, made it in 1979 for GRID Systems Corporation. It was 5 kg and had a 340 kilobyte memory. It was very expensive, about $9,000, but the US government liked the small computer and bought a lot of them. NASA used a GRID Compass on the Space Shuttle in the early 1980s.

The first personal music player
A German-Brazilian, Andreas Pavel, made the Stereobelt in 1972. It had headphones and used cassettes. Pavel wanted people to have music everywhere they went. He met directors of electronics companies and they listened to the Stereobelt but said, "People don't want to wear headphones and listen to music in public." So Pavel never sold his idea, but his personal music player was the first. Sony's Walkman was the second, and people loved it.

Singular	Plural
thing year cassette	things years cassettes
university company	universities companies
person	people

Grammar reference and practice, p135

3   Read the article again and complete the notes.

The first mobile phone
Name: DynaTAC 8000X
Inventor:
Year:
Price: $3,995
Company: Motorola

The first laptop
Name:
Inventor:
Year:
Price:
Company:

The first personal music player
Name:
Inventor:
Year:

> Well, cameras are very different now. They're very small and ...

4 Mobiles, laptops and music players are very different now. What other things are different from twenty or thirty years ago? How are they different?

Talking about the past

GRAMMAR

Past simple verbs

Irregular verbs, p160

1 a Find the past forms of these verbs in the article.

regular (-ed)		irregular	
1	use _used_	7	make _made_
2	work _____	8	go _____
3	like _____	9	cost _____
4	want _____	10	have _____
5	listen _____	11	buy _____
6	love _____	12	meet _____
		13	say _____
		14	sell _____

b 🔴 **1.45** Listen to check. **P** Practise saying the past forms.

2 Complete the paragraphs with the past forms of these verbs.

> use   work   want   listen   go   cost   have   make   buy   meet

A

Moggridge ¹_____ for GRID Systems Corporation. His laptops ²_____ about \$9,000 but the American government ³_____ them and ⁴_____ them on the Space Shuttle.

B

Pavel ⁵_____ the Stereobelt in 1972. He ⁶_____ to some electronics companies and he ⁷_____ the directors. They ⁸_____ to the personal stereo but said it was a bad idea because it ⁹_____ headphones. They said no one ¹⁰_____ to listen to music with headphones.

VOCABULARY

Past time expressions

3 a 🔴 **1.46** Listen to Sang-mi. Is she good with new technology?

b 🔴 **1.46** Listen again. Answer the questions with expressions from the box.

> last week   last month   last year
> in 1993   in 1998   in 2003
> six months ago   six or seven years ago   about 25 years ago

When was the first time Sang-mi:
1 had a mobile phone?
2 sent a text message?
3 used a computer?
4 bought a CD?
5 bought music online?
6 used a digital camera?

SPEAKING

4 a Think about the first time *you* did the things in 3b. What expressions can you use with in, last and ago?

b Tell each other when you first did the things.

c Do you use the same technology now? Are you good with new technology?

Sang-mi from South Korea talks about technology in her life.

4.2 goals
- talk about past events ♻
- talk about trips

Going away

VOCABULARY

Things for a trip

1 Ask and answer the questions.

1 How often do you travel?
2 Do you go on business trips? other trips?
3 Do you like flying? driving? taking the train?

2 a Match the things on the list with 1–12 in the picture.

> Remember...
>
> keys
> sunglasses
> money
> address book
> mobile
> map and directions
> tickets
> passport
> driving licence
> toothbrush
> comb
> pen

b 🔴 **1.47** Listen to check. ℗

3 a Make a list of things you take with you when you:

- go out for an evening with friends.
- go to work, school or university.
- go away for a week.

b Compare with a partner.

4 What things do you sometimes forget when you go out or travel?

LISTENING

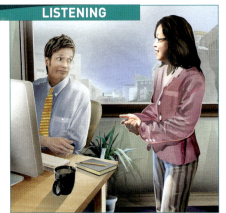

Sang-mi works for an engineering company in Seoul, Korea. She travels a lot in her job.

5 a 🔴 **1.48** Listen to Sang-mi talking to Mick, her assistant, about a business trip.

1 Where does she plan to go? 2 What day does she plan to come back?

b 🔴 **1.48** Listen again. Write down three things Mick gives Sang-mi for her trip.

6 a 🎧 **1.49** Listen to Sang-mi talking to Mr Donovan in Seattle. Write T (true) or F (false) next to each sentence.

1 Sang-mi's flight was very comfortable. ☐
2 The office wasn't very easy to find. ☐
3 Mr Donovan's directions weren't very good. ☐
4 Sang-mi enjoyed the meal in the restaurant. ☐

b 🎧 **1.50** Now listen to Sang-mi's conversation with Tom, her husband. Answer questions 1–4 again.

7 a 🎧 **1.51** Read and listen.

1 Here's your ticket.
2 Yes, the money's in the packet with the tickets.
3 Your directions were very good.
4 It was great, thank you. We had a lovely meal.
5 I have a new client!

b Which words do we usually stress, A or B?

A information words, for example nouns (*ticket*), verbs (*travel*) and adjectives (*good*)
B grammar words, for example *and*, *the*, *in*

c Practise saying the sentences with the correct stress. 🄿

Did you have a good time?

1 Match the questions and answers from Sang-mi's conversations.

1 What did you do last night?
2 What did you think of the restaurant?
3 Did you have a good journey?
4 Did you find the office OK?

a No, I didn't. You know I hate flying.
b Yes, thanks. Your directions were very good.
c I went out for dinner.
d It was great, thank you. We had a lovely meal.

2 a Complete the questions and answers in the table with **did** and **didn't**.

❓	➕
What **did** you do last night?	I went out for dinner.
	➖
_____ you have a good time?	Well, I _____ like the restaurant.
	✔️ ✖️
_____ you have a good journey?	Yes, I _____ / No, I didn't.

b 🎧 **1.52** Listen to check. 🄿

3 Put the words in order to make questions.

1 have / good / a / you / weekend / Did ?
2 did / What / do / you / at the weekend ?
3 on Saturday / you / go / did / Where ?
4 you / Did / out / go / last night ?
5 get up / What time / did / this morning / you ?
6 watch / you / this morning / Did / TV ?
7 for breakfast / What / have / you / did ?
8 go / you / to bed / last night / What time / did ?

4 a Look at the questions in 3 and think of three more questions.

b Ask and answer all the questions.

Did you have a good weekend?

Yes, I did. It was very nice.

Target activity

Talk about an important event

Onyinye was born in Nigeria but grew up in the UK. She talks about her memories of moving to Scotland when she was a child.

TASK LISTENING

1 Read about Onyinye and look at the photos. What differences between NIgeria and Scotland do you think she will talk about?

2 🔊 **1.53** Listen to Onyinye and (circle) the right words.

1 Onyinye moved when she was five / fifteen years old.
2 She says everything was difficult / different.
3 She remembers / doesn't remember the first time she saw snow.
4 She enjoyed / didn't enjoy playing in the snow.

TASK VOCABULARY

Good and bad experiences

3 Which expressions are about good experiences? Which are about bad experiences? Which can be about both?

It was really It was very	exciting interesting difficult boring strange
I had	a great time lots of fun a terrible time a lovely time a very bad time

TASK

4 a Write down one or two important events in your life. For example, when you:

• got married   • moved into a new house or flat   • went on a trip
• had a baby   • got a new job   • met an important new person
• started school / university / a new course ...

b Think about each event.

When did it happen? *last month, many years ago ...*
Where did it happen? *at work, in Tokyo, in a club ...*
What happened? *We got married, We met ...*
How was it? *It was exciting, I had a terrible time ...*

5 Ask and answer questions about each other's events.

So, when did you get married?

It was three years ago.

And where was that?

Keyword *have*

1 Put the words in the correct group.

~~breakfast~~   lunch   a bath   a cat   a meal   a break   two brothers
something to eat   a digital camera   a sandwich   a shower   a lot of friends
a nice flat   a meeting   a drink   a coffee   a lesson   a conversation

Possessions	Activities	Food and drink	Relationships
have a new car	have a party	have dinner, *breakfast*	have a big family
_____	_____	_____	_____

2 a Talk to other people in the class and find someone who:

1 has a big family.
2 has breakfast after 10 in the morning.
3 had a conversation online yesterday.
4 sometimes doesn't have a lunch break.
5 has a cat.
6 often has long meetings at work.

> Do you have a big family?

> What time do you have breakfast?

b Compare your information.

3 Talk in pairs. When was the last time you had:

1 a bad morning?
2 a long journey?
3 a great night out?
4 a terrible weekend?
5 a nice meal in a restaurant?

> I had a terrible morning on Monday.

> Why? What happened?

What happened?

Independent learning Self-study

1 a Think about these things. Answer the questions about your English studies.

reading   writing   speaking   listening
pronunciation   vocabulary   grammar

1 Which do you like working on?
2 Which don't you like?
3 Which are the most important for you?

b Compare your ideas with a partner.

2 a Match these self-study materials with pictures A–F.

1 A dictionary
2 The *English Unlimited* e-Portfolio
3 The *English Unlimited* Self-study Pack
4 The Internet
5 Books
6 Magazines in English

b Do you use these self-study materials now? Which ones would you like to try?

> I use …

> I don't use …

> I'd like to try …

4 EXPLORE Writing

1 Read the emails between two friends. Answer the questions.

1 Where did Judy go? What three things did she do there?
2 What did Mari's daughter do?
3 What's Mari's other news?

From: Judy
Sent: 30 July
To: Mari

Hi Mari,

How are you? I hope you're well. We're fine.

I enjoyed Thailand. It was my first trip so it was really exciting. The hotel and the food were wonderful. We had some bad weather but we went swimming in the sea most days. We also went on a boat trip and visited the Rose Garden. We had a lovely time.

We plan to visit my sister in Melbourne in September. What about you? Do you have any travel plans?

Love, Judy

Judy,

Hi. It's good to hear from you. Glad you enjoyed your trip to Thailand. No, we have no travel plans. Maybe in the autumn.

Our news: Life is busy, as usual. My daughter Miki moved to France last month. She got a job in a bank there and likes it. We bought a new car – a silver Toyota. It's great. I started French lessons two weeks ago. It's very difficult but the teacher and the other students are really nice.

That's all for now. Hope to hear from you soon.

Best wishes, Mari

2 a Cover the emails. Make sentences.

1	How	a from you.
2	I hope	b for now.
3	We're	c from you soon.
4	It's good to hear	d are you?
5	That's all	e you're well.
6	Hope to hear	f fine.

b Read the emails to check.

c Which sentences in 2a can you use to start an email? Which can you use to finish an email?

3 a Can you remember the past verbs?

1 It _____ my first trip.
2 The <u>hotel</u> and the <u>food</u> _____ wonderful.
3 We _____ some <u>bad</u> weather.
4 We _____ <u>swimming</u>.
5 My <u>daughter</u> _____ to France.
6 She _____ a job in a <u>bank</u>.
7 We _____ a <u>new car</u>.
8 I _____ <u>French</u> lessons.

b Check your answers in the emails.

c Look at the <u>underlined</u> words in 3a. What other words can you use?

It was my second / third trip.

4 a *Punctuation* Cover the emails. Add full stops (.), question marks (?) and CAPITAL letters to these sentences.

we also went on a boat trip and visited the rose garden we had a lovely time we plan to visit my sister in melbourne in september what about you do you have any travel plans

b Check your answers in Judy's email.

5 Plan an email to another student. Make a list of things you did recently.

6 a Write the email and give your news.

b Read each other's emails. Ask questions to find out more.

> Oh, you bought a new computer. What kind?

Review

GRAMMAR Questions and negatives

1 a Read the questions. Add them to the table.

1 What did you study at university?
2 Does your family have a pet?
3 Can you play the piano?

question word	auxiliary verb	subject	verb	
What time	did	you	get	home?

b Write three more questions to ask another student. Ask and answer the questions.

c Write the negative sentences in the table.

1 She doesn't enjoy watching TV.
2 I can't get up early in the morning.
3 My camera didn't cost a lot.

subject	auxiliary verb+n't	verb	
I	didn't	see	my family last weekend.

d Talk in pairs and write three more negative sentences that are true for both of you.

VOCABULARY Past verbs, *last* and *ago*

2 a 🔊 1.54 Listen to Andrew's story about the first time he went swimming. Answer the questions.

1 When was it?
2 Where was he?
3 Who was he with?
4 How did he feel?

b Read the script on p151 to check. Underline the past verbs.

c Think about the first time you did something.

When was it?   Who were you with?
Where was it?   How did you feel?

d Talk about your experiences. Ask questions to find out more.

> I first went to the cinema 20 years ago.

> What film was it?

CAN YOU REMEMBER? Unit 3 – Free time activities

3 a Which activities go with the highlighted verbs?

computer games	a walk	restaurants	films
family	the radio	books	shopping

1 watch TV
2 listen to music
3 go dancing
4 go to parties
5 read newspapers
6 play the drums
7 see friends
8 go for a coffee

b Talk about when you do the activities.

> I usually watch TV in the evening.

SPELLING AND SOUNDS *th*

4 a 🔊 1.55 Read and listen to these words. Notice the two different sounds.

/θ/	/ð/
things	the
thanks	these

b Add the words from this unit to the correct group.

think   that   bath   toothbrush   other

c 🔊 1.56 Spellcheck. Close your book. Listen to eight words and write them down.

d Check your spelling on p151.

NOTICE Ordinal numbers

5 a You use ordinal numbers as adjectives and for dates. Match the numbers with the words.

Pavel's personal music player was the first. (1st)
Sony's Walkman was the second. (2nd)

On April 3rd, he went for a walk in New York.
(April the third *or* the third of April)

seventh   thirty-first   ninth   twelfth
twenty-third   sixth   eighth   sixteenth
twenty-seventh   tenth   twentieth   fifth   ~~fourth~~

4th *fourth*   9th _____   20th _____
5th _____   10th _____   23rd _____
6th _____   12th _____   27th _____
7th _____   16th _____   31st _____
8th _____

b Write down three important dates for you. Ask questions about each other's dates.

> Is January 25th your birthday?

> No, it's my mother's birthday.

Self-assessment

Can you do these things in English? Circle a number on each line. 1 = I can't do this, 5 = I can do this well.

	1	2	3	4	5
talk about past events	1	2	3	4	5
talk about first times	1	2	3	4	5
talk about trips	1	2	3	4	5
talk about important events in your life	1	2	3	4	5
write a personal letter or email giving news	1	2	3	4	5

• For Wordcards, reference and saving your work → e-Portfolio
• For more practice → Self-study Pack, Unit 4

Place to place

A Province of San Luis, Argentina

B Buenos Aires, Argentina

C Paceville, Malta

D London, UK

VOCABULARY
Places

Vocabulary reference
Places, p143

1 a Find six of these things in pictures A–D.

> an airport   a beach   a bridge   a bus stop
> a farm   a forest   a hospital   a lake
> a market   a motorway   mountains
> a river   a school   the sea   a train station

b 🔘 **2.1** Listen to check. ℗

2 a How far are the things in 1a from where you are now? Talk in groups.

b Compare your ideas with other groups.

READING

3 Read the article about José Luis and Lawrence. Where do they live and work?

I live here but I work 800 kilometres away

José Luis Garcia, a father of four from Argentina, lives in a small village in the province of San Luis but works in Buenos Aires, 800 kilometres away.

"I grew up in my village and I love it here but the good jobs are in Buenos Aires," he says. "I have to travel for fourteen hours on the bus on Friday and Sunday nights but it's OK. I don't want to live in Buenos Aires. It's an exciting place but it's quite polluted and parts of it can be dangerous. The village is on the Chorrillos river, near the mountains. It's safe and quiet – a great place for my wife and kids."

There are more and more people like José Luis all over the world. Many people now live and work in very different places as cities become more expensive.

Lawrence Wood, an English businessman, works in London but lives in another country. He flies to London on Monday mornings and flies back to Malta on Thursday evenings, where his wife Samantha and two young children live in a family apartment in Paceville.

"Our new place in Malta is next to the sea, and bigger than our house in London," says Lawrence. "We have a beautiful view of the Mediterranean, it's five minutes from the kids' school and seven kilometres from the airport. The flying's OK. It's three or four hours but I only do it twice a week."

4 Read again. Answer the questions about José Luis and Lawrence.

1 How long are their journeys?
2 How many times a week do they travel?
3 When do they travel?
4 What do they have near their homes?
5 Who do they live with?
6 Why do they live and work in different places?

5 Do you know anyone like José Luis or Lawrence? Do you live near the place where you work or study?

6 a Find the opposites of the adjectives in the article.

boring / *exciting*	_____ / cheap
_____ / dangerous	ugly / _____
noisy / _____	_____ / clean

b 🔊 **2.2** Listen to check. ℗

7 a Think of five places you really like or don't like. Why do you like or dislike them?

b Listen to each other's ideas. Give your opinions about the places you know. Use the words in 6a.

I really like la Boca in Buenos Aires ...

Where I live

1 a Complete the sentences with the prepositions.

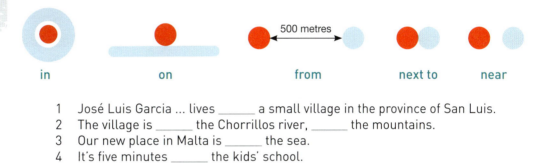

in   on   from   next to   near

1 José Luis Garcia ... lives _____ a small village in the province of San Luis.
2 The village is _____ the Chorrillos river, _____ the mountains.
3 Our new place in Malta is _____ the sea.
4 It's five minutes _____ the kids' school.

b Look at the article to check.

2 Which groups of expressions go with **in**? Which expressions go with **on**?

I live...

1 _____ a village	a town	a city	the city centre	the country
2 _____ the north / south of Argentina		the east / west of the city		
3 _____ the road to Mendoza		a river	the metro line	
4 _____ a flat	an apartment	a house		
5 _____ the ground floor		the tenth floor		

3 Write five or six sentences about where you live, work or study.

4 a Think about your answers to the questions.

1 Where do you live? Do you like it? Why? / Why not?
2 Where do you work or study? Do you like it? Why? / Why not?
3 Where would you like to live, work or study?

b Ask and answer the questions.

Where do you live?

I live in Chengdu.

Where's that?

Carole's flat

VOCABULARY

Things in the home

1 Look at the pictures of Carole's flat. What rooms can you see?

a bathroom   a bedroom   a dining room   a kitchen   a living room   a study

2 **a** Match the things with a–q in the pictures.

a bath   a computer   a cooker   a cupboard   cutlery   a drawer
a fridge   a toaster   a plant   a shelf   a sofa   a wardrobe
a washing machine   bedclothes   plates   pots and pans   towels

What's this?   A shelf.

b 🎵 **2.3** Listen to check. ℗

c Look at the pictures and test each other.

SPEAKING

3 **a** 🎵 **2.4** Listen to Carole. What's her favourite room? What does she do there?

b Read the script on p151 to check.

4 Ask and answer the questions.

1   What rooms do you have in your home?
2   What's your favourite room? Why?

House-sitting

LISTENING

1 Look at the definition and answer the questions.

1   Do you ever house-sit for friends or family? Do they house-sit for you?
2   Do you think house-sitting is a good idea? Why? / Why not?

house-sit /ˈhaʊs sɪt/ *verb* to stay in someone's home when they are away to keep it safe: *My friend always house-sits for me when I'm on holiday.*

Estrella from Spain is in the UK for an English course. Her friend Carole wants Estrella to house-sit for her.

2 🔊 **2.5** Listen to Carole and Estrella. Match parts 1–4 of their conversation with the things they talk about.

the kitchen ☐1☐   the living room ☐   the bedroom ☐   things near the flat ☐

3 a Can you remember the answers to these questions?

1   What's in the fridge?
2   Where are the extra bedclothes?
3   What's the problem with the computer?
4   How often does the big plant need water?
5   Are there any shops near the flat?
6   Is there an internet café?

b 🔊 **2.5** Listen again to check.

GRAMMAR
There is, there are

4   Look at the pictures and complete the sentences.

| microwave   yoghurts   ~~computer~~   shops   DVDs |

➕
There's a *computer* in the living room.
There's / There are a couple of [1]_____ in the fridge.
There's / There are a lot of [2]_____ .

➖
There's no [3]_____ .
There are no [4]_____ near here.

❓
Is there an internet café?
Are there any shops near here?

✔️✖️
Yes, there is. / No, there isn't.
Yes, there are. / No, there aren't.

5   Circle the correct words.

1   There are no radios / a couple of radios in the house. One's in Cheryl's room.
2   There are a lot of eggs / no eggs in the fridge, so please use them.
3   There's no / a microwave in the kitchen. It's a bit old but it's OK.
4   There are a lot of plates / a plate in this cupboard – on the top shelf.
5   There's a towel / a couple of towels in the wardrobe. They're for you.
6   There's no / a computer in the flat, but there's an internet café on the corner.
7   "Is / Are there any pens in that drawer?" "No, there isn't / aren't."
8   "Is / Are there a washing machine in here?" "Yes, there is / are."

Grammar reference and practice, p136

PRONUNCIATION
Sentence stress 2

6 a Can you remember which words are usually stressed in sentences, 1 or 2?

1   information words: nouns (*bed*), verbs (*walk*), adjectives (*big*) ...
2   grammar words: *there, is, are, in, on, the* ...

b Guess the stressed words in the sentences in 5.

There are a couple of radios in the house.

c 🔊 **2.6** Listen and read the script on p151 to check. 🅟 Practise saying the sentences.

WRITING AND SPEAKING

7 a In the sentences in 5, find:

1   nine expressions with **in**: *in the house, ...*
2   two expressions with **on**: ...

b Write five sentences about your home for a house-sitter. Use these and your own ideas.

- food and cooking   • washing clothes   • towels and bedclothes
- plants   • pets   • useful things near your home

There's a microwave in the kitchen.

8 a You're going to house-sit for a friend. Decide what questions you want to ask.

Is there a ...? Are there any ...? Where's ...? Where are ...? Can I ...?

b Talk in A/B pairs. You're both in A's home. B is the house-sitter.

c Change roles and talk again.

Vocabulary reference
Homes, p143

5.3 Target activity

Rent a room

5.3 goals
- talk about cities and neighbourhoods ♻
- talk about homes ♻
- find information in adverts for rooms

TASK READING

1 Read the adverts. Which place is best for someone who:

1 doesn't smoke and has a car?
2 doesn't like noisy places and doesn't have a car?
3 doesn't have furniture?

---

http://www.dublincapitalrentals.com

DUBLINCAPITALRENTALS.COM

A

Oxmantown Road, Dublin 7, North Dublin City

Apartment to let – €135 weekly

Single studio apartment with toilet and shower. Quiet house. Near Phoenix Park, on main bus route. Rent includes central heating.

Available: from 8 February
Contact: Max, 01 355 01 26

B

Collins Avenue West, Dublin 9, North Dublin City

Single bedroom to let – €100 weekly

Share 3-bed house with two women. Looking for males or females. Modern, non smoking. Parking included. 4.3 km from city centre.

Available: immediately
Contact: C Kerrigan, 0868 58 75 77

C

Hazelwood, Dublin 9, North Dublin City

Room to let – €600 monthly

Students only! Furnished single room on 10th floor. Own bathroom. Shared living room and kitchen. Near Dublin City University.

Available: immediately
Contact: Jess Keyes, 087 259 08 62

TASK VOCABULARY

Adverts for rooms

2 Find words or expressions in adverts A–C which mean:

A 1 money you pay to live somewhere – *rent*
2 for one person – s_____
3 system for making a place warm – c_____ h_____
B 4 men / women – m_____ / f_____
5 ready to live in – a_____
6 now, without waiting – i_____
C 7 with bed, wardrobe, chairs etc. – f_____
8 only for you – o_____
9 for you and other people – s_____

TASK LISTENING

3 **2.7** Listen to Alicja calling about one of the rooms. Which one is she interested in?

4 a Match the questions and answers.

1 **Does the room have** its own bathroom and kitchen?
2 **Is there a** washing machine?
3 **Is it near** a bus stop for the city centre?
4 **Is** heating **included** in the rent?
5 **Can I** see the room this evening?

a Yes, it's five minutes from the bus stop.
b Yes, any time after six.
c It has a bathroom with a shower, but you'll share the kitchen.
d Yes, it's in the kitchen, and there's a dishwasher.
e Yes, it's a hundred euros a week for everything, except the telephone.

b **2.7** Listen again to check.

TASK

5 a Work in A/B pairs.

A, you're interested in the apartment on Oxmantown Road.
B, you're interested in the room in Hazelwood.

Think of four questions you want to ask about the flat or apartment.

b A, phone B. B, look at p124 and answer A's questions.

c Change roles. B, phone A. A, look at p128 and answer B's questions.

Keyword *on*

1 Add the highlighted expressions to the table.

> 1 Plates and mugs and stuff are up here on the shelf. Unit 5
> 2 Please use the wardrobe on the left. Unit 5
> 3 Talking to my husband and watching something good on TV with him. Unit 3
> 4 We have two New Years, one on January 1st and Seollal, in January or February. Unit 3
> 5 And can he come on Friday? Unit 3
> 6 On Sofasurfing.com you can read people's profiles, email them and go and stay in their homes. Unit 2
> 7 You can stay on a sofa or spare bed for one or two nights. Unit 2
> 8 I'm often on planes or trains and in hotels and offices around the world. Unit 1

places	days, dates	transport	media and communication
on the second floor	on March 25th	on the bus	on the phone

2 a Add *on* to the questions.

           on

1 What did you do ∧ Friday evening?
2 How often do you go the internet?
3 What's your favourite programme TV?
4 What do you listen to the radio?
5 When was your first trip a plane?
6 Do you always work Mondays?

b Write four more questions with on.

c Ask and answer all the questions.

Across cultures Personal space

1 Read the article. How much personal space does it say people prefer:

1 in the Far East?
2 in North America and northern Europe?
3 in South America and southern Europe?
4 in Arab countries?

EDWARD T. HALL wrote that different cultures have different ideas of personal space. For example, colleagues having a conversation in East Asia can feel uncomfortable if someone stands closer than about a metre. However, in North America and northern Europe, most people feel that a metre is too far away: a distance of 50−90 cm is normal. In the south of Europe and South America, people often prefer to stand closer than this. In Arab countries, personal distance can be 30 cm or less. Of course, people sometimes need to stand very close together, for example on crowded trains and buses. When this happens, some people listen to music or read a newspaper to make a different kind of 'personal space'.

2 Match the highlighted expressions in the text with their opposites.

empty   feel comfortable   too close

3 Think about the questions. Then discuss your ideas with other students.

1 Do you think the information in the article is correct?
2 In your culture, how close do people stand when they talk to friends? colleagues? strangers?
3 Do you know any places where people have different ideas about personal space?

4 a Do the *Personal space quiz* on p124.

b Compare your answers to the quiz with other students. Can you explain your answers?

Estrella tells her friend Mike about her old flat in Barcelona.

> There was this really big crack in the ceiling …

ESTRELLA	A couple of years ago, I lived in this flat in Barcelona. It was on the third floor of an old house, big, really beautiful.
MIKE	That's great.
ESTRELLA	Yes, well, it was beautiful but it was also very old, and in my bedroom there was this really big crack in the ceiling.
MIKE	Right.
ESTRELLA	It didn't look very nice of course but I didn't really think it was dangerous.
MIKE	OK.
ESTRELLA	Anyway, everything was fine and after a couple of years I left the flat and a friend of mine went to live there.
MIKE	Right.
ESTRELLA	And then, about a month later, it was quite early in the morning I think, she was in the kitchen cooking, when she heard this amazing 'crash!' and the whole flat shook.
MIKE	Really? It was the bedroom, yeah?
ESTRELLA	Yeah, the bedroom ceiling fell down. On the bed.
MIKE	That's terrible. Was she OK?
ESTRELLA	Yes, she was fine. She was in the kitchen.
MIKE	So what did she do?
ESTRELLA	I can't really remember, I was so shocked when she told me! But I know she moved out of the flat.
MIKE	And that was your bedroom!
ESTRELLA	Yes.
MIKE	It's a good thing you moved out when you did.
ESTRELLA	Yeah, that's what I thought.

1 a Look at the photos of the building where Estrella lived in Barcelona. Would you like to live there?

b 🎧 2.8 Listen to the first part of Estrella's story.

1 Where was the crack in the ceiling?
2 What did Estrella think about it?
3 How long did Estrella live in the flat?
4 Who went to live in the flat after Estrella?

2 a What do you think happened next?

b 🎧 2.9 Listen to the rest of the story. Were you right?

c Read the script to check.

3 a Which of the highlighted expressions in the conversation does Mike use:

1 to say he understands? *OK*, …
2 to show he's surprised?
3 when Estrella tells him about something good?
4 when Estrella tells him about something bad?

b Add these expressions to the groups 1–4.

> Oh no!   That's wonderful.   That's awful.   Yeah.

c 🎧 2.10 Listen to check.

4 a Complete this conversation with expressions from 3. Then compare your ideas.

SIMON	Hi, Ana. How was the festival?
ANA	Well, the music was great.
SIMON	1 _____
ANA	But we didn't have a very good time.
SIMON	2 _____ What happened?
ANA	It rained the whole time.
SIMON	3 _____ What did you do?
ANA	Well, we couldn't camp, so we slept in the car. All four of us!
SIMON	4 _____ How long did you stay?
ANA	Not long – we left after one night!

b Practise the conversation in pairs.

5 a Think of a topic you want to talk about and plan what to say. Use these or your own ideas.

- what you did last weekend
- someone you met   • a surprising event
- a really good / bad day

b Talk about your topics together. Use expressions to show interest.

5 Look again ♻

Review

VOCABULARY Places, describing places

1 **a** Which is the odd one out in each group?

1 sea lake (forest) river
2 school mountains museum hospital
3 dangerous exciting safe clean
4 farm flat house airport

b Compare and explain your ideas. Do you agree?

Forest is the odd one out. All the others are water.

c In pairs, write three more 'odd one out' questions with words from this unit.

d Read your questions to another pair. Can they find the odd one out?

VOCABULARY Things in the home, prepositions of place

2 **a** 🎧 **2.11** Listen. Name the four rooms.

1 *bathroom* 2 ...

b Work in groups. How many things can you think of for each room in 2a? Make four lists.

1 bathroom: *shower, cupboard, shelf, ...*

c Who has the longest list for each room?

d Look at the picture of the spare room on p124 for 30 seconds only.

e What can you remember about the room? In teams, take turns to make sentences like this:

There's a plant. (= 1 point)
There's a plant *near the window*. (= 2 points)

Who can get the most points?

CAN YOU REMEMBER? Unit 4 – Past simple

3 **a** Can you remember the past simple of the verbs?

buy cost go have like listen love
make meet use want work

b Choose past simple verbs to complete the questions. Then think of two more questions.

When was the last time you:
had a holiday?
_____ a DVD?
_____ to the cinema?
_____ a cake?
_____ an old friend?

c Use the questions to start conversations.

When was the last time you had a holiday?

Six months ago, last December.

Really? Where did you go?

Extension

SPELLING AND SOUNDS Final *e*

4 **a** 🎧 **2.12** Read and listen to the words in the table. Notice the long vowel sound before final *e*.

a...e /eɪ/	i...e /aɪ/	o...e /əʊ/
plan > plane	win > wine	not > note
pl**a**ce l**a**ke	l**i**ke dr**i**ve	h**o**me ph**o**ne
s**a**fe	M**i**ke	sm**o**ke

b Add the words to the table. Practise saying them.

age invite male date life mobile note
plane postcode Rome write wrote

c 🎧 **2.13** Some common verbs with –ve have a short vowel sound. Practise saying them.

have give live love

d 🎧 **2.14** Spellcheck. Close your book. Listen to ten words and write them down.

e Check your spelling on p152.

NOTICE *away*

5 **a** What was the title of the article about José Luis and Lawrence? Put the words in order, then check on p42.

800 km   away   but   here

I   I   live   work

You can use away with distances and times.

800 km away   13 hours away

b In groups, ask and answer questions about different places, like this:

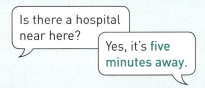

Is there a hospital near here?

Yes, it's five minutes away.

Listen to each other's answers. Do you agree?

Self-assessment

Can you do these things in English? (Circle) a number on each line. 1 = I can't do this, 5 = I can do this well.

⊚ talk about cities and neighbourhoods	1	2	3	4	5
⊚ talk about homes	1	2	3	4	5
⊚ find information in adverts for rooms	1	2	3	4	5
⊚ show interest in a conversation	1	2	3	4	5

• For Wordcards, reference and saving your work → e-Portfolio
• For more practice → Self-study Pack, Unit 5

What would you like?

Do you like shopping?

1 **a** **2.15** Listen to Andrew and Dorien talking about shopping. Do they like shopping?

b **2.15** Listen again. Who shops:

1 on the internet?
2 after work?
3 for food once a week?

2 Talk together. Find out about each other's shopping habits.

1 Do you like shopping? Why? / Why not?
2 How often do you buy books? What about magazines and music?
3 What do you enjoy buying? What don't you enjoy buying?
4 Do you use the internet for shopping? What do you usually buy?

3 **a** Match shops 1–8 with A–H on the plan of the shopping centre.

1	a bookshop	9	the toilets
2	a pharmacy	10	a lift
3	a shoe shop	11	an escalator
4	a sports shop	12	the entrance / the exit
5	a computer shop	13	the stairs
6	a music shop	14	information
7	a clothes shop	15	a cash machine / an ATM
8	a newsagent		

b Now match places 9–15 with I–O on the plan.

c **2.16** Listen to check. **P**

4 **a** Where can you go to:

1	buy boots?	5	buy a football?
2	buy maps?	6	wash your hands?
3	get money?	7	buy medicine?
4	buy trousers?	8	buy a magazine?

b What other things can you buy in each shop?

Shopping trip

LISTENING

1 **a** 🔘 **2.17** Listen to Jon shopping. Which three shops does he go to?

b 🔘 **2.17** What does he buy? Listen again to check.

VOCABULARY
Buying things

2 **a** Who asks questions 1–7? Write J (Jon) or A (the shop assistant).

1 Do you need some help? ☐
2 How many would you like? ☐
3 Is that everything? ☐
4 Do you have any street maps? ☐
5 How much is this one? ☐
6 How much are they? ☐
7 Would you like anything else? ☐

b Match questions 1–7 with these answers.

a Yes, they're over there.
b It's 5.99.
c I'd like a new tennis racket.
d They're 79.95.
e Yes, I think so.
f I'll have six, please.
g No, that's fine, thanks.

c Read the script on p152 to check.

3 Look at how much and how many in the conversations. Which expression do you use to ask about the *price* of something? Which expression do you use to ask about the *number* of things?

4 Test each other. Take turns to say the questions in 2a and remember the answers.

PRONUNCIATION
Sentence
stress 3

5 **a** 🔘 **2.18** Listen and <u>underline</u> the stressed words in these questions.

1 How much is this one?
2 How many would you like?
3 Do you have any street maps?
4 Would you like anything else?

b Which words, 1 or 2, do you usually stress at the beginning of questions?

1 words like *would*, *do*, *does*, *are*, *is*, *am* ...
2 words like *how much*, *how many*, *when*, *what*, *where*, *who* ...

c Practise saying the questions. 🅟

SPEAKING

6 **a** Work in pairs. Choose a shop and think of three things you want to buy.

b Take turns to be the shop assistant and the customer. Have a conversation.

Can I help you?

Yes, please. I'm looking for a map of Lisbon.

7 Listen to each other's conversations. Can you guess the shops?

Shopping list

6.2 goals
- talk about shopping and food
- talk about preferences and give reasons

VOCABULARY
Food

Vocabulary reference
Food, p144

> Potatoes are good for you.
>
> No, they're not.

1 Which of the foods on the shopping list do you like? Tell each other.

2 a Find one more food in the list that:

is **sweet**: bananas, …
is **good for you**: carrots, …
has a **skin**: onions, …
is **round**: watermelon, …
is good if you're **on a diet**: chicken, …
is **high in carbohydrates**: potatoes, …
is **low in carbohydrates**: lettuce, …

b Compare your ideas. Do you agree?

bananas	apples
prawns	chocolate
chicken	carrots
potatoes	cheese
butter	watermelon
onions	beef
bread	lettuce
salmon	lemon
yoghurt	rice
lamb	broccoli

READING

3 Read the article. Which of the pictures A–H does Charlie talk about?

Weird fruit and veg

Greengrocer Charlie Hicks looks at some of the unusual fruit and vegetables you can buy in supermarkets today.

Purple carrots
Did you know that people in the past didn't eat carrots because they didn't taste good? They used them for medicine, and they were white, purple, red, yellow or black. People only grew the first orange carrots about 500 years ago. Now supermarkets sell carrots with purple or yellow skins, but they're still orange inside. I don't see the point. Close your eyes and it's a carrot.

Strawmatoes
It's a silly name but I like strawmatoes. It's not a strawberry mixed with a tomato because you can't do that. It's just a different type of tomato. They're nice and sweet so you can put them in desserts.

Low-carb potatoes
These are special potatoes that are very low in carbohydrates, so they're good for you if you're on a diet. Again, what's the point? I'd rather have normal potatoes. If you don't want to eat carbohydrates, have some lettuce.

Square watermelons
I don't like these. I think they're silly. The Japanese first made square watermelons in about 2001, because round watermelons are difficult to keep in fridges. You can buy them in a few supermarkets these days. No fruit or vegetable is naturally square. I eat a lot of watermelon and I prefer a nice, round one.

Red bananas
I eat a lot of these too. I like them because they're very sweet. Go and buy some, but eat them quickly because they're only good for a few days.

4 Read the article again. Which fruit and vegetables does Charlie like? Which ones doesn't he like? Why?

VOCABULARY

Talking about preferences and giving reasons

5 **a** Cover the article. Match 1–4 with a–d.

1 **I prefer**   a **because** they're very sweet.
2 **I'd rather**   b a nice, round one.
3 I like them   c have normal potatoes.
4 I don't like these.   d **I think** they're silly.

b Check your answers in the article.

SPEAKING

6 Give your opinions about these fruit and vegetables.

> I prefer normal potatoes.

- normal potatoes / low-carb potatoes
- yellow bananas / red bananas
- tomatoes / strawmatoes
- round watermelons / square watermelons
- orange carrots / purple carrots

Some carrots

GRAMMAR

Countable and uncountable nouns

1 **a** Which food in pictures A–E can you count? These are *countable* nouns. Which can't you count? These are *uncountable* nouns.

A   B   C   D   E

b Match pictures A–E to sentences 1–5 in the table.

Countable	Uncountable
How many bananas do you want? ¹ I prefer **a** nice, round watermelon. ² I'd like **some** carrots, please. ³ I eat **a lot of** bananas.	**How much** lettuce would you like? - ⁴ Have **some** lettuce. ⁵ I eat **a lot of** watermelon.

c Make three rules.

1 You can use **many**, **a / an** and numbers with   a   countable and uncountable nouns.
2 You can use **much** with   b   countable nouns.
3 You can use **some** and **a lot of** with   c   uncountable nouns.

2 **a** Circle the correct words.

1 How many / much tomatoes would you like?
2 How many / much milk do you have in your tea?
3 Would you like a / some rice?
4 I'd like an / some apple, please.
5 I buy a lot of / a bread every week.
6 Can you buy some banana / bananas?
7 I'd like some lettuce / lettuces in my sandwich.
8 I need six tomato / tomatoes.

b 🔴 **2.19** Listen to check. **P**

Grammar reference and practice, p137

3 What food do you buy every week? What do you eat a lot of? Write five sentences.

I usually buy a chicken every week and a lot of vegetables. I eat a lot of fish.

SPEAKING

4 Ask and answer the questions.

1 What's your favourite food? What's your favourite drink? Why?
2 Do you eat and do other things at the same time? What?
3 Is there something you especially like eating in winter? in summer? What?

Target activity

Order a meal

6.3 goals
◎ talk about shopping and food ♻
◎ order a meal

TASK LISTENING

1 **Answer the questions.**

1 Do you like eating out in cafés or restaurants?
2 Where do you usually eat when you're travelling?

HOT MEALS		
Steak and chips	€8.50	
Fish with potatoes	€7.50	
Chicken with rice	€6.50	
Pasta with seafood sauce	€6.50	
Tomato and cheese pizza and salad	€6	
All hot meals are served with side salad or vegetables		

LIGHT MEALS	
Vegetable soup	€4.50
Mixed salad	€3
Green salad	€3
Hot and cold sandwiches	€4.50
Cakes	€3

HOT DRINKS	
Tea	€1.50
Coffee	€1.50

COLD DRINKS	
Fruit juice	€2
Mineral water	€1.50

Indra is travelling in Europe. She's ordering food in an airport café.

2 a **Indra is hungry but she doesn't eat meat. What can she order from the menu?**

b 🔴 **2.20** **Listen and tick (✓) the things Indra orders on the menu.**

TASK VOCABULARY

Ordering food

3 a 🔴 **2.20** **Listen again and complete Indra's sentences.**

1 Mm, I'm not sure. What's _____ ?
2 I'll _____ , thanks.
3 Thanks. Does it _____ anything?
4 Could I have some of _____ , please?
5 Can I _____ , please?
6 How _____ ?

b **Read the script on p153 to check.**

TASK

4 a **You're in the airport restaurant. Choose one of these roles.**

• You don't like vegetables, and you're very hungry.
• You're hungry, but you don't have much money.
• You're not very hungry, but you don't want to eat on the plane.
• You're thirsty, and you want a healthy snack.
• You're hungry, but you're on a low-carbohydrate diet.

b **Work in A/B pairs. A, you're the customer.**

1 Look at the menu, and decide what to have. Remember your role in 4a.
2 Order the food from B and pay for your meal.

B, you work in the restaurant.

1 Answer A's questions, and serve the food and drink.
2 Tell A how much it costs.

c **Change roles and have another conversation.**

5 **Listen to each other's conversations. Guess what the customers' roles in 4a are.**

Keyword *this, that, these, those*

1 Match sentences 1–4 with pictures A–D.

1 How much is this one?
2 They're over there, on that wall.
3 Could I try these shoes on, please?
4 Could I have some of those carrots, please?

2 a Cover the sentences and look at the pictures. Can you remember the sentences?

b In pairs, ask each other about the names of things in your classroom. Use this, that, these and those.

> What are those in English?
>
> They're windows.

3 a Match the expressions with the <u>underlined</u> words in the conversations.

That's right. No, that's fine, thanks. that's a good idea.
That's all right. / That's OK. something like that. That's great!

1 A Are you a student?
  B <u>Yes, I am. *That's right.*</u>
2 A Sorry I'm so late.
  B <u>No problem.</u>
3 A I passed my driving test this morning.
  B Really? <u>You did very well!</u>

4 A How many books do you have in your home?
  B 200, <u>maybe 150, maybe 250.</u>
5 A Do you want anything else?
  B <u>No, thank you.</u>
6 A Would you like to go for a coffee?
  B Yes, <u>I'd love to.</u>

b Test each other. Take turns to say the first lines of the conversations and give answers using the expressions with that.

Independent learning Using a dictionary

1 What kind of dictionary do you use in class? at home? at work?

- monolingual (in English)   • bilingual (your language and English)
- electronic   • CD-ROM   • internet   • mobile phone

2 a Why do *you* usually use a dictionary? Tick (✓) the list.

1 to check the spelling of a word
2 to find out what a word means
3 to find out how to say a word
4 to see an example of the word in a sentence
5 to check the kind of word (noun, adjective, verb)

b Read the dictionary entries for live. Match A–E with the reasons in 2a.

c Now answer questions 1–4 about live.

1 What kind of word is it?
2 How do you say it?
3 How many meanings does it have?
4 What words often go with it?

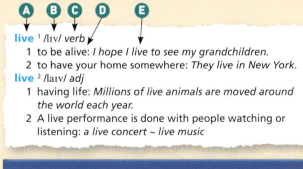

A B C D E

live ¹ /lɪv/ *verb*
  1 to be alive: *I hope I live to see my grandchildren.*
  2 to have your home somewhere: *They live in New York.*
live ² /laɪv/ *adj*
  1 having life: *Millions of live animals are moved around the world each year.*
  2 A live performance is done with people watching or listening: *a live concert ~ live music*

3 a Work in A/B pairs. A, find the word book in your dictionary or on p146. B, find the word match. Answer the questions in 2c.

b Tell each other about your words.

File Edit View Favorites Tools Help
Address

SEARCH [live]

[English > French] [French > English]

live ¹ *verb* /lɪv/
1 vivre
2 habiter > **to live together / apart** vivre ensemble / séparés

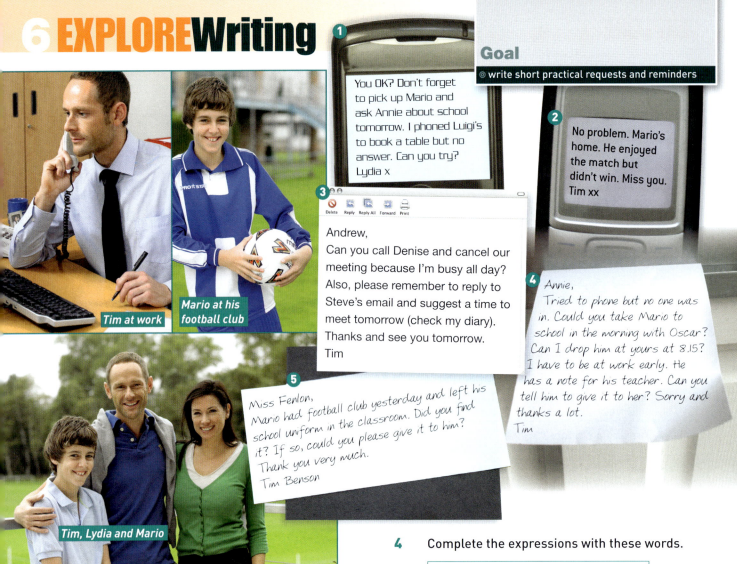

Goal
◎ write short practical requests and reminders

1. You OK? Don't forget to pick up Mario and ask Annie about school tomorrow. I phoned Luigi's to book a table but no answer. Can you try? Lydia x

2. No problem. Mario's home. He enjoyed the match but didn't win. Miss you. Tim xx

3. Andrew,
Can you call Denise and cancel our meeting because I'm busy all day? Also, please remember to reply to Steve's email and suggest a time to meet tomorrow (check my diary). Thanks and see you tomorrow.
Tim

4. Annie,
Tried to phone but no one was in. Could you take Mario to school in the morning with Oscar? Can I drop him at yours at 8.15? I have to be at work early. He has a note for his teacher. Can you tell him to give it to her? Sorry and thanks a lot.
Tim

5. Miss Fenlon,
Mario had football club yesterday and left his school uniform in the classroom. Did you find it? If so, could you please give it to him? Thank you very much.
Tim Benson

Tim at work

Mario at his football club

Tim, Lydia and Mario

1 Look at the pictures and notes. Who are they from? Who are they to?

Tim   a teacher   a neighbour
Tim's wife, Lydia   a colleague

2 Complete Tim's 'to do list' from the messages above.

To Do
• pick up **Mario** from football
• ask _____ to take Mario to school
• write note to _____ about uniform
• tell _____ to cancel meeting with Denise
• book a table at _____
• buy something for dinner

3 <u>Underline</u> requests and reminders in the notes beginning with:

1 Don't forget to ...
2 Can you ... ?
3 Could you ... ?
4 Can I ... ?
5 Please remember to ...

4 Complete the expressions with these words.

| pick up | reply | take | book | cancel |

1 _____ a meeting
2 _____ a table at a restaurant
3 _____ someone from football club
4 _____ someone to school
5 _____ to an email

5 **and, but** Read the examples. Then add and or but to sentences 1–6.

Can you call Denise and cancel our meeting?
I phoned to book a table but there was no answer.

1 Could you please cancel the meeting reply to Ahmed's email?
2 Remember to buy the chicken carrots for dinner.
3 I enjoyed the meal I didn't like the fish.
4 I wrote a nice email to Carolina she didn't reply.
5 Can you call the restaurant book a table?
6 I went to pick up Johan he wasn't there.

6 a Choose three people to write notes or text messages to. Then choose one or two things you want each person to do. You can use the ideas in 4 if you want.

• a neighbour   • your flatmate
• your husband / wife   • your boss / employee
• your friend   • your tutor

b Write three messages.

c Read each other's messages and guess who they're for.

Review

VOCABULARY Food

1 a Find the 'odd one out' in each group.

meat	chicken ~~apples~~ beef
seafood	salmon tuna yoghurt
fruit	bananas watermelon lamb *apples*
vegetables	prawns potatoes carrots
dairy products	cheese onions butter

b Add the odd words out to the correct group.

c How many more words can you think of for each group?

GRAMMAR Countable and uncountable nouns

2 a Look at the food in the market. Which things are countable? Which are uncountable?

b Choose things from the market to buy for a meal.

c Work in A/B pairs.

A, you're the customer. Ask for the food you want. B, you work at the market. Ask *how much* or *how many* A wants.

> Hello. Can I have some lamb, please?

> Yes, of course. How much would you like?

d Change roles and have another conversation.

CAN YOU REMEMBER? Unit 5 – Adverts for rooms

3 a Look again at the adverts for rooms on p46. Write an advert for a place to live in your home town.

b Look at other students' adverts. Which place would you prefer to live in? Why?

Extension

SPELLING AND SOUNDS *ou*

4 a 🔴 **2.21** Read and listen to these words. Notice the different sounds.

/aʊ/	/ɔː/	/uː/
tr**ou**sers	y**ou**r	s**ou**p

b Add these words from previous units to the correct groups.

course   round   group   accountant
fourteen   sound   bought

c 🔴 **2.22** Spellcheck. Close your book. Listen to eight words and write them down.

d Check your spelling on p153.

NOTICE Shopping expressions

5 a Complete the sentences from the shop conversations with *in* (x3), *on*, *for* or *with*.

1 They're _____ packets of three.
2 I'm looking _____ the new book by Paulo Coelho.
3 Sorry, it's not _____ at the moment.
4 Could I try these shoes _____, please?
5 Do you have them _____ a size 10?
6 Does it come _____ anything?

b Read 🔴 **2.17** and 🔴 **2.20** on p152–3 to check.

c Write a conversation in a shoe or clothes shop. Practise your conversation with another student.

> Hello. Would you like some help?

> Yes, please. I'm looking ...

Self-assessment

Can you do these things in English? Circle a number on each line. 1 = I can't do this, 5 = I can do this well.

◎ buy things in shops	1	2	3	4	5
◎ talk about shopping and food	1	2	3	4	5
◎ talk about preferences and give reasons	1	2	3	4	5
◎ order a meal	1	2	3	4	5
◎ write short practical requests and reminders	1	2	3	4	5

• For Wordcards, reference and saving your work → e-Portfolio
• For more practice → Self-study Pack, Unit 6

7

Work-life balance

What do you do?

1 a Match each picture A–E with a job and study subject.

Jobs	an accountant	a chef	a doctor	an engineer	a musician
Study subjects	catering	accounting	engineering	medicine	music

 **A**  **B**  **C**  **D**  **E**

b What other jobs and subjects do you know?

2 a What jobs and subjects are good for people who like:

1 working with their hands? with numbers? with words?
2 thinking of new ideas? finding out new things?
3 working with people? helping people?

You can find more words for jobs and study subjects on p145.

> I really like working with numbers. I love maths.

b What things in 2a do you like doing?

3 a Which sentences are about working? Which are about studying?

1 I have a **full-time** job.
2 I'm **a doctor**.
3 I work for Alstom / at home / in **an office**.
4 I'm doing a **part-time** course in catering.
5 I'm studying **languages** at Berlin University.
6 I look after **my home**.
7 I'm **unemployed**.

b Replace the highlighted expressions in 1–7 with these words to make sentences.

a bakery   a chef   full-time   history   my children   part-time   self-employed

c 🔊 **2.23** Listen to check. ℗

4 a Write five sentences about your work and studies, now and in the past.

I worked in a bookshop when I was a student.

b Give the sentences to your teacher. Listen and guess who wrote them.

Work-life balance

1 a 🔊 **2.24** Listen to some sounds from Pete's and Dagmara's lives. Can you guess:

1 what kind of work they do?   2 what they do in their free time?

b In A/B pairs, read to check your ideas. A, read about Pete. B, read about Dagmara on p125.

SO WHAT DO YOU DO ALL DAY?

Pete Chappell, 19, catering assistant, North Sea oil platform

⏱ *Work 12 hours*

I work 12 hours on, 12 hours off. Every day, I help prepare three meals – breakfast, lunch and dinner – for 300 people. I make ten different fresh salads, peel a 50kg bag of potatoes and wash up hundreds of dishes. I carry a lot of heavy boxes of food to the kitchen and it's very hot in there, so by the end of the day I'm very tired, but the time goes fast.

⏱ *Me 1 hour*

After work, I spend 45 minutes in the gym doing weight training. This helps build the strength you need for the job. Then I have a shower.

⏱ *My evenings 3 hours*

There's always a film to see in the platform's 'cinema'. This is in a small room, so only about 30 people can see a film. I go maybe twice a week. Everyone knows everyone else and it's good fun. We also spend a lot of time talking and some of the guys tell amazing stories. I'm learning a lot about life out here!

⏱ *Sleep 7–8 hours*

Last thing at night, I read in bed or chat with my room mate for around an hour. This is my time to relax. I need around seven hours' sleep a night, and I always sleep well because I'm so tired after my day's work.

Time off 2 weeks

We work on the platform for two weeks, then have two weeks off. Travelling home takes a whole day. It's great seeing my friends, but the time goes too fast. Next year, I'm planning to go to a catering college in Aberdeen and train to become a chef. I don't always want to work on an oil platform. It's too hard.

2 **a** B, read Dagmara's article again and answer the questions on p125.
A, read Pete's article again. What does he do:

1 every day?
2 twice a week?
3 before going to sleep?
4 every two weeks?

b Tell each other about Pete and Dagmara.

3 Who do you think has the best 'work-life balance', Pete or Dagmara? Why?

VOCABULARY
spend

4 **a** Add the expressions to the table.

on the bus   sleeping   driving   with friends   with my girlfriend   at home
with my husband   watching TV   at work

I	spend	45 minutes	**in** the gym / _____ / _____ / _____ .
We	spend	a lot of time	talk**ing** / _____ / _____ / _____ .
I	don't spend	time	**with** my family / _____ / _____ / _____ .

b Write three sentences about a typical day in your life. Use spend.

SPEAKING

5 🔊 **2.25** Dorien works for a publisher and likes rowing in her free time. Listen to her talking about her week. How much time does she spend:

1 working?
2 rowing?
3 sleeping?
4 with her mates (friends)?

Is she happy with her work-life balance?

6 Talk about your typical week. How much time do you spend doing different things? What would you like to do more? What would you like to do less?

> ❝ I would like to work a bit less, but who doesn't? ❞

I'm just watching the news

7.2 goals
◎ describe present activities
◎ say why you can't do things

Dean at work

Dean at home

LISTENING

1 Ask and answer the questions in pairs.

> When I'm busy, I don't enjoy …

1 How many phone calls do you usually get every day?
2 Who calls you?
3 What kind of calls do you enjoy? Which don't you enjoy?
4 How do you feel when you're busy and get a lot of calls?

2 a Look at the pictures of Dean. What kind of life do you think he has?

b 🔴 **2.26** Dean gets five telephone calls. Listen and number the calls in the order you hear them.

☐1☐ a colleague ☐ his daughter ☐ a friend
☐ a colleague in Madrid ☐ a telephone salesperson

3 a Who does he say these things to?

1 I'm sorry, but I'm working on the report for our conference.
2 Sorry, but I'm not interested.
3 I'm just watching the news.
4 I'm quite busy right now. Can we talk when I get home?
5 Sorry, but I'm in the middle of dinner.

b 🔴 **2.26** Listen again to check.

VOCABULARY

Saying you're busy

4 a Add these expressions to the right group.

studying for an exam   on the internet   busy   writing an essay
making dinner   in a meeting   tired   watching a film   not feeling well

Sorry, but I'm I'm afraid I'm Well, actually, I'm	in the middle of dinner.	+ preposition
	not interested.	+ adjective
	working on a report.	+ -ing

b Can you think of more ideas?

PRONUNCIATION

The schwa
sound 1

5 a 🔴 **2.27** You usually say grammar words like and, the, of, etc. without stress and with a schwa /ə/. These are *weak forms*. Listen and notice the words with /ə/.

CARLA Hi, Dean. This is Carla. Listen, can you talk now? I'm planning my seminar and I want your advice.

DEAN Sorry, Carla, but I'm in the middle of dinner. Can I call you later?

CARLA Yes, no problem. Talk to you later.

b Practise the conversation with the weak forms. 🅟

6 a In pairs, plan four short telephone conversations. Say why you can't do these things.

    1   Your colleague asks: *Can you drive me to the airport?*
    2   Your friend asks: *I'm going to the gym now. Do you want to come?*
    3   Your boss says: *I'd like you to work late tonight.*
    4   A salesperson says: *We're having a special sale of carpets.*

b Practise your conversations.

Talking about now

Present progressive

1 Match 1 and 2 with A and B.

    1   I **work** for a bank. (present simple)   A   Now.
    2   I**'m planning** my seminar. (present progressive)   B   All the time.

2 a Complete the sentences.

Present progressive: *be + -ing*	
➕ I**'m planning** my seminar. Dean _____ **working** on a report.	➖ He **isn't watching** the news. They _____ **working** at the moment.
❓ _____ you **feeling** OK? **Is** he **working** hard? What _____ you **doing** these days? What _____ they **studying**?	✔️❌ **Yes**, I **am**. **No**, he _____ .

Grammar reference and practice, p137

b 🔴 **2.28** Listen to check. 🅿️

3 a Work in A/B pairs. A, look at the picture on p125. B, look at the picture on p129. Write six sentences about your picture. Think about these questions.

    1   Who are the people?
    2   Where are they?
    3   What are they doing?

> There are six people in an office. A woman is talking to the others ...

b In pairs, take turns to describe your pictures to each other. How many differences can you find?

4 a Think about what you're doing these days in your work, studies or free time.

b In pairs, tell each other what you're doing.

> I'm reading a really good book by ...

> I'm repairing a motorbike.

> I'm working on a design project at work.

5 Work in new pairs. Tell each other about your first partner.

> Leo's working on a design project at work.

Target activity

Explain what you do

7.3 goals
- talk about work and studies ♻
- describe present activities ♻

TASK LISTENING

1 Find these things in the photographs.

fashion designs   a library   costumes   a theatre

Liam from Dublin, Ireland

Dmitri from St Petersburg, Russia

2 🔊 **2.29** Listen to Dmitri and Liam talking at a party.

1 Do they know each other well?
2 Who works?
3 Who studies?

3 **a** Complete the sentences with the correct name, Dmitri or Liam.

1 _____ designs and makes clothes.
2 _____'s doing a Master's degree in business administration.
3 _____ works at home.
4 _____'s working on two projects.
5 _____'s working on his dissertation right now.

b 🔊 **2.29** Listen again to check.

c Which verbs in 3a are present simple? Which are present progressive? Why?

TASK VOCABULARY

Work and studies 2

4 Add these expressions to the right groups.

> websites   to conferences   essays   my professor
> clients   emails   on business trips

design clothes / furniture / _____
work on a project / my dissertation / a few different things
have meetings with my tutor / colleagues / _____ / _____
go to classes / _____ / _____
read / write reports / _____ / _____

TASK

5 **a** Prepare to talk about your own job or course of study, or one you'd like to do. Think about answers to these questions.

- What do you do?
- Where do you work or study?
- What kind of things do you do on a usual day? Do you enjoy them?
- What are you working on now? Are you enjoying it?

b Talk together. Ask and answer the questions.

c Would you like to change jobs or courses with anyone?

Keyword *of*

Containers and quantities

1 Complete the sentences with these words.

a lot   bit   bottle   couple   lots   pair

1   I'm looking for a _____ of <u>black shoes</u>.
2   I always have a _____ of <u>water</u> <u>on my desk</u>.
3   I can speak English and a _____ of <u>French</u>.
4   There are _____ / _____ of <u>interesting shops</u> near here.
5   I had a _____ of <u>meetings</u> yesterday.

2 What other words can you use in place of the <u>underlined</u> words?

a pair of socks, a pair of trousers

Places and times

3 Which sentences are about places? Which are about times?

1   There's a beautiful park in the centre of town.
2   Gdansk is a city in the north of Poland.
3   People always phone me when I'm in the middle of dinner.
4   There's a table in the corner of my bedroom.
5   I get my salary at the end of the month.
6   I usually have one or two meetings at the start of the week.

4 Ask and answer the questions.

1   What are your favourite places in the centre of your home town? in the north of your country? in the south of your country?
2   What do you always/usually do at the start of the week? at the end of the month? at the end of the year?

Across cultures Workplaces

1 🔊 **2.30** Listen to Annabel and Geoff talking about their workplaces. Do they like where they work?

2 a Who says what? Write A (Annabel) and G (Geoff).

1   All the men **wear a suit and tie**. ☐
2   Everyone **wears casual clothes**, usually. ☐
3   The company president ... **makes all the important decisions**. ☐
4   It's important to **work as a team**. ☐
5   It's good to **have a strong leader**. ☐
6   We can go and **ask him for help**. ☐
7   Everyone can **say what they think** in meetings and things. ☐

b 🔊 **2.30** Listen again to check.

c Where would you prefer to work, Annabel's or Geoff's workplace? Why?

3 a Think about your workplace or a workplace you know. Discuss these questions.

1   What do people usually wear at work?
2   Who makes the important decisions?
3   Who do employees ask for help with problems?
4   Are people happy to say what they really think in meetings?
5   Is it an international workplace? Does this make a difference to how people work?

b Do you have experience of working anywhere very different? Talk about it.

7 EXPLORE Speaking

1 🔘 **2.31** Listen to Andrew talking about how he spends his time.

    1 How much time does he spend working, sleeping, and with his family?

    2 What would he like to do more? What would he like to do less?

2 a 🔘 **2.31** You can use these expressions to say you aren't sure. Listen again and tick (✓) the expressions Andrew uses.

    a I'm not sure.   c I don't know exactly.

    b I don't know.   d I think …

b Read the script to check.

3 Find words in the script to use when you're not sure about an exact number.

    1 I don't know, _____ 40 hours …

    2 … _____ 45.

    3 … _____ six or seven hours every day.

4 a Match the questions with the answers.

    1 How many hours do you work?

    2 How long do you sleep?

    3 How much time do you spend at home?

    4 How much time do you spend with family or friends?

    5 How much time do you spend on public transport?

    a I'm not sure. Probably about five hours a week with friends.

    b I don't know exactly. Probably six or seven hours a night.

    c Oh, about eight hours. I leave the office at about 5.30.

    d About two or three hours. The buses are slow.

    e I don't know. Maybe about 13 hours a day, and most of that is sleeping.

b 🔘 **2.32** Listen to check. ℗

5 a Work alone. Write three more questions like these for other students.

    How many people work in your company?
    How many people study in your college?
    How many people live in your city?
    How many people live in your country?
    How many people speak your language?
    How far is it from … to …?
    How old …?

b Ask and answer all the questions.

> How many people work in your company?

> I'm not sure. About 250, I think.

Andrew from Wales.

> **ANDREW** I think in a normal week I spend, I don't know, maybe 40 hours working, more than 40 hours working …
>
> **ONYINYE** That's a long time.
>
> **ANDREW** I know, 45, maybe …
>
> **ONYINYE** Okay.
>
> **ANDREW** … about 45. Erm, sleeping, erm, probably six or seven hours every day…
>
> **ONYINYE** Right.
>
> **ANDREW** Erm, I don't know exactly. But with family, I don't live with my family, so zero hours usually in an average day. Erm, alone or with friends, that's the rest of my time. So …
>
> **ONYINYE** Right.
>
> **ANDREW** I think I would like to work less. That would be nice, and sleep more.

Review

VOCABULARY Work and studies

1 **a** Match the verbs with the expressions.

> look after   work   go   write   work on
> have meetings with   study

1 _____ a project
2 _____ for a bank / at home
3 _____ a language / history
4 _____ my children / my home
5 _____ colleagues / my tutor
6 _____ on business trips / to classes
7 _____ reports / a book / my dissertation

b Choose a job from Vocabulary Reference, Jobs on p145. Write five sentences about what the person does.

c In groups, listen to each other's sentences. Guess the jobs.

GRAMMAR Present simple or present progressive

2 **a** Circle the correct words from Dmitri and Liam's conversation.

1 I design / am designing clothes.
2 At the moment I work / am working on two projects.
3 I design / am designing costumes for a theatre company.
4 I do / am doing some work for a restaurant.
5 I do / am doing a Master's degree in business administration.
6 I work on / am working on my dissertation right now.

b Read script ● 2.29 on p153 to check.

c Talk about three people you know well. What do they do? What do you think they're doing now?

> My sister works in a bank. I'm not sure what she's doing now but maybe she's having lunch.

CAN YOU REMEMBER? Unit 6 – Food

3 **a** How many food words can you remember?

meat and seafood: fish, …
vegetables: carrots, …
fruit: bananas, …
carbohydrates: rice, …
dairy products: butter, …

b What do you have at home at the moment? What do you need to buy?

> I have a lot of vegetables right now but I need to buy some rice.

Extension

SPELLING AND SOUNDS c

4 **a** ● 2.33 Read and listen to these words. Notice the two different sounds.

/k/	/s/ (c + i or e)
colleague activity subject	cinema receive twice

b Add more words from this unit to the right group. Practise saying the words.

> advice   college   doctor
> accountant   project   exercise

c ● 2.34 Spellcheck. Close your book. Listen to ten words and write them down.

d Check your spelling on p153.

NOTICE so

5 **a** Look at the sentence beginnings from the articles about Pete and Dagmara. Can you remember how they continue?

1 It's very hot in there, **so** by the end of the day …
2 This is in a small room, **so** only about …
3 I live in Zabrze and work in Bytom, **so** I spend about …
4 I get back from work quite late most days, **so** I don't …
5 But sometimes I do extra work, like writing reviews, **so** I lose …
6 I need to get up at six in the morning to get to work, **so** I'm …

b Read the articles on p59 and p125 to check.

c Complete these sentences with your own ideas.

1 I'm on a diet, so …
2 The summers here are hot, so …
3 My flat's very small, so …
4 I often work late, so …
5 There isn't much milk in the fridge, so …

d Compare your ideas with another student.

Self-assessment

Can you do these things in English? Circle a number on each line. 1 = I can't do this, 5 = I can do this well.

◎ talk about work and studies	1 2 3 4 5
◎ describe present activities	1 2 3 4 5
◎ say why you can't do things	1 2 3 4 5
◎ say you're not sure about facts and numbers	1 2 3 4 5

• For Wordcards, reference and saving your work → e-Portfolio
• For more practice → Self-study Pack, Unit 7

8

What's she like?

8.1 goals
- ⊚ talk about your family
- ⊚ describe people's personality

Family

VOCABULARY

Family

Vocabulary reference
Family, p145

1 a Which of these family members are male? Which are female? Which can be either?

> aunt brother child children cousin daughter father/dad grandfather grandmother mother/mum niece nephew parents sister son twins uncle

b 2.35 Listen to check. ℗

LISTENING

2 2.36 Listen to Onyinye talking about her family. Match questions 1–3 with parts A–C of the conversation.

1 How many people are there in your family? ☐
2 Who are you closest to? ☐
3 Where does your family live? ☐

3 a Can you complete Onyinye's sentences?

1 I have four _____ .
2 Most of my family live in _____ .
3 My uncle and aunt have _____ children, or eight children.
4 I live with my _____ , so I see her a lot of the time.
5 I see my _____ quite often.
6 The member of my family that I'm closest to is my _____ .
7 We _____ very similar and we have similar style.

b 2.36 Listen again to check.

4 Do you think Onyinye has a large family? Think about families you know.

PRONUNCIATION

The schwa
sound 2

5 a Words or syllables without stress often have a schwa /ə/ sound. Can you find six more /ə/ sounds in these expressions?

most of my family   a lot of the time
another part of England   a member of my family

b 2.37 Listen and read the script on p154 to check. ℗ Practise saying the expressions.

SPEAKING

6 a Look again at the questions in 2 and think about your own answers.

b Tell each other about your families.

Friends

READING

1 Read the information about two friends. How do you think they met?

ED SMITH was born in England in 1977, the son of the novelist and teacher Jonathan Smith. He went to Tonbridge School and Cambridge University, and is now a well-known cricketer and journalist.

Poet and novelist VIKRAM SETH was born in India in 1952. He went to schools in India and England, and studied at universities in England, the USA and China. His novels include *A Suitable Boy* and *An Equal Music*.

2 a In A/B pairs, read to check how Vikram and Ed met.
A, read Vikram's article on this page and answer questions 1–6.
B, read Ed's article on p126 and answer questions 1–6 there.

1 How old was Ed when Vikram met him?
2 Where did they meet?
3 Why did Vikram write a poem for Ed?
4 When and where did they meet for the second time?
5 What's Ed like? *He's outgoing and ...*
6 What does Vikram say about his friendship with Ed?

Ed Smith

How we met

VIKRAM SETH ON ED SMITH

I first met Ed when he was about sixteen. I was at his father's house but I don't remember much about Ed then – he was just the son of my old English teacher. His dad invited me to stay the night so I had Ed's room and I think Ed slept on the sofa. The next morning I wrote him a poem to say thank you.

Years later I was in Australia and I got a call saying, "Can I meet you? I'm Ed Smith, Jonathan Smith's son." And I said, "Of course you can." In India, if your friend's child phones up and asks if they can meet you, the answer is "yes", no question. So I couldn't say no and I'm happy I didn't. I like Ed and I admire him in many ways.

Ed is young and old at the same time. He's outgoing and adventurous and also very independent and hard-working. He wants to do his best in life. It's difficult to say why we're friends. We don't ask a lot of each other, we just enjoy our friendship. Whenever I meet him it's interesting.

Vikram Seth

b Tell each other about your articles. Find out two new things about Ed and Vikram's friendship.

VOCABULARY
Personality

3 a Tick the adjectives you know from the articles about Ed and Vikram. Then check the meanings in a dictionary or on p146.

adventurous	creative	funny	hard-working
independent	intelligent	outgoing	serious

b 🔊 **2.38** Practise saying the words. 🅟

SPEAKING

4 a Write the names of five people in your life: friends, family or colleagues. What are they like? Use personality adjectives from 3a.

b Show each other your names. Ask questions to find out about the people.

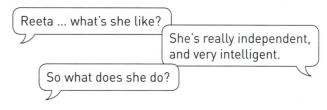

Reeta ... what's she like?

She's really independent, and very intelligent.

So what does she do?

Fashion sense

READING

1 Find these things in pictures A–C.

1 a wig
2 jewels
3 a beauty spot
4 a necklace
5 make-up

2 Read the guide to an exhibition on the history of fashion. Which part, 1 or 2, talks about:

1 fashions today?
2 fashions in the past?
3 clothes?
4 hairstyles?
5 skin?

CHANGING IMAGE

This exhibition shows how ideas of beauty and fashion change with culture and time and are often connected to money, beliefs and lifestyle.

❶ In 1624, King Louis XIII of France started wearing a wig because he was bald. Soon fashionable men in Northern Europe started wearing wigs, like the man in this picture. Under the wig, his hair is shaved or tied back.

This 18th-century woman has got a large white wig with jewels in it. She is wearing white make-up and has got a black beauty spot to show her pale skin. Pale skin was fashionable for hundreds of years in Northern Europe because it showed that you didn't work outside in the fields. Then, in 1923, fashion designer Coco Chanel came back from holiday with a tan. Suddenly a tan showed you had a lot of money and could travel to hot countries. By the 1970s, tans were very popular in Europe.

❷ Today, Indian fashions change from place to place. This woman is wearing a *sari*, the traditional dress of Indian women. The type of sari often shows a woman's age, occupation and religion and where she comes from. She's got a special necklace to show that she's married, and a red dot on her forehead, often called a *bindi*. Traditionally, the bindi also shows that someone is married, but nowadays a lot of unmarried women and even children have bindis because they are fashionable.

Most Indian women wear traditional dress but men in towns and cities in all regions of India usually wear western-style clothing, like shirts and trousers. In villages, however, many men are still more comfortable in traditional clothing.

3 Read again and answer the questions.

1 Why did people in Northern Europe want to wear wigs? have pale skin? have a tan?
2 What can a *sari* often show about the person who wears it? What about a *bindi*?
3 What's the difference between the way women and men dress in India?

SPEAKING

4 Talk in groups.

1 What current fashions do you like? What fashions do you dislike?
2 What colours and styles suit you?
3 Do you wear special clothes for special occasions? What?
4 Do you like make-up, or jewellery?
5 Do you think the things people wear show their personality? What else can they show?

5 Which of these words can you use to describe the people in the exhibition guide? What about people in your class?

She's / He's	very tall short medium height beautiful bald
She's / He's wearing	make-up jewellery glasses high heels trousers a jacket a dress
She's / He's got	long / short hair blue / brown / green eyes dark / pale skin a tan a beard a moustache glasses

6 a Think of a famous person in your country or around the world. Write a description.

He's an ...   He's very ...   He usually wears ...   He's got ...

She's a singer.
She's very beautiful.
She's got long black hair.

b Listen to each other's descriptions. Guess who the people are.

He's got a beard

1 a In these sentences, *have got* means the same as *have*.

They **have got** pale skin. = They **have** pale skin.
She **has got** a special necklace. = She **has** a special necklace.

Complete the sentences in the box with the correct form of have got.

I / you / we / they	he / she / it
1 ❓ _____ you **got** glasses? 2 ✓✗ Yes, I **have**. / No, I **haven't**. 3 ➕ They**'ve got** pale skin. 4 ➖ I _____ _____ a lot of jewellery.	5 ❓ _____ she **got** a tan? 6 ✓✗ Yes, she **has**. / No, she **hasn't**. 7 ➕ She _____ _____ a *bindi*. 8 ➖ He _____ _____ a beard or moustache.
In conversation, use the short forms: have got > 've got has got > 's got	

b 🔘 **2.39** Listen to check. ℗

2 Complete this paragraph about another picture in the exhibition. Use the correct form of **have got**.

In the mid-1800s in Northern Europe, it was important for people to look clean and tidy. In this picture of a British couple, they aren't wearing wigs and they ¹_____ plain and simple clothes. The man ²_____ short hair, a beard and a moustache. The woman ³_____ long hair, tied back, and she ⁴_____ any make-up. They ⁵_____ any jewellery.

3 Choose a picture on p126. Take turns to describe a person. Listen and guess which picture it is.

I think this is in the 1970s, probably in Europe.

4 a Look at all the pictures together. Guess where the people are from and when they lived.

b Check your ideas on p129.

Describe someone you admire

8.3 goals

◉ describe people's personality ♻
◉ describe people's appearance ♻
◉ describe relationships

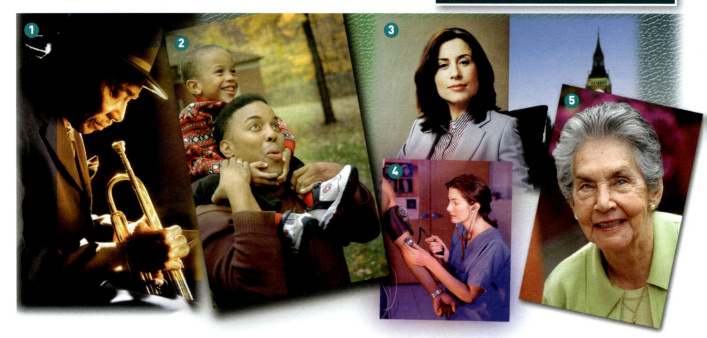

TASK LISTENING

1 🔴 2.40 Listen to Lesley talking about someone she admires. Which person in photos 1–5 does she talk about?

2 a 🔴 2.40 Listen again. What does Lesley say about Sybil? Circle the correct words.

1 She's a relative / a neighbour.
2 She loves going out / talking.
3 She wants to live alone / with her daughter.
4 She's happy / not happy with her home and her life.
5 Her father / uncle trained her for a car race.
6 She won the race and still has the silver car / cup.

b Read the script on p154 to check.

TASK VOCABULARY

Relationships

3 a Look at sentences a–i. Which is about:

1 how often you see or contact each other?
2 how close your relationship is?
3 how similar your interests are?

a We don't **see each other** a lot.
b We **get on** really **well**.
c We're interested in **the same things**.
d We can **talk about** everything **together**.
e We **get in touch** maybe twice a year.
f We like **different things**.
g We **spend** a lot of **time together**.
h We're very **close**.
i We don't **know each other** very well.

b 🔴 2.41 Listen to check. **P**

TASK

4 a Plan a short description of someone you admire. Think about these questions.

1 How did you meet?
2 What kind of relationship do you have?
3 What's he/she like?
4 What does he/she look like?
5 Why do you admire him/her?

OK, a person I really admire is my friend Kenji. I first met him at ...

b In groups, tell each other about the people. Ask some questions to find out more.

Keyword *like*

1 a Look at sentences A–D from previous units. Then add *like* to sentences 1–8.

> A I like Ed and I admire him in many ways. Unit 8
> B I'd like to go to Cuba and Ireland. Unit 2 (= want)
> C Our mum says we're like twins, just born ten years apart. Unit 8 (= are similar to)
> D Soon fashionable men ... started wearing wigs, like the man in this picture. Unit 8 (= for example)

like
1 Would you ⋀ anything from home? Unit 2
2 I don't bad news. Unit 3
3 We all play yunnori. It's chess. Unit 3
4 There are more and more people José Luis all over the world. Unit 5
5 How many would you? Unit 6
6 But sometimes I do extra work, writing reviews. Unit 7
7 I going to bed late. Unit 7
8 Men in towns and cities in all regions of India usually wear western-style clothing, shirts and trousers. Unit 8

b Are sentences 1–8 like sentences A, B, C or D?

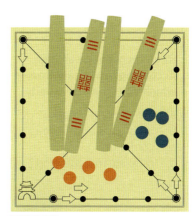

yunnori

2 a Complete the sentences with your own ideas.

1 I'm like my .... We're both ...
2 I like going ...
3 I usually wear ... , like ...
4 I'd like to buy ...

I usually wear smart clothes to work, like a jacket and tie.

b Listen to each other's sentences. Ask questions to find out more.

Independent learning Reading the phonemic script 1: consonants

1 a You can use the *Sounds of English* chart on p160 to help you with the pronunciation of new words. Match the symbols 1–8 with the sounds in these words.

adventurous /əd'ventʃ*ə*rəs/ *adj*
liking to try new or difficult things:
I'm going to be more adventurous with my cooking.

Cambridge Essential English Dictionary

short ☐ outgoing ☐ children ☐ usually ☐ brother ☐
jewellery ☐ thanks [1] yellow ☐

p	t	k	f	θ¹	s	ʃ³	tʃ⁵
b	d	g	v	ð²	z	ʒ⁴	dʒ⁶
h	l	m	n	ŋ⁷	r	j⁸	w

b ● 2.42 Listen to check.

2 Complete the pronunciation of these words. Use the consonant symbols.

big /_ɪ_/   listen /'_ɪ_ə_/   forest /'_ɒ_ɪ__/   colleague /_ɒ_iː_/ job /_ɒ_/
kitchen /'_ɪ_ɪ_/ reading /'_iː_ɪ_/ passport /_ɑː__ɔː_/ maths /_æ__/

3 a Can you read these words from units 0–8? How do you say them?

/'ælfəbet/ /bɪ'kɒz/ /nekst/ /'ɒfɪs/ /tə'geðə/

b ● 2.43 Listen to check.

4 a Find out how to say these words from unit 8. Use a dictionary, or check on p146.

necklace exhibition traditional image fashionable

b ● 2.44 Listen to check.

1 How many people in the class are:

1 first-born children?
2 middle children?
3 last-born children?
4 only children?

Goal
◉ write a web posting giving an opinion

2 Read the website article. According to Michael Grose, which children are usually:

a artistic and creative?
b ambitious and serious?
c confident?
d relaxed and outgoing?

3 Read four web postings about the article. Who agrees with Michael Grose? Who disagrees?

MEDIAWATCH

First borns 'are more ambitious'

First-born children are more ambitious than their brothers and sisters, says parenting expert Michael Grose in his new book *Why first-borns rule the world and last-borns want to change it*. First-borns are serious and hard-working and many become lawyers or doctors. He says only children are similar to first borns. They are confident but need to learn to share with other people. Middle children are relaxed and outgoing, have more friends and are good at meeting new people. Last-born children are often artistic and creative but need to learn to take responsibility. He believes a child's position in the family is connected to personality, behaviour, learning and work.

Your comments

W Chen, Hong Kong
Today, 12.25 pm
I agree with Michael Grose. Here, first-born children have to look after younger brothers and sisters so they're usually more serious. The last-borns are more creative because they can do what they want. Middle children need to be good with people because they're less popular than the 'important' first child and 'special' last child!

Erika, Ljubljana
Today, 11.46 am
I don't agree with the writer. I think the important thing is that our brothers and sisters are happy and we look after each other. We all need to learn to share and be responsible for ourselves and help other people. Your position in the family isn't important.

Sapna, Mumbai
Today, 9.15 am
Personally, I think Michael Grose is right. I was the first-born child so I had to work hard to help our family when we had problems. My younger brother didn't do anything! My parents said he was too small.

Eduardo Lopez, Mexico City
Yesterday, 10.02 pm
I'm the fifth of six children so what about me? Am I a 'middle child'? My eldest brother's a writer, I'm an architect and have my own company and my youngest sister's a very good doctor. I agree with some of Grose's ideas, but I don't think the job you get is connected to birth order. You can't become a lawyer or doctor if your family's too poor to pay for the education and training.

---

4 a *so* Cover the web page. Add **so** to the sentences below.

1 Here, first-born children have to look after younger brothers and sisters they're usually more serious.
2 I'm the fifth of six children what about me?
3 I was the first-born child I had to work hard to help our family when we had problems.

b Look at the web page to check your answers.

5 Complete the expressions for giving opinions.

1 I _____ with Michael Grose.
2 I don't agree _____ the writer.
3 I _____ the important thing is that …
4 _____ , I think Michael Grose is right.
5 I agree with some of Grose's ideas, _____ I _____ think …

6 a Write a web posting giving your opinion about the article. Use expressions from 4 and 5.

b Read other students' web postings. Do you agree with each other?

8 Look again ♻

Review

VOCABULARY Appearance

1 a Complete the profile of Nicky on a social networking website. Use **be** or **have got** in the correct form.

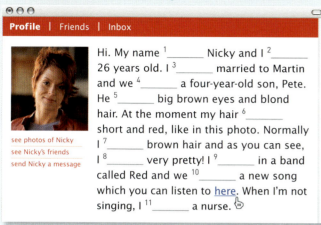

Profile | Friends | Inbox

see photos of Nicky
see Nicky's friends
send Nicky a message

Hi. My name ¹_____ Nicky and I ²_____ 26 years old. I ³_____ married to Martin and we ⁴_____ a four-year-old son, Pete. He ⁵_____ big brown eyes and blond hair. At the moment my hair ⁶_____ short and red, like in this photo. Normally I ⁷_____ brown hair and as you can see, I ⁸_____ very pretty! I ⁹_____ in a band called Red and we ¹⁰_____ a new song which you can listen to here. When I'm not singing, I ¹¹_____ a nurse.

b Write a profile of yourself for a website. Think about:

- family   • appearance   • personality
- work   • free time   • other interesting facts

c Read each other's profiles. Find out three new things about each person.

GRAMMAR *have got*

2 a Write a list of five of your favourite possessions.

my car, my iPod, my bed, my music collection ...

b Look at another student's list. Write one or two questions with **have got** about each possession.

*What kind of ... have you got? Has it got a ...?
How many ... has it got?*

c Ask and answer your questions in pairs.

CAN YOU REMEMBER? Unit 7 – Work and studies

3 a Complete the questions with the correct prepositions.

at (x2)   in   for   on (x2)   to

1 What was your favourite subject _____ school?
2 Do you work _____ an office?
3 Do you ever go _____ business trips?
4 Do you often work _____ home?
5 Who do you work _____ ?
6 What are you working _____ at the moment?
7 How often do you go _____ meetings or conferences?

b Write two more questions to ask another student about work or studies.

c Ask and answer the questions in pairs.

Extension

SPELLING AND SOUNDS *ee, ea, ie*

4 a 🔊 **2.45** Listen to these words from unit 8. Notice the different spellings of /iː/.

agr**ee**   t**ea**cher   n**ie**ce

b Work in pairs. Complete these words with **ee**, **ea** or **ie**.

1 He always wears j_ _ns.
2 How did you m_ _t?
3 I don't bel_ _ve you.
4 I don't eat m_ _t.
5 I've got thr_ _ children.
6 I love r_ _ding.
7 She's got gr_ _n eyes.
8 We don't see _ _ch other often.
9 I like working in a t_ _m.
10 Are you fr_ _ tonight?

c 🔊 **2.46** Spellcheck. Close your book. Listen to ten words and write them down.

d Check your spelling.

NOTICE *to* for giving reasons

5 a Make three sentences. Then check in the articles on p68 and p126.

1 He visited Tonbridge
2 She's got a black beauty spot
3 She's got a special necklace

a **to show** that she's married.
b **to give** a reading.
c **to show** her pale skin.

b Change the underlined words so the sentences are true for you.

1 I'm learning English to get a good job.
   I'm learning English to travel.
2 I use the internet to buy music.
3 I go to the city centre to meet my friends.
4 To keep fit, I go swimming every weekend.
5 To relax, I watch TV.

c Compare your sentences in groups.

Getting around

How do you get there?

Vijay from London, England

1 Match the questions with Vijay's answers a–e.

1 How do you get to the city centre?
2 How do you get to the shops?
3 How do you usually get to work?
4 How do you get to your closest friend's home?
5 How do you get to the airport?

a Well, it's a bit difficult to get there by public transport, so I usually walk. He rides a motorbike and that's how he gets to my place.

b Well, I usually get the underground because it's cheaper. But if it's a business trip, I get a taxi.

c I drive because I usually buy more than I can carry.

d I get the train. I hate driving on crowded roads and it's difficult to park in the centre.

e I cycle most days but if I'm late, I get the bus.

2 a Match the highlighted verbs and expressions with pictures 1–8.

b ◉ 2.47 Listen to check. ℗

c What other kinds of transport do you know? *scooter, the Metro*

3 In groups, ask and answer the questions in 1. Find out who:

1 walks the most.
2 drives the most.
3 uses public transport the most.
4 cycles the most.

A visitor in Lucknow

Vijay is visiting his cousin Meera in Lucknow, India.

1 ◉ 2.48 Listen to Vijay talking to Meera. Is this his first visit to Lucknow?

2 a ◉ 2.49 Listen again. Are these sentences true or false?

1 There are cash machines near Meera's house.
2 Vijay wants to buy an English book.
3 Universal Booksellers opens very early.
4 It takes about twenty minutes to walk to the centre of Lucknow.
5 Meera and Vijay decide to walk to the city centre.

b Read the script on p154 to check your answers.

an auto-rickshaw
or 'auto'

VOCABULARY

Getting
information

3 a Complete the questions from Meera and Vijay's conversation with these words.

| best   know   near   nearest   take   can |

Asking where something is

Is there a cash machine _____ here?

Are there any bookshops here?

Where's the _____ rickshaw stop?

Asking how to get there

What's the _____ way to get there?

_____ we walk?

Is there a bus?

Asking how far away it is

How long does it _____?

Asking when it's open

Do you _____ when it's open?

b Add these questions to the correct groups in 3a.

Is it far?   What time does it open?
Where can I buy some shoes?
How far is it?

4 a Complete the questions in the conversations.

1
A Where's the nearest bus stop?
B It's on Station Road.
A What's _____?
B Oh, you can walk.
A How _____?
B About half a kilometre.

2
A Is _____ a bank _____?
B Not really. The nearest one is next to the train station.
A Is _____?
B It's better to get the metro.
A How _____?
B About fifteen minutes.

3
A Where _____?
B The best shoe shop is Porter's.
A Is _____?
B No. It's a ten-minute walk.
A What _____?
B It opens at nine-thirty.

b 🔊 **2.49** Listen to check.

PRONUNCIATION

Sentence stress and /ə/

5 a Underline the stressed syllables in 4a, conversation 1. Then mark the schwa sounds with /ə/.

A *Where's the nearest bus stop?*

b Look at the script on p154 to check. 🅟 Practise saying the conversation in pairs.

6 Practise all the conversations in 4a, changing the highlighted words.

> Where's the nearest cinema?
> It's on 127th Street.

SPEAKING

7 a Think of three places you might need to find when you're visiting a new place. For example:

• a bank   • a post office   • a supermarket   • gift shops
• a hotel   • the tourist information office   • a train station

> Excuse me. Where's the nearest train station?
> It's on Park Street.

b You leave the building you're in now. Stop another student to ask for information.

c Ask your questions again to another student. Are the answers the same?

King of the road

READING

1 a Look at the picture of Joe Marshall.
Why do you think he rides a unicycle to work?

1 He enjoys it.
2 It's quick and safe.
3 He likes people looking at him.
4 It's good exercise.
5 It's good in traffic jams.
6 It's cheap.

b Read the article to check your ideas.

One-wheeled wonder

The unicycle is the real king of the road

Forget public transport. For computer programmer Joe Marshall, the daily journey to work across one of the most crowded cities in the world is fun. "It's like playing on the way to work," he says.

It takes Joe 50 minutes to travel the nine-mile journey across London by unicycle. That's about the same as it takes on the bus or the underground, and ten minutes quicker than by car. "Unicycles are slower than bikes," he says, "but they're the best thing in traffic jams because you can turn in a really small space. It's great exercise, too, because you can't stop moving. I have to jump up and down at traffic lights."

But aren't unicycles more dangerous than bikes? Marshall doesn't think so. "Unicycles are safer than they look and easier to ride," he says. "And drivers are more careful with me than with cyclists." Long-distance unicycling is more common than many people think. "Someone rode across America a few years ago," Marshall says. "That's the longest trip ever on a unicycle. And last year a group of people rode across Norway."

But what about all the looks you get? "You can't worry about what people think," he says. "Most of them are all right but I get a lot of comments, like 'Where's the other wheel?' A few days ago, an old lady came up to me and said, 'That's really stupid. Buy a car!'"

2 Read the article again. Who thinks unicycles are fun? dangerous? stupid?

3 What do you think of Joe's form of transport?

Comparing

GRAMMAR
Comparatives and superlatives

1 Read the second paragraph again and answer the questions.

To get across London, what's:
1 **quicker** than a unicycle?
2 **slower** than a unicycle?
3 **the best** form of transport when there's a lot of traffic?

2 a Complete the table with comparative and superlative adjectives from the article.

	comparative	superlative
1 syllable quick safe long	+er _____ _____ longer	+est the quickest the safest the _____
2 syllables or more careful crowded dangerous **2 syllables -y** easy	more ... _____ more crowded _____ +ier _____	the most ... the most careful the _____ the most dangerous +iest the easiest
irregular good bad far	better worse further	the _____ the worst the furthest

b 🔴 **2.50** Listen to check. 🅿

c What are the comparative and superlative forms of these adjectives? Use the table to help you.

cheap   busy   clean   expensive   interesting   nice   comfortable

3 Practise conversations 1–5 in pairs. Then use the adjectives in brackets to change the conversations.

1
- **A** How can I get into town?
- **B** Well, you could get a bus but it's easier to walk. (interesting, nice)

2
- **A** I think I'll get a taxi to the airport.
- **B** Well, the subway's quicker than a taxi. (cheap)

3
- **A** What's the quickest way to get to the shopping centre? (easy)
- **B** The underground. It only takes 10 minutes.

4
- **A** Do you always cycle to work?
- **B** Yes. It's the cheapest way to get there. (nice, best)

5
- **A** How do I get to the train station?
- **B** The best way is to get the bus. (quick, comfortable)

Grammar reference and practice, p138

Journeys

VOCABULARY

Prepositions of movement

1 Read Jaynie's description of a journey she likes.

"One of my favourite journeys is walking ¹from my house in Lower Sydenham ²to the shopping area in Lewisham. I go ³out of my front door and ⁴across Southend Lane and then, after a few minutes, I go ⁵down some steps and ⁶into a quiet, riverside park. It's really beautiful, with lots of trees, flowers and green grass. I walk for about forty minutes near the river and then go ⁷through Ladywell Fields, a large park. Then I go ⁸up some steps and right at the top is Bardsley's, my favourite café, and some nice shops."

2 Match the prepositions in Jaynie's description with pictures A–H.

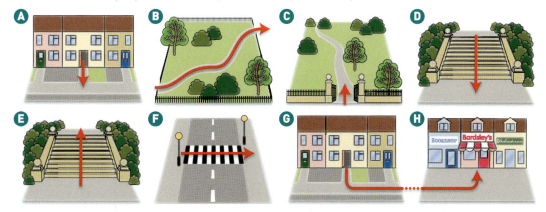

WRITING AND SPEAKING

3 Write a short description of a journey you like.

4 Listen to each other's journeys. Which do you think is the most interesting?

Target activity

Buy a ticket

9.3 goals
◎ get information in places you visit
◎ compare ways of travelling
◎ buy a travel ticket

TASK LISTENING

EXPRESS*Coach*

PASSENGER TICKET

From: London Victoria
To: Basingstoke
Type: OPEN RETURN
Service: 022
19 May
Adult: 01 Child: 00

Total Fare: £15.45

1 Vijay wants to visit a friend at his new house in Basingstoke, England. Look at his coach ticket.

1 Where's he travelling from?
2 Where's he going?
3 Is it a single or a return ticket?
4 What's the departure date?
5 How much did the ticket cost?

2 🔴 **2.51** Listen to Vijay buying his ticket. Circle the correct words.

1 He wants to go to Basingstoke today / tomorrow.
2 With a day return ticket, he comes back today / tomorrow.
3 With an open return, he can come back any time / at the weekend.
4 The day return is more expensive / cheaper.
5 The 4.15 coach is faster / slower than the 4.30 coach.

TASK VOCABULARY

Buying a ticket

3 a Match the questions and answers.

1 How much does an open return ticket cost?
2 What time does the next coach leave?
3 Is it direct?
4 How long does it take to Basingstoke?
5 Which coach do I get?
6 Where do I get it?

a The direct coach? About an hour and a half.
b Number 342.
c It leaves at 4.15, in fifteen minutes.
d To Basingstoke? It's £15.45.
e Just outside those doors. You'll see the sign.
f No. You need to change coaches once.

b 🔴 **2.51** Listen again to check.

c Use these words to make five new questions using the highlighted expressions in 3a.

bus a single train a day return Birmingham

TASK

4 a You want to buy a ticket. Work in A/B pairs. A, read your role cards on p127. B, read your role cards on p129.

b Think of questions to ask about prices, times and other travel details.

5 a Take turns to buy a ticket. Have conversation 1 first, then conversation 2.

b Change role cards and have two more conversations.

Keyword *get*

get = *receive, obtain, buy*

1 **Get** with a noun usually means *receive*, *obtain* or *buy*. Complete the sentences from previous units with these words.

job   dollars   newspapers
comments   salary   calls

> 1 I get a lot of _____, like 'Where's the other wheel?' Unit 9
> 2 How many phone _____ do you usually get every day? Unit 7
> 3 I get my _____ at the end of the month. Unit 7
> 4 Did you get some US _____ for me? Unit 4
> 5 I want to get a good _____ and learn salsa. Unit 2
> 6 Can you get some _____ ? Unit 2

2 Ask and answer the questions.

1 How many emails, texts and phone calls do you get every day?
2 How often do you get magazines or newspapers?
3 How much holiday do you get every year?
4 What presents did you get for your last birthday?
5 Where's the best place to get a good cup of coffee near you?

get = *travel, arrive*

3 In which sentences does get mean *arrive*? In which sentences does it mean *travel on*?

> 1 You can get the number forty-three bus. Unit 5
> 2 Can we talk when I get home? Unit 7
> 3 I usually get the underground because it's cheaper. Unit 9
> 4 It's a bit difficult to get there by public transport. Unit 9

4 Talk in pairs. How do you get to:

* your doctor?
* your hairdresser?
* your nearest cinema?
* your workplace?
* your favourite café or restaurant?

5 What's the first thing you do when you:

* get to work?
* get home after work?

Across cultures Transport culture

1 **a** Which cities do you think the pictures show?

b 🔘 **2.52** Listen to Marike and Hasan talking about their cities and check your ideas.

2 **a** What do Marike and Hasan say about these things?

1 the government	3 the price of petrol	5 roads
2 traffic lights	4 taxis	6 bike lanes

b 🔘 **2.52** Listen again to check.

3 Match 1–6 with a–f. Which sentences are about which cities?

1 We don't have a big
2 The city has
3 Everyone I know
4 The government thinks about
5 We're really
6 People really

a bike lanes and bike traffic lights.
b bicycles first and cars second.
c bicycle-friendly.
d car culture.
e uses a car.
f love their cars.

4 In groups, discuss the questions.

1 Do you think you live in a car culture, a bike culture, or a public transport culture?
2 Does your town or city have bike lanes? What's the public transport like?
3 What forms of transport do most people use where you live?
4 Was it different ten years ago? What about twenty years ago?
5 Do you prefer private transport or public transport? Why?
6 Do you know any places with a very different 'transport culture' from where you live?

1 ⏺ **2.53** Listen to the first part of Vijay and Sara's conversation. Answer the questions.

1 What day are they meeting?
2 What do they decide to do?

2 ⏺ **2.54** Listen to the rest of the conversation. What time will they meet, and where?

3 a Look at the highlighted expressions in the conversation. Which expressions are for:

1 checking information?
2 correcting yourself?
3 correcting other people?
4 summarising information?

b What are these expressions for? Match them with 1–4 in 3a.

> So, just to repeat, …
> Sorry, I'm wrong. It's …
> No, it's …
> Do you mean …?

4 a ⏺ **2.55** Listen. Which two words in each line have the strongest stress?

1 Was that Campie Street? P for Peter?
2 No, Cambie Street. B for Bob.
3 Sorry, not the Palace Theatre. I mean the Royal Theatre.
4 Sorry, is that 393 or 353?
5 Well, it's not next to the theatre, exactly. It's near it.

b Look at the script on p155 to check. Practise saying the sentences. ⓟ

5 a You make a mistake and want to correct it. Add a correction after the first sentence, using the word in brackets.

1 Her name's Tracey <u>Clarence</u>. (Claremont)
   No, not Clarence. I mean Claremont.
2 The meeting's at the Hotel <u>Astoria</u>. (Astor)
3 Catch the number 42 bus and get off at <u>East</u> Broadway Station. (West)
4 His number's 356<u>332</u>. (342)

b Someone makes a mistake and you correct it. What do you say?

1 Is your name spelled <u>J-a-n-i-e</u>? (J-a-y-n-i-e)
   No, it's …
2 OK, see you on <u>Thursday</u> at 6.00. (Tuesday)
3 He's on Flight AC914 from <u>Ottawa</u>. (Toronto)
4 Is your surname <u>Walton</u>? W for west? (Malton)

Goals
◎ correct yourself and other people
◎ check and summarise information

VIJAY …Well, there's a café in Cambie Street that has good food. I can't remember the name but it's really nice.

SARA [1]Was that Campie Street? [2]P for Peter?

VIJAY [3]No, Cambie Street. [4]B for Bob … you know, it's where the Palace Theatre is. [5]Sorry, not the Palace Theatre. I mean the Royal Theatre.

SARA Oh, right. I know the Royal Theatre.

VIJAY Well, the café's near the theatre. It has lots of big photos of actors on the walls.

SARA It sounds interesting. Shall we meet at eight?

VIJAY Yes, that's fine. Anyway, call me if you get lost. Do you have my mobile number?

SARA I don't know. Tell me and I'll write it down.

VIJAY OK, it's, er, 0791 334 4353.

SARA [6]Sorry, is that 393 or 353?

VIJAY [7]It's 353.

SARA [8]So, just to check, we're meeting at eight in the café next to the Royal Theatre, [9]right?

VIJAY [10]Well, it's not next to the theatre, exactly. It's near it.

SARA No problem. See you there.

6 Look at the information. In pairs, take turns to check the main points.

1 Next direct train for Basingstoke, leaves from Platform 2, 4.00

> So, just to check, the next direct train for Basingstoke leaves from Platform 2 at 4.00, right?

2 Bus number 15, goes to Central Station. Next one leaves 1.30
3 Open return ticket, £16.00, but day return ticket, £11.00
4 Party at Golden Lion Café, Fourth Avenue, near Green Park

7 a Work in pairs. A, look at the cards on p127. B, look at the cards on p129. Have two conversations.

b Change roles and repeat.

Review

GRAMMAR Comparatives

1 a Work in pairs. Write four forms of transport in a square.

b Take turns to compare them. For each comparison, draw a line. Try to use different adjectives.

OK, the bus is cheaper than a plane.

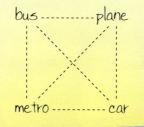

bus - - - - - - - - plane

metro - - - - - - - - car

c Choose a different topic and repeat.

- cities
- rooms
- activities
- films
- furniture
- food
- animals
- free time
- shops

GRAMMAR Superlatives

2 a Complete the sentences with the superlative form of the words.

1 What's *the best* restaurant you know? (good)
2 What's _____ way to travel? (dangerous)
3 What's _____ city you know? (crowded)
4 What's _____ car? (fast)
5 What's _____ shopping area? (busy)
6 What's _____ city to live in? (expensive)
7 What's _____ form of transport? (slow)
8 What's _____ free time activity? (boring)

b Ask and answer the questions. Express your opinions and give reasons.

I think The Golden Lion is the best restaurant.

Why?

Well, it has great food, like …

CAN YOU REMEMBER? Unit 8 – Personality adjectives

3 a Complete the personality adjectives with vowels.

_dv_nt_r__s   _nd_p_nd_nt
cr__t_v_   _nt_ll_g_nt
f_nny   _nt_r_st_ng
h_rd-w_rk_ng   s_r___s

b Think of one person for each adjective. The person can be from the past or present, someone you know or someone famous.

c Talk about the eight people in pairs.

My brother Henri is really adventurous. He likes mountain climbing and paragliding.

Extension

SPELLING AND SOUNDS Double consonants

4 a Which of these one-syllable words ends in *one* vowel + *one* consonant?

big   hot   quick   cheap

Now look at the comparative and superlative forms.

comparative	superlative
bigger, hotter *but* quicker, cheaper	biggest, hottest *but* quickest, cheapest

b How do you spell the comparative and superlative forms of these adjectives?

1 fat   3 old   5 long   7 safe
2 nice   4 wet   6 fit   8 fast

c You can use the same rule for other endings:

sun > sunny   stop > stopped
run > running   shop > shopping

d 🔲 2.56 Spellcheck. Close your book. Listen to ten words and write them down.

e Check your spelling on p155.

NOTICE *safer than it looks*

5 a Read the sentences. Do unicycles look safe or dangerous? Do many people think unicycling is common?

Unicycles are safer than they look.
Unicycling is more common than many people think.

b Complete the sentences with your own ideas.

1 … is easier than it looks.
2 … is safer than it looks.
3 … is more difficult than it looks.
4 … is more expensive than people think.
5 … is more interesting than people think.

c Compare sentences with a partner and explain your ideas.

Self-assessment

Can you do these things in English? Circle a number on each line. 1 = I can't do this, 5 = I can do this well.

get information in places you visit	1	2	3	4	5
compare ways of travelling	1	2	3	4	5
buy a travel ticket	1	2	3	4	5
correct yourself and other people	1	2	3	4	5
check and summarise information	1	2	3	4	5

• For Wordcards, reference and saving your work → e-Portfolio
• For more practice → Self-study Pack, Unit 9

Getting together

10.1 goals
- talk about films
- find information in a cinema programme
- make and respond to suggestions

World cinema

VOCABULARY

Films

1 a 🔊 **3.1** Listen to eight short extracts from films. Match each extract with a kind of film.

| a documentary   a comedy   an action film   an animated film |
| a drama   a science fiction film   a horror film   a romantic film |

> Well, *Shrek*'s an animated film ...

b Think of some examples of each kind of film.

c What kinds of film do you like? What kinds don't you like? Why?

READING

2 Read the cinema programme. What kind of film is on each day?

Monday: Annarth, an action film; Tuesday ...

THE PICTURE HOUSE
International Film Week
See a selection of great films from around the world.

ANNARTH *India, 180 min, Mon 30 Oct, 7.00 pm*
A great action film. Sameer comes home to his village after ten long years and meets his old friend Jimmy (Sunil Shetty). Then Jimmy's brother kills Bandya, a member of a local criminal gang …

FAMILY LAW *(DERECHO DE FAMILIA) Argentina, 102 min, Tue 31 Oct, 7.30 pm*
Family Law is about the difficult relationship between a father and son, both lawyers in Buenos Aires. A comedy with a serious message. Excellent music by Cesar Lerner.

THE OTHERS *Spain, 100 min, Wed 1 Nov, 2.30 pm & 7.30 pm*
It is 1945, and Grace Stewart (Nicole Kidman) and her children live alone in a huge house. Strange things start to happen, and one of the children sees people no one else can see. Are Grace and her children really alone?

2 DAYS IN PARIS *France, 96 min, Thu 2 Nov, 7.30 pm*
Written, directed by and starring Julie Delpy, this is an intelligent romantic comedy about a French photographer and her American boyfriend on a two-day visit to her family in Paris. It also stars Delpy's real-life parents and her cat, Max.

YEELEN *Mali, 105 min, Fri 3 Nov, 8.00 pm*
The classic 1987 drama by Malian film-maker Souleymane Cissé. Yeelen is set in the 13th century and tells the story of Niankoro, a young man who uses magic to fight his father, a dangerous magician.

🎬 **FAMILY FILM** 🎬

RATATOUILLE *USA, 111 min, Saturday 4 Nov, 11.30 am, 3.00 pm & 6.30 pm*
Rémy, a rat, wants to be a chef. He comes to Paris and makes friends with Alfredo Linguini, a young man who works in the kitchen of a famous restaurant. Animated fun for all the family.

Box Office The Picture House, Hay Street, Perth   **Ticket Prices** Adults $13.50. Over 60s / students / under 15s $9.00

3 Read the programme again. What films can you see if you:

1 like serious films?
2 want to have a good laugh?
3 are busy in the evening?
4 want to take your children to the cinema?
5 enjoy long films?

Choosing a film

Jon and Mia from Perth, Australia

VOCABULARY

Suggestions

1 a Jon and Mia decide to go to the cinema. Complete their conversation.

> Why don't we ...   Would you like to ...   OK.   We could ...   I don't know.

MIA Some of these films look quite interesting.
JON Yeah, that's true. _____ go and see one some time this week?
MIA Yeah, _____. _____ see *Family Law*? I heard it's really good.
JON Hm, _____. It sounds a bit boring. _____ see *The Others*.
MIA Well, I don't usually like horror films, but that one sounds good.

b 🔊 **3.2** Listen to check.

2 a Put the expressions from 1a in the correct groups.

Making suggestions *Why don't we ...*	Saying yes	Saying no / not sure

b Add these expressions to the correct groups in 2a.

> Good idea.   Fine with me.   I don't really want to.   Let's ...
> That sounds good.   I'm not sure.   No, thanks.

3 Practise the conversation in 1a with different expressions. Take turns to be Jon and Mia.

SPEAKING

4 a You're going to The Picture House with a group of friends. Choose two films from the programme you'd like to see, and two films you don't want to see.

b In groups, decide which film to see together.

5 In pairs, ask and answer the questions.

1 How often do you watch films at the cinema?
2 When was the last time you saw a film? What was it? Did you enjoy it?
3 Do you ever watch films more than once? Give examples.
4 Do you like watching films from other countries? Give examples.

What are you doing tonight?

10.2 goals
◎ make and respond to suggestions ♻
◎ make arrangements to meet

READING

1 a Look at the picture and read the first email. Can you guess how Kimiko answers Jon's questions?

Kimiko from Perth

Hi Kimiko,
How's your day going? And what are you doing tonight? I'm going to the cinema with Mia. Want to come with us?
Jon.

Delete Reply Reply All Forward Print

Hello Jon,
Not a good day at the office – I'm having lots of problems. Yes, let's go out tonight. Text me – I'm in a meeting this afternoon.
K.

b Read Kimiko's reply. Check your ideas.

2 Read the texts Jon and Kimiko send later. Put them in order from 1–6.

Sorry, stuck in traffic. Call me after film.

Hi. Going to see *The Others* at Picture House. Having coffee first 6.15. Can you come?

7.30. Meet 7.00 outside cinema?

Can't come for coffee. Stuck at work until 6.30. What time's the film?

Where are you? We're waiting for you!

7.00, OK.

Jon and Mia

3 Who:

1 invited Kimiko to the cinema?
2 had coffee together?
3 had a difficult day?
4 saw the film?
5 couldn't get to the cinema on time?

LISTENING

4 🔊 3.3 Listen to Jon and Kimiko's phone call after the film. Can they meet this week?

5 🔊 3.3 Listen again.

1 Where are Jon and Mia going now?
2 Does Kimiko want to go with them? Why? / Why not?
3 What are Kimiko's plans for Friday? What are her plans for Monday?

Arrangements

GRAMMAR

Present progressive for future arrangements

Meet Kimiko at airport MONDAY 11PM

Tues.
shopping: chicken, mushrooms, cream, fruit.
8.00 - cook dinner for Mia.

Meet Mia Thursday lunchtime, 1pm. Get present for Gillian.

Silver Court Dental Practice

Name: Jon Ellis
Date & time: Thursday 9th Nov., 4pm
Dentist: Dr Vernon

Friday: Gillian's birthday party, Royston cafe (from 6pm)

Grammar reference and practice, p139

1 Look at sentences 1–8 in the table and answer the questions.

a Which **two** sentences are about now?
b Which **six** sentences are about future arrangements?

> ❓
> ¹ What **are you doing** tonight?
>
> ➕
> ² **I'm going** to the cinema with Mia.
> ³ **We're having** coffee first at 6.15. Can you come?
> ⁴ Where are you? **We're waiting** for you!
> ⁵ **We're walking** to Delmonico's now for a pizza.
> ⁶ **I'm flying** to Singapore this Friday.
> ⁷ **I'm coming** back on Monday night.
>
> ➖
> ⁸ **You're not going** for work, I hope.

2 Look at the underlined future time expressions in the table. Add these expressions to the correct groups. Some can go in more than one group.

12 March	year	tomorrow	11 o'clock	December	evening

-	**at**	**on**	**this**	**next**	**in**
tonight	6.15	Monday night	Friday		

3 **a** Work in A/B pairs. A, look at Jon's arrangements for next week on the left. B, look at Kimiko's diary on p123.

b Tell each other about Jon's and Kimiko's arrangements. How many times will Jon and Kimiko see each other next week?

> Jon's meeting Kimiko at the airport on Monday at 11 pm.

PRONUNCIATION

Compound nouns

4 **a** 🔊 **3.4** Listen to these compound nouns (nouns made from two different nouns). Notice that the stress is on the *first* word. ℗ Practise saying the words.

a phone call   a sales meeting   football practice   a birthday party

b Underline the stress in these compound nouns.

a coffee break   a yoga class   a guitar lesson   a tennis match   a cinema programme

c 🔊 **3.5** Listen to check. ℗ Practise saying the compound nouns.

SPEAKING

5 **a** You want to go for a coffee with friends. Write down four times when you're free.

1 tomorrow, 11am
2 Monday, 8pm
3 Tuesday, 2pm
4 Friday evening

> What are you doing tomorrow lunchtime?

> I think I'm free.

> I'm not, sorry. I'm going to the shops.

b In groups, arrange a time to meet.

c When are you meeting? Tell the class.

Target activity

Arrange a film night

10.3 goals

◉ talk about films ♻
◉ make and respond to suggestions ♻
◉ make arrangements to meet ♻

Reeta Jane Matthew

TASK LISTENING

1 How often do you watch films at home? When? Who with?

2 ▶ **3.6** Listen to Jane, Reeta and Matthew arranging a film night at Reeta's home.

1 When are they going to meet?
2 Tick (✓) the films they talk about.
   Pan's Labyrinth ☐ Casablanca ☐ The Bourne Supremacy ☐ Yeelen ☐
3 Which film do they decide to watch?

TASK VOCABULARY

Talking about films

3 a Match 1–4 with a–d.

1 What's it like?
2 Who's in it?
3 What's it about?
4 It's about this young man with magical powers.

a It's about a young girl and it's set in Spain … in the 1940s, I think.
b That sounds interesting.
c Matt Damon.
d Well, it's an action film, I guess.

b Read the script on p155 to check.

c In pairs, test each other. Take turns to say 1–4 and remember a–d.

TASK

4 a You want to watch a film at home with some friends. Think about:

• when you're free this week.
• two films you'd like to see.
• how to describe the films.

b Talk in groups. Decide:

• when to meet.
• where to meet.
• which film to watch.

c Tell other groups what you decided.

Keyword *about*

1 Which sentences use about with a topic? Which use it with a number? <u>Underline</u> the topics and numbers.

> 1   *Family Law* is **about** the difficult relationship between a father and son. **Unit 10**
> 2   I've got an idea. I read **about** this film called *Yeelen*. **Unit 10**
> 3   I first met Ed when he was **about** sixteen. **Unit 8**
> 4   So, Min, what do you think **about** <u>New Year</u>? **Unit 3**

about with topics

2 a Match 1–7 with a–g to make conversations.

1 "You look stressed. Is there a problem?"	a "Hmm. I don't know. **I'll think about it**."
2 "Can I see the room this evening?"	b "Yes, there is! **Do you know anything about** computers?"
3 "Do you know that Dave's getting married?"	c "Sure. **How about** six thirty?"
4 "Don't forget the party on Friday."	d "It was terrible! **I don't want to talk about it**."
5 "Hello, can I help you?"	e "What party? **No one told me about that**."
6 "How was your day?"	f "Yes, please. **I have a question about** my ticket."
7 "So, do you want to buy these jeans?"	g "Yes, **I heard about that**."

b 🔊 **3.7** Listen to check. Practise the conversations.

c Test each other in pairs. Take turns to say 1–7 and remember a–g.

about with numbers

3 a Talk in teams. Guess the answers. Use about.

1   When did Yuri Gagarin go into space?
2   How many teeth does an adult elephant have?
3   When were the first modern Olympics?
4   How high is Mount Everest?
5   How many people are there in a cricket team?
6   How long is the Great Wall of China?
7   How long does it take for light to travel from the sun to the earth?
8   When did people start writing?

b 🔊 **3.8** Listen to check. Which team has the best guesses?

> Gagarin went into space in **about** 1960, I think.

> Was it 1962?

Independent learning Reading the phonemic script 2: vowels

1 a You can use the *Sounds of English* chart on p160 to help you with the pronunciation of new words, for example when you find them in a dictionary. Match symbols 1–12 with the sounds in these words.

¹æ	²ɑː	³e	⁴ɜː	⁵ɪ	⁶iː	⁷ɒ	⁸ɔː	⁹ʌ	¹⁰ʊ	¹¹uː	¹²ə

bl**a**ck **1**   b**u**t ☐   f**i**rst ☐   l**o**t ☐   g**oo**d ☐   h**e**lp ☐
p**a**rk ☐   f**oo**d ☐   s**i**st**er** ☐   s**i**x ☐   m**ee**t ☐   sp**or**t ☐

documentary /ˌdɒkjəˈmentˀri/ *noun*
(*plural* **documentaries**)
a film or television programme that gives facts about a real situation

Cambridge Essential English Dictionary

b 🔊 **3.9** Listen to check.

2 a Can you read these words from units 8–10? How do we say them?

1   /ˈhɒrə/   4   /ˈbjuːtɪfəl/
2   /ˈmɔːnɪŋ/   5   /ˈmʌðə/
3   /ˈkɒmədiː/   6   /məˈstɑːʃ/

b 🔊 **3.10** Listen to check.

3 a Match the words with the same vowel sound.

b Use a dictionary to check your answers, or look at the key on p127.

boot   car   floor   fruit   full   good   got   learn   love   met   niece   short   speak   start   sun   wash   went   worse

10 EXPLOREWriting

Goals
⊚ write and reply to an invitation
⊚ write a thank-you note

1 In pairs, ask and answer the questions.

1 When was the last time you got together with old friends? What did you do?
2 How do you usually invite people to your home: by email, phone, text, or face to face?

2 a Put emails A–C in order.

A
Thank you so much for Saturday. We had a fantastic time and it was great to see Paul and the kids again. You organised everything so well – I hope you had a good time too! I must invite you and Paul to dinner soon.

Love, Ana.

B
This is to invite you (and your families) to my 30th birthday party on December 15th. I'd like to book Toni's restaurant for the afternoon and evening (have a look at their website). Please let me know if you can come (and how many) so I can book it as soon as possible. I'll ask you again nearer the time. I hope you can come.

Claudia. X

C
Sounds absolutely fantastic, Claudia. Toni's looks lovely. We'd love to come.

Ana.

b Put text messages D–H in order.

D

Friday's good. See you then.
C

E
Lovely evening. Thanks Ana. Let's get together again soon.
Cx

F

Can you and Paul come to dinner this Saturday (17th)? About 8?
Ana

G

Going away (rock climbing!), but free on Friday evening, 23rd. OK?
Ana

H
Sorry, Paul's away this weekend. Are you free next weekend?
Claudia

3 Read all the emails and text messages again. Which are invitations? replies? thank-you notes?

4 a Cover the emails and text messages. Match the beginnings and endings of the invitations.

1 This is to invite you to   a if you can come.
2 I'd like to   b next weekend?
3 Please let me know   c this Saturday?
4 I hope you   d book Toni's restaurant.
5 Are you free   e my 30th birthday party.
6 Can you and Jon come to dinner   f can come.

b Look at the invitations to check. Can you think of more ways to complete 1–6?

This is to invite you to my flat for dinner.

5 Complete these expressions from the replies and thank-you notes.

1 We had a …   3 Sounds …   5 Friday's …   7 Let's get together …
2 It was great …   4 We'd love …   6 Lovely …   8 Sorry, …

6 ***Ellipsis*** In emails and texts, we often don't use words like *I*, *we*, *be*, *do*, *that*, *the*, etc.

~~That was a~~ Lovely evening.
~~We're~~ Going away (rock climbing!) but ~~we're~~ free on Friday evening.

Make these sentences shorter for an email or text. Cross out the words you don't need.

1 That sounds absolutely fantastic.
2 I'm very busy this weekend. I can't come to the picnic. I hope you have a good time.
3 It was lovely to see you. Do you want to meet again next weekend?
4 We're going to see *The Others* at the Picture House. We're having coffee first.

7 a Choose an event and write an email invitation.

• a birthday party   • a graduation party   • a picnic   • something else

b Read another student's invitation. Write a reply.

c Imagine it's after the event. Write a short note to say thank you.

Review

VOCABULARY Suggestions

1 a 🎧 **3.11** Listen to Suzi and Michelle. What do they want to do?

b 🎧 **3.11** Listen two more times. Write down as many words as you can.

SUZI	So Michelle, _____ _____ _____ _____ _____ _____ tomorrow?
MICHELLE	Hm, not really. _____ _____ _____ _____ _____ Heidelberg?
SUZI	That _____ _____ . _____ _____ _____ some shopping.
MICHELLE	Hm, _____ _____ _____ . _____ _____ _____ the castle.
SUZI	All right. _____ _____ _____ _____ _____ a coat.

c Work together to complete the conversation. Then read the script on p156 to check.

d Find expressions in the conversations for:
  • making suggestions
  • saying yes   • saying no

e You're going to plan a day trip to another town or city. Think about:
  • where to go   • what to do
  • how to get there   • when to go

f Plan your trip in groups. Then tell the class what you decided.

GRAMMAR Present progressive for arrangements

2 a What questions can you ask about this sentence?

I'm going to Brno this weekend.
Why ...? Who ...? Where ...? How long ...? How ...?

b Take a piece of paper and:
  1 Write four of your arrangements for this month. Exchange papers with a partner.
  2 Write one or two questions about each of your partner's sentences. Give back the paper.
  3 Write answers to the questions.

c Put away the paper and tell a group about your partner's arrangements. Can you remember all the information correctly?

CAN YOU REMEMBER? Unit 9 – Getting information

3 a Put the words in order to make questions.
  1 here / Are / there / any bookshops / near ?
  2 get there / to / What's / way / the best ?
  3 long / it / take / does / How ?
  4 What / it / open / does / time ?

b Ask and answer the questions.

c Change the word *bookshops* in 1 and have two more conversations.

Extension

SPELLING AND SOUNDS g

4 a 🎧 **3.12** We can say g in two ways. Read and listen to the words in the table.

/g/	/dʒ/ g + e, i, y
go again big good great grammar	arrangements page magic religion gym Egypt

b Add these words to the correct group.

agree colleague college dangerous engineer green group message technology

c Some common words don't follow the rule. Practise saying them.

begin get forget girl give together

d 🎧 **3.13** Spellcheck. Close your book. Listen and write twelve words. Check your spelling on p156.

NOTICE sounds + adjective

5 a Find the conversations from this unit (on p156) and complete the expressions with sounds.

  1 MIA   Would you like to see *Family Law*?
    JON   It sounds a bit _____ .
  2 JON   We could see *The Others*.
    MIA   Well, I don't usually like horror films, but that one sounds _____ .
  3 REETA Would you like to come over to my place and watch a film?
    JANE   Yeah, that sounds _____ , Reeta.
  4 JANE   It's about this young man with magical powers.
    MATTHEW That sounds _____ .

b Which expressions are positive? Which are negative? Think of more adjectives you can use.

c In groups, make a list of films which are on at the cinema at the moment, or are coming soon.
  1 Tell each other what you know about the films.
  2 Guess what the films are like. Use sounds.

Self-assessment

Can you do these things in English? Circle a number on each line. 1 = I can't do this, 5 = I can do this well.

◉ talk about films	1	2	3	4	5
◉ find information in a cinema programme	1	2	3	4	5
◉ make and respond to suggestions	1	2	3	4	5
◉ make arrangements to meet	1	2	3	4	5
◉ write and reply to an invitation	1	2	3	4	5
◉ write a thank-you note	1	2	3	4	5

• For Wordcards, reference and saving your work → e-Portfolio
• For more practice → Self-study Pack, Unit 10

Journeys

At the airport

VOCABULARY

Airports

1 Do you ever travel by plane? Do you like flying? Why? / Why not?

2 a Match these places with pictures A–F.

> boarding gate   check-in   security
> baggage collection   customs   passport control

b What parts of the airport do you have to go through before you fly? What about when you arrive? Put the places in order.

> OK, you go to the check-in, then ...

3 a Look at Belinda's boarding pass.

  1 Where's she travelling to?
  2 What airline is she using?
  3 What time's her flight?

b Find Belinda's flight on the board.

  1 Is her flight on time?
  2 What time's it leaving?
  3 What gate's it leaving from?

Belinda from Spain

Destination			Departure			
Code	City	Flight	Scheduled	Actual	Gate	Status
DUB	Dublin	EI 153	11:50 AM	-	-	Cancelled
FCO	Rome	BA 548	12:20 PM	12:20 PM	4	Boarding
BOM	Mumbai	AI 119	12:20 PM	12:40 PM	11	Delayed
KUL	Kuala Lumpur	MH 329	12:25 PM	12:25 PM	21	On time
NRT	Tokyo	BA 0059	12:35 PM	12:45 PM	20	Delayed
YYC	Calgary	AC 851	12:45 PM	12:45 PM	18	On time

Getting a flight

1 a **3.14** Listen to Belinda checking in. What does she give the person?

   b **3.14** Listen again. Complete 1–5.

   1 Can I see your _____ , please?
   2 Do you have any _____ luggage?
   3 Did you pack your _____ yourself?
   4 Are you carrying _____ for anyone else?
   5 Boarding is at _____ from _____ 20.

   c Match 1–5 with Belinda's answers a–e.

   a Here you are.   b Thanks.   c Just this bag.   d Yes, I did.   e No.

   d **3.15** Listen to the sentences in b and give answers.

2 a **3.16** Listen to Belinda. Where is she now?

   b **3.16** Listen again. Tick (✓) every time you hear these things.

   | bag | belt | keys | laptop | shoes | wallet | mobile |

   c Complete the conversation with words from 2b. Write them in the gaps on the right.

OFFICER 1	1?	1 _____
BELINDA	I've put them in my 2.	2 _____
OFFICER 1	OK. Is there a 3 in here?	3 _____
BELINDA	No.	
OFFICER 1	And your 4, please.	4 _____
BELINDA	Oh, OK.	
OFFICER 2	Come forward, please. 5? 6?	5 _____ 6 _____
BELINDA	Uh, they're in my 7.	7 _____
OFFICER 2	8?	8 _____
BELINDA	That too.	
OFFICER 2	Are you wearing a 9?	9 _____
BELINDA	Oh yes, sorry.	
OFFICER 2	That's fine, thank you.	
BELINDA	Thanks.	
OFFICER 3	Could you open your 10, please?	10 _____
BELINDA	OK.	
OFFICER 3	That's fine. Enjoy your trip.	
BELINDA	Thanks.	

   d **3.16** Listen again to check.

3 a **3.17** Listen to each of these expressions, said twice. Which one sounds more polite, A or B? Why?

   1 Oh yes, sorry. A / B
   2 That's fine, thank you. A / B
   3 Thanks. A / B
   4 That's fine. Enjoy your trip. A / B

   b Practise saying the expressions politely. **P**

4 a In pairs, practise Belinda's conversation at security.

   b Cover the words 1–10 and practise again.

5 a Work in groups of three. You're at an airport. Look at your role cards and complete them.

   A, you work at **check-in**. Look on p123.
   B, you work for **airport security**. Look on p128.
   C, you're a **passenger**. Look on p130.

   b Have two conversations: one at check-in, and the other at security.

6 Change roles and have the conversations again.

A traveller's tale

1 a Match the pictures and the words.

a bear   a snake   a pigeon   a spider   a rat   a bat

b Do you have these animals in your country? How do you feel about them?

2 Read the story. What was Belinda frightened of? What was the receptionist frightened of?

TRAVELLERS' TALES

Help!

Belinda Ramos works for a large IT company and travels whenever she can. She's visited Belgium, Lebanon, England, France, Germany, Japan and Mexico. She'd love to go to Africa one day.

I was in the south of Japan at the time. One morning, I woke up in my hotel room, opened my eyes and looked around my room. The first thing I saw was a huge spider on the wall. It was about ten centimetres across. I hate spiders! I ran out of the room to the reception desk and shouted for help. "Kuma!" I remembered from my Japanese lessons that 'kuma' means 'spider'.
"Kuma?" the receptionist said.
"Kuma!" I shouted again. "In my room!"

"Kuma?"
"KUMA!!!"
The receptionist looked really frightened. She picked up the phone and said something quickly in Japanese. About a minute later – and I'm not joking – a policeman with a gun ran into the hotel and went into my room. For a minute there was silence but then we heard a laugh, so we went in. When the receptionist saw the spider on the wall, she started laughing too.
In Japanese, spider is 'kumo'. 'Kuma' means 'bear'.

3 Read the story again. Who:

1 took Japanese lessons?
2 shouted 'Kuma'?
3 made a phone call?

4 looked frightened?
5 went into Belinda's room first?
6 laughed?

4 What words in your language do learners sometimes mix up?

5 Look at the examples from Belinda's story and (circle) the correct form in the grammar box.

> Use *a / the /* no article when you talk about a person or thing for the first time:
> The first thing I saw was **a** huge spider on the wall.

> Use *a / the /* no article when the reader or listener knows *which* thing:
> When the receptionist saw **the spider** on the wall, she started laughing too.

> Use *a / the /* no article when you talk about things in general.
> I hate **spiders**!

6 You use **the** in a lot of fixed expressions and before some adjectives. Add expressions 1–3 from Belinda's story to the table on p93.

I was ¹in the south of Japan ²at the time.
³The first thing I saw was a huge spider on the wall.

Time expressions	Place expressions	Before some adjectives
in the morning	in the middle of ...	the best, the worst, the most
at the weekend	in the corner of ...	the same
at the moment	at the end of ...	the last, the next

7 a Complete the sentences with a, an, the, or no article.

1 When was _the_ last time you saw a spider?
2 Do you like _____ pasta?
3 Is there _____ art gallery near here?
4 Can you open _____ door, please?
5 Have you got _____ pen I can use?
6 What's _____ name of the person next to you?
7 Do you like _____ cats?
8 What's _____ easiest language to learn?

b 🎧 **3.18** Listen to check. How do you usually say a, an and the? How do you say the in sentence 8? Why? ❷

Grammar reference and practice, p140

c Write two or three more questions with expressions from the table in 6.

d Ask and answer all the questions.

Telling a story

VOCABULARY

Storytelling expressions

1 a Which expressions in the box:

1 start a story?   2 link a story?   3 end a story?

> Later, ...   It was two in the morning.   It was really strange.
> ... and then ...   I was with some friends.   In the end, ...   After that, ...
> I had a great time.   Well, this was a few weeks ago.

b 🎧 **3.19** Listen to check. ❷

SPEAKING

2 a Work in A/B pairs. A, look at these pictures and read Holly's story here. B, look at the pictures and read Jack's story on p128.

> in my car in the Rocky Mountains in Canada ➜ lots of mountains and trees ➜ see a family of bears, mother and two cubs ➜ stop car ➜ get out and take photos ➜ cubs look frightened, mother gets angry ➜ walks towards me ➜ can't open car door ...

b Think of a good ending for Holly's story. Imagine you are Holly. Prepare to tell the story. Think about:

- the past simple of the verbs (see > saw).
- where to use the (stop the car; the mother bear).
- where to use storytelling expressions. (Later, ...)

> Well, this was a couple of years ago. I was in my car in the Rocky Mountains ...

3 Work in A/B pairs. Tell your stories.

4 🎧 **3.20** Now listen to both stories. Are the endings like yours?

Describe a journey

11.3 goals
- tell a story ♻
- talk about a journey

TASK LISTENING

1 a Look at the pictures of Sam's journey. What do you think happened?

b 🔊 **3.21** Listen to the story of Sam's journey. Were you right?

TASK VOCABULARY

Talking about a journey

2 a Circle the correct words in the sentences about Sam's journey.

1 He drove to / flew to the airport.
2 The flight was delayed / cancelled.
3 He booked a seat on another flight / a room in a hotel.
4 He spent two hours / all night at the airport.
5 The airport was comfortable / uncomfortable.
6 He caught / missed the plane to Dublin.
7 The plane took off / landed at nine o'clock.
8 It had to go to Cork, in the north / in the south of Ireland.
9 He stayed in a five-star hotel / a youth hostel.
10 He had a great time / a terrible time there.

b 🔊 **3.22** Listen to check. **P**

TASK

3 a Think of two or three of your own journeys. For example, a time when:

- you missed a flight or a train.
- something interesting happened.
- you saw something interesting.
- you had a very long journey.

b Prepare to tell your stories. Think about the questions.

1 When was it?
2 What was the reason for your journey?
3 What happened?
4 How did you feel?

4 Tell each other about your journeys. Which journeys were fun? Which were difficult?

Keyword *at*

1 Add the highlighted expressions to the table.

```
1  I was in the south of Japan at the time. Unit 11
2  Middle children are good at meeting new people. Unit 8
3  I met Ed when he was about 16. I was at his father's house. Unit 8
4  I watch the fireworks at midnight from the window. Unit 3
5  We were best friends at school. Unit 1
6  She wasn't at the party. Unit 1
```

times	places	group events	*good at ...*
at 7.00 at the moment	at home at work at John's flat	at a lecture at a match	good at English not very good at driving

2 a Add at to sentences 1–8.

Find someone who ...

1 was a party last night.
2 met their husband or wife school.
3 works home a lot.
4 is reading a good book the moment.

5 often works the weekend.
6 was a wedding recently.
7 is good sport.
8 isn't very good geography.

> Were you at a party last night?
>
> Yes, I was.
>
> Where was it?

b Use the sentences in 2a to ask questions to other students. Try to find out more information.

Across cultures Saying sorry

1 The word **sorry** has a lot of different uses in English. Match pictures A–E with situations 1–5.

A Sorry, but there's a problem with my shower.

B Sorry, is this the train to Bristol?

C Oh, I'm sorry!

D Sorry?

E I'm very sorry, your card's not working.

You can use **sorry** when:
1   you want to apologise.
2   you don't understand or can't hear someone.
3   you ask for information from people you don't know.

4   you want to complain about something.
5   you give bad news.

2 Read what people from different countries say about saying **sorry**, and discuss the questions in pairs.

> In Spain you use different words to say *sorry*. When you can't hear something you say *perdón?* or *qué?* When you want to complain you say *lo lamento* or *discúlpame* or *lo siento*. MANUEL

> In Britain, people apologise a lot. When you bump into someone, or when someone bumps into you, both people usually say *sorry*. MATTHEW

> In Sudan if you are not happy about something you just complain about it, you don't say *sorry*. KHALID

> In Switzerland the word for sorry is *Entschuldigung* but if we can't hear someone we don't normally say *sorry*, we just say *what? uh?* NATHALIE

1   Does your language have one word for saying sorry, or different words for different situations?
2   Do you think people apologise a lot in your country? What about other countries you know?
3   What do you say in situations 1–5?

Goals
- ask questions to develop a conversation
- change the topic of a conversation

Ben

Nina

NINA	Hi, Ben. ¹How are you?
BEN	Fine thanks. Are you okay?
NINA	Yes, not bad. ²Did you see *The Family* on TV last night?
BEN	Yeah.
NINA	³What happened? I missed it.
BEN	Erm, Dario left his job and Jon asked Anna to marry him. It was, er, pretty boring actually.
NINA	Jon asked Anna to marry him? Really? ⁴What did she say?
BEN	Erm, I don't know.
NINA	What do you mean you don't know? Did she say yes?
BEN	Well, actually, I stopped watching before the end. ⁵Anyway, ⁶what did you do last night?
NINA	Oh, we went out for a meal. It was really nice. But I forgot my credit card and we didn't have any cash.
BEN	Oh no, ⁷what did you do?
NINA	I had to drive home and get the credit card while Sam and the kids had dessert.
BEN	Oh, that's too bad.
NINA	Yeah.
BEN	⁸So, ⁹how's your family?
NINA	Oh, fine. Adriana starts school next week …

1 Look at the picture. Where do Nina and Ben work?

2 🔊 **3.23** Listen to their conversation. Tick (✓) the things they talk about.

a TV programme ✓ friends the cinema
last night a meal a concert a wedding

3 Read the script. Complete the notes with the highlighted expressions from the script.

Starting a topic
- How are you?
-
-
-

Developing a topic
- What happened?
-
-

Changing the topic
- Anyway, …
-

5 a It's Monday morning. You're going to have a conversation with your colleague.
- Think about the questions you can ask to start the conversation.
- Think about your answers to the questions.

b Start the conversation. Try to keep your conversation going for one or two minutes.

6 How long were your conversations? What was the most popular topic?

4 a Complete this conversation with expressions from 3, and your own ideas.

A Hi. How are you?
B Good, thanks. Are you okay?
A Yes, fine thanks. _____ ?
B No, I was too tired.
A _____ ?
B Just watched TV.
A Oh, _____ ?
B Yes, I always watch it but I missed the ending. _____ ?
A Well, the wedding didn't happen in the end.
B Oh, you're joking.
A No, and that was the last show. _____ , what have we got to do today?
B Well, we need to check all these …

b In pairs, practise the conversation. Take turns to start.

11 Look again ♻

Review

VOCABULARY Airports

1 a Complete the words with vowels.

1 b_ _rd_ng g_te
2 ch_ck-_n
3 s_c_r_ty
4 b_gg_ge c_ll_ct_ _n
5 c_st_ms
6 p_ssp_rt c_ntr_l

b Where can you hear these sentences?

1 Do you have any hand luggage?
2 Are you wearing a belt?
3 Could you open your bag, please?
4 Are you carrying anything for anyone else?
5 Come forward, please.
6 Boarding is at 12.15 from gate 20.
7 Did you pack your bag yourself?
8 Can I see your boarding pass, please?

c Ask and answer the questions in b.

GRAMMAR Articles

2 a Complete the questions with a, an, the, or no article.

1 How many _____ international airports are there in your country? Where are they?
2 What's _____ biggest one? How many terminals does it have?
3 Do you have _____ central train station in your city? What's the name of _____ station?
4 Do people use _____ buses to travel around your city? What about your country? How comfortable are they?
5 Does your city have _____ underground? How many lines does _____ underground have?
6 What other _____ kinds of transport do people use where you live?

b Ask and answer the questions.

CAN YOU REMEMBER? Unit 10 – Suggestions

3 a Look at the suggestion. Think of other expressions to replace Why don't we ...?

Why don't we go out for a meal?

b Think of suggestions for a person in these situations.

1 I want to drive to the airport but my car is at the garage.
2 I'm bored. I have no money to go out.
3 My neighbour is playing very loud music.
4 I'm in an English lesson and I feel ill.
5 It's 4 o'clock in the morning and I can't sleep.
6 I'm hungry, but I don't have any food at home to cook.

c Compare your suggestions. Say what you think about each other's ideas.

Extension

SPELLING AND SOUNDS ng

4 a ⊙ 3.24 You can say -ng in two ways. Listen and practise saying the words.

/ŋ/	/ŋg/
fly**ing**	E**ng**land

b Add these words to the correct groups. What's the rule?

skiing   long   longer   running
thing   stronger   youngest

c ⊙ 3.25 Listen to check. Practise saying the words.

d ⊙ 3.26 Spellcheck. Close your books. Listen to six words and write them down.

e Check your spelling.

NOTICE start and stop

5 a After start and stop, you can often use a verb + -ing:

When the receptionist saw the spider on the wall, she started laughing.
Well, actually, I stopped watching before the end.

Complete sentences 1–5 with these words:

running   shouting   boarding
eating   playing

1 Can you ask your children to stop _____ around the airport lounge?
2 Passengers with children can start _____ now.
3 Please start _____ before your meal gets cold.
4 Could you stop _____ and talk more quietly?
5 I started _____ the guitar when I was about eight years old.

b Talk about your present and past interests or habits.

1 When did you start doing them? Did you stop? When? Why?
2 Is there anything you would like to start doing, or stop doing?

Self-assessment

Can you do these things in English? Circle a number on each line. 1 = I can't do this, 5 = I can do this well.

◎ check in and board a flight	1	2	3	4	5
◎ tell a story	1	2	3	4	5
◎ talk about a journey	1	2	3	4	5
◎ ask questions to develop a conversation	1	2	3	4	5
◎ change the topic of a conversation	1	2	3	4	5

• For Wordcards, reference and saving your work → e-Portfolio
• For more practice → Self-study Pack, Unit 11

12 Are you OK?

12.1 goals
- ◉ talk about health
- ◉ buy things in a pharmacy
- ◉ understand instructions on medicines

I've got a headache

VOCABULARY

The body and health

1 **a** Do the quiz. (Circle) your answers.

BODY SENSE: *Test your knowledge*

1 Your head weighs about 3.5 / 5.5 / 8.5 kilos.
2 The stomach can hold four / six / eight litres of food.
3 You use 5 / 12 / 20 muscles to smile. You use about 50 / 70 / 80 muscles to speak.
4 Our eyes never grow / stop growing. Our nose and ears never grow / stop growing.
5 The body loses half a kilo / more than half a kilo / a kilo of skin every year.
6 Over 20% / 40% / 50% of the bones in your body are in your hands and feet.
7 The smallest bone is in your ear / nose / little toe. It's the size of a grain of rice.
8 Your thumb is the same length as your nose / big toe / ear.
9 Children have 18 / 20 / 22 first teeth. Adults have 28 / 30 / 32 teeth.
10 Your heart beats about 50,000 / 100,000 / 200,000 times every day.

b **3.27** Listen to check.

Vocabulary reference, *The body*, p147

2 Look at the highlighted words in the quiz. What other body words do you know? Check in Vocabulary reference, *The body*, p147.

3 **a** Match problems 1–8 with pictures A–H.

I've got a	¹headache. ²cold . ³sore throat. ⁴temperature. ⁵pain in my back. ⁶problem with my knee.
I feel (really / a bit)	⁷sick. ⁸tired.

b **3.28** Listen to check. **P**

4 Make conversations. Talk about different problems from 3a.

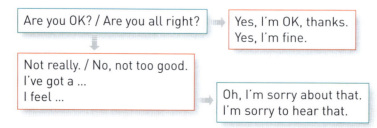

Are you OK? / Are you all right? ➡ Yes, I'm OK, thanks. / Yes, I'm fine.

Not really. / No, not too good. / I've got a … / I feel … ➡ Oh, I'm sorry about that. / I'm sorry to hear that.

What are your symptoms?

LISTENING AND READING

Marc, from Lyons in France, is in the UK on a work trip. He goes to a pharmacy.

1 🔴 **3.29** Listen to the first part of Marc's conversation with the pharmacist. What problems does Marc have?

2 Match the pharmacist's questions with Marc's answers.

1 What are your **symptoms**?	a Just dairy products.
2 Are you **allergic to** anything?	b No, not at the moment.
3 Are you **taking** any other **medicine**?	c I've got a pain in my back.

3 a Read the medicine packages below. Which medicine is best for Marc? Why?

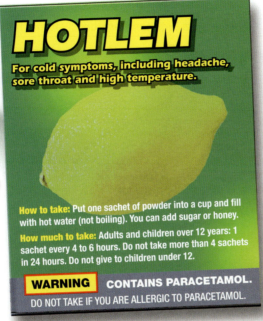

HOTLEM

For cold symptoms, including headache, sore throat and high temperature.

How to take: Put one sachet of powder into a cup and fill with hot water (not boiling). You can add sugar or honey.

How much to take: Adults and children over 12 years: 1 sachet every 4 to 6 hours. Do not take more than 4 sachets in 24 hours. Do not give to children under 12.

WARNING CONTAINS PARACETAMOL.
DO NOT TAKE IF YOU ARE ALLERGIC TO PARACETAMOL.

Paracetamol

500 mg tablets

For the relief of aches and pains, including headache and toothache.

KEEP AWAY FROM CHILDREN
Do not take with alcohol.
If symptoms continue, go to your doctor.

DOSE: Adults and children over 12 years: 1 to 2 tablets every 4 to 6 hours. Do not take more than 8 tablets in 24 hours. Children 6 to 12 years: half to one tablet every 4 to 6 hours. Do not take more than 4 tablets in 24 hours. Not for children under 6.

b 🔴 **3.30** Listen to the second part of Marc's conversation. Does he buy Hotlem or paracetamol?

4 Read the packages again. Are these sentences true or false?

1 You shouldn't give Hotlem to a ten year-old.
2 Hotlem has paracetamol in it.
3 An adult can take six sachets of Hotlem in 24 hours.
4 You can drink wine with paracetamol.
5 An adult shouldn't have more than eight tablets in 24 hours.
6 You can give paracetamol to a five year-old.

PRONUNCIATION
Linking consonants and vowels 1

5 a 🔴 **3.31** Listen to sentences from Marc's conversation. Notice how a consonant at the end of a word links to a vowel at the beginning of the next word.

1 Do you need‿any help?
2 What‿are your symptoms?
3 I've had the headache for‿about‿an hour.
4 I've got‿a pain‿in my back.
5 This‿is the best thing.

Do you need‿any help?

consonant   vowel

b Practise saying the sentences.

SPEAKING

6 a Work in A/B pairs. A, you're the pharmacist. B, you feel ill. Have a conversation and buy some medicine.

Hello. Can I help you?

Yes. I'd like something for ...

b Change roles and have another conversation.

Home remedies

READING

1 What do you do in situations 1–4? Do you:

- take a day off work?
- ask someone for advice?
- see a doctor or dentist?
- go to a pharmacy?
- take some medicine?
- do nothing?
- do something else?

1 You've got toothache.
2 You feel tired and you have no energy.
3 You've got a temperature.
4 You've got a really bad pain in your back and you don't know why.

> Maybe onions can help stomach ache.

2 a Pictures A–D show different remedies. Can you match them with these problems?

headache   toothache   a high temperature   stomach ache

A

black toast with honey

B

an onion

C

a wet teabag

D

salt water

b Read the web postings to check your ideas.

KNOWLEDGE.COM

http://www.knowledge.com/homeremedies

The world's best advice site ... written by you.

Home Remedies

💬 Monica, Canada
April 24 10.41

Black toast with honey
A friend of mine stayed in a hotel in India and the manager gave this to her for stomach ache. It really works. Just take a piece of bread and toast it until it's black. Then put honey on the toast and eat it. You don't really need the honey but it makes it taste better! It doesn't look good, but it can really help. So if you get stomach ache, try this remedy.

💬 Norma, USA
April 24 9.52

An onion
If you get a high temperature, use an onion. It sounds strange but it helps. Cut one large onion in half and tie half an onion to the bottom of each of your feet. You shouldn't wear socks of course, just bare feet! I use this on my kids and it works every time. The remedy came from a relative from down south.

💬 Heli, Finland
April 23 18.03

A wet teabag
Here are my tips for toothache. You should put a wet teabag on the sore tooth. I always have a wet teabag in the fridge so it's there when I need it. Another idea: take a garlic clove and put it on the tooth. Both these ideas help me nine times out of ten. But if they don't work for you, you should go to a dentist.

💬 Lameed, Egypt
April 23 16.15

Salt water
When I was a child, I got a lot of headaches and my grandmother always did this for me. Put a few drops of warm salt water in your ears. Don't use really hot water. Do this three or four times for both ears. Then lie down and close your eyes for about ten minutes.

3 What do you think of these home remedies? Would you like to try them? Why? / Why not?

VOCABULARY
Giving advice

4 **a** You can use the imperative or should to give advice. Complete the sentences with *socks, teabag, water, feet, garlic*.

	✓		✗	
You should	Take a _____ clove and put it on the tooth.	**Don't**	use really hot _____.	
	put a wet _____ on the sore tooth.	**You shouldn't**	wear _____ of course, just bare _____.	

> You should take a paracetamol and lie down for half an hour.
>
> Is that for a headache?

b Read to check. **3.32** Listen to the sentences. **P**

5 **a** Think of advice for each of these problems:

a high temperature   headache   stomach ache   backache   toothache

b Talk in groups. Listen to each other's advice and guess the problem.

If you get stomach ache …

GRAMMAR
Giving advice with *if*

1 **a** Look at the *if* sentences in the table. Then put the words of this sentence in order and add it to the box.

If / an onion / get / a temperature, / you / use .

> **If + present simple, imperative**
> **If** you **get** stomach ache, **try** this remedy.
> **If** you **try** the salt water remedy, **don't use** really hot water.
> _____
>
> **If + present simple, *should / shouldn't* + infinitive**
> **If** they **don't work** for you, you **should go** to a dentist.
>
> You can change the order of *if* sentences:
> **If** you get stomach ache, **try** this remedy. *or* **Try** this remedy **if** you get stomach ache.

b **3.33** Listen to the sentences. **P**

> If you've got a very bad cold, don't go to work.

Grammar reference and practice, p140

2 **a** Match problems 1–6 with advice a–f. There's more than one correct answer.

1	you've got a very bad cold	a	you shouldn't eat a large meal
2	you're allergic to paracetamol	b	be careful what medicine you take
3	your feet hurt	c	don't go to work
4	you've got stomach ache	d	don't go for a run
5	you feel very tired	e	put them in hot water with mustard
6	you've got a problem with your knee	f	you should go to bed early

b Now say the six sentences with *if*.

SPEAKING

3 **a** **3.34** Listen to Amina from Lebanon, Angharad and Nathalie from Switzerland, and Ruth from England talk about their own remedies for a cold. Tick (✓) the remedies they talk about.

- eat oranges   • eat chicken soup   • drink hot honey and lemon juice
- drink black tea with honey   • get on with work   • go to the doctor
- take paracetamol   • inhale steam from hot water

b Read the script on p157 to check.

4 Talk about these questions in groups.

1 What do you think of their remedies?
2 What do you do when you've got a cold? What about people you know?
3 What's the most popular remedy? What's the most unusual remedy?

> " I put my head over a bowl of hot water and inhale the steam. "

Target activity

Give advice

TASK READING

1 Read the magazine article.
What's the main topic?

   a   better relationships with colleagues
   b   a better office environment
   c   exercising at work

 **Tips of the week** Stay healthy in the workplace

Offices are not always healthy environments. Here are some tips for improving your office and your health.

✓ Try to sit near a window. Natural light makes you feel happier.

✓ Fresh air is good for you, so you should open the window if possible.

✓ If you want to improve the appearance of your office, get some plants.

✓ Get a good chair and make sure the top of your computer screen is at eye level. A bad sitting position can give you headaches and back pain.

✓ Don't sit near an air-conditioner. It dries out your eyes and skin.

✓ If you feel bored, change the colour of your office walls. The right colour improves your mood and helps you to be more creative. White, blue or green offices are better than dark or bright-coloured offices.

✓ Don't use the lift. You should always use the stairs. This keeps you fit.

2 Read the tips again. Find:

   • seven things you should do.
   • two things you shouldn't do.

3 Do you do any of the things in the article? Why? / Why not?

TASK VOCABULARY

Giving reasons for advice

4 **a** Cover the article. Complete the sentences with these words.

Fresh air   The right colour   Using the stairs   Plants   Natural light

   1   _____ **makes you feel** happier.
   2   _____ **is good for** you.
   3   _____ **improve** the appearance of your office.
   4   _____ **helps you to** be more creative.
   5   _____ **keeps you** fit.

   b Check your ideas in the article.

TASK

5 **a** You want some advice. Choose one of these topics or use your own ideas.

How to:
   ◦ improve your home cheaply
   ◦ give a talk to a large audience
   ◦ work at home effectively
   ◦ cook a meal for a large group of people
   ◦ entertain a group of children
   ◦ organise a party for 50 people

b You're going to ask for and give advice. Think about how to:

   • ask for advice: *I want to improve my home, but I'm not sure what to do.*
   • give advice: *You should / shouldn't ...   Don't ...   If you ...*
   • give reasons for advice: *Fresh air's good for you.*

6 Ask other students for advice.

7 Did you agree with the advice you got? Why? / Why not?

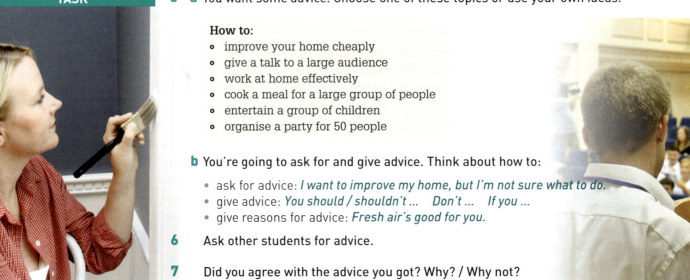

Keyword *take*

take with nouns

1 a Complete the sentences with these words.

boat trip message medicine
photos tablets

> 1 OK, and do you prefer taking _____ in a drink or tablets? **Unit 12**
> 2 Do not take more than four _____ in 24 hours. **Unit 12**
> 3 My mobile phone doesn't take _____. **Unit 3**
> 4 Sorry, he isn't here at the moment ... Can I take a _____? **Unit 3**
> 5 And would you like to take a _____ on the Bosphorus? **Unit 2**

b You can use take to talk about travel and medicine. Find examples in 1a. Can you think of more examples?

2 Can you remember the last time you:

- took a train?
- took a taxi?
- took a message?
- took a really good photo?
- took a trip to somewhere new?
- took a tablet for a headache?

Talk together.

take with time

3 a Underline an activity and circle a time in these sentences.

> 1 Travelling home takes a whole day. **Unit 7**
> 2 It takes about twenty minutes to walk to the centre of Lucknow. **Unit 9**
> 3 It takes 50 minutes to travel the nine-mile journey across London by unicycle. **Unit 9**

b Complete these sentences so that they're true for you. Then compare with a partner.

1 It takes _____ to do my food shopping.
2 It usually takes about _____ to get home from work.
3 Starting up my computer takes _____.
4 It usually takes _____ to cook my dinner.
5 Cleaning my home takes _____.
6 It takes _____ to read the newspaper.
7 It takes _____ to answer my emails.
8 Flying to Australia takes about _____.

Independent learning Learning collocations

1 🎧 **3.35** Listen to Yukio. What is a collocation?

a It's a kind of word.
b It's two words that go together.
c It's a kind of sentence.

watch TV have lunch
spend money
take a message go for a walk
see you soon

2 🎧 **3.35** Listen again. What two mistakes did he make when he first started learning English? Why did he make them?

3 a When you try to learn new words and expressions, do you write them down?

b Do you write:

a single words? *watch*
b collocations? *watch TV, watch films*
c sentences? *I usually watch TV on Friday evenings.*

4 When you read in English, try to notice and learn new collocations. Read A–C and find collocations with take, spend, and have.

A

Too busy?

British actress, Tanya Hoxton, said in an interview last week that she needs to take a break. Speaking to *Hello* magazine, she said she wants to spend more time with her friends and family. The first thing she wants to do is have a party for her

B

Stress busting tips for working parents

- Take a break from work. Spend time with your kids in the open air – go for a walk every day.
- Every few months, let the kids stay with their grandparents and have a party for your adult friends.

C

HARRY'S BLOG 💬

We had a great party last weekend to celebrate the end of the academic year. I spent a lot of time preparing for it – more than I did preparing for exams ... Anyway, now it's time to take a break from university and think about doing some real work and getting some money for next term. This summer, I'm working at

A

Hi Marc,

I'm writing to say I'm really sorry for not meeting you yesterday. I had a very bad headache and sore throat. I wanted to call you but I haven't got your home or mobile numbers.

I'm really sorry and hope you're not angry with me. Could we meet another time? I promise to be there! And please give me your number!

Write when you have a moment,

Abby

B

Hello Joseph,

Thanks very much for the invitation. I'm very sorry but I don't think I can come. I've got an exam on Sunday (!) so I really should stay at home on Saturday and do some studying.

Thanks again and sorry to be so boring! Hope you have a great time. Let's meet up for coffee some time soon.

All the best,

Abby

C

Hi Mum & Dad,

Hope you had a great holiday, and thanks for letting us stay. Mum, I'm afraid Sammy broke your mug, the one with cats on it. I'm really sorry. I know it was your favourite. Can we buy you another one? Or take you (and dad, of course) out to dinner some time? I'll give you a call at the weekend.

Love, A. xxxxx

1 a What are the names of the people in photos 1–3? Read A–C to find out.

b What do you find out about Abby? Read A–C again and make a list.

She's studying something.

2 How did Abby say sorry? Cover the emails and notes and match 1–5 with a–e. Then read again to check.

1 I'm writing to say **I'm really sorry for**
2 **I'm really sorry**
3 **I'm afraid** Sammy broke your mug.
4 **I'm very sorry, but**
5 **Sorry to**

a I'm really sorry.
b be so boring.
c and hope you're not angry with me.
d not meeting you yesterday.
e I don't think I can come.

3 When we say sorry, we usually say why. Look at A and B and find out:

1 why Abby didn't meet Marc.
2 why Abby didn't phone Marc.
3 why Abby can't go to Joseph's.

4 Complete the sentences with these words.

Could   Hope (x2)   Can   Thanks (x2)   Let's

1 _____ we meet another time?
2 _____ we buy you another one?
3 _____ meet up for coffee some time soon.
4 _____ you have a great time.
5 _____ you had a great holiday.
6 _____ very much for the invitation.
7 _____ again.

5 a Choose one situation for an email.

It's Sunday afternoon. You have a very bad cold. Tomorrow you have a meeting with a colleague at work, but you think you should stay in bed.

You're on holiday and you're using your friend's car. Yesterday you had a small accident. You broke one of the lights at the back of the car. Your friend loves his car.

You visited a friend in another city at the weekend. On Monday morning, you remember that another friend had her birthday party on Saturday.

b Discuss ideas for your emails in pairs.

1 Who are you writing to?
2 How can you say sorry?
3 What reasons can you give?
4 Can you use any expressions from 2 and 4?

6 a Work alone and write your email.

b Look at another student's email. Can you improve your emails together?

7 Read other students' emails. What do you think of their reasons?

Review

VOCABULARY Health and advice

1 **a** Make sentences from the words in the table.

I've got	toothache	a cold
I feel	a sore throat	tired
	a high temperature	stomach ache
	a problem with my knee	sick

b Make sentences giving advice from these words.

You should/shouldn't …

go to	a day off work
take	a doctor
eat	work
try	hot lemon juice with honey
drink	black toast and honey
	coffee
	some tablets

c In pairs, take turns to say a problem and give advice. Do you agree with the advice?

> I've got a cold.   You should take some tablets.

GRAMMAR Giving advice with *if*

2 **a** Complete the sentences with your own advice.

1. If you like chocolate, …
2. If you want to buy a new computer, …
3. If you're looking for a good restaurant, …
4. If you're interested in films, …
5. If you need travel information, …
6. If you'd like to go to a relaxing place, …
7. If you want to read a good book, …
8. If you can't sleep well at night, …

b Compare your sentences. Who has the best ideas?

CAN YOU REMEMBER? Unit 11 – Articles

3 **a** Add *a*, *the* or no article to Holly's story.

> " Well, I was in my car in the Rocky Mountains in Canada and I was on ¹_____ highway with lots of beautiful mountains and trees nearby. It was ²_____ sunny day and everything was perfect. Suddenly I saw ³_____ family of bears – ⁴_____ mother bear and two cubs – near the side of ⁵_____ road. I love ⁶_____ bears! So I stopped ⁷_____ car, got out and started taking ⁸_____ photos. I wasn't very close to ⁹_____ bears, but ¹⁰_____ cubs got frightened and ¹¹_____ mother looked angry … "

b Check your answers in 🔴 3.20 on p156.

Extension

SPELLING AND SOUNDS *ay, ai*

4 **a** 🔴 3.36 We usually say *ay* and *ai* in the same way: /eɪ/. Listen and repeat.

d**ay**   st**ay**   w**ay**
p**ai**n   m**ai**n   gr**ai**n

1. Which spelling is usually at the *end* of a word?
2. Which spelling is usually in the *middle* of a word?

b 🔴 3.37 Spellcheck. Close your book. Listen to eight words from this unit and write them down.

c Check your spelling on p157.

NOTICE *it, they*

5 **a** In the first sentence, *it* means 'a piece of bread'. Look at 1–4. Does *it* mean 'honey', or 'black toast with honey'?

> Just take <u>a piece of bread</u> and toast <u>it</u> until it's black. Put honey on the toast and eat ¹it. You don't really need the honey but ²it makes the toast taste better. ³It doesn't look good, but ⁴it can really help.

b Read the advice about toothache. What do *it* and *they* mean in 5–8?

> 💬 I always have a wet teabag in the fridge so ⁵it's there when I need ⁶it. Another idea: take a garlic clove and put ⁷it on the tooth. Both these ideas help me nine times out of ten. But if ⁸they don't work for you, you should go to a dentist.

Self-assessment

Can you do these things in English? Circle a number on each line. 1 = I can't do this, 5 = I can do this well.

⊚ talk about health	1 2 3 4 5
⊚ buy things in a pharmacy	1 2 3 4 5
⊚ understand instructions on medicines	1 2 3 4 5
⊚ give advice	1 2 3 4 5
⊚ write an email or note apologising	1 2 3 4 5

• For Wordcards, reference and saving your work → e-Portfolio
• For more practice → Self-study Pack, Unit 12

13

Experiences

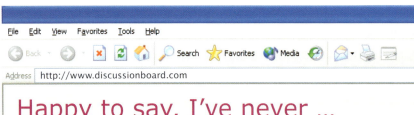

13.1 goals
◉ talk about experiences
◉ say what you've never done and always wanted to do

I've never …

SPEAKING

1 Talk in pairs. When was the last time you:

1. used a mobile phone?
2. went to a gym?
3. worked after eleven at night?
4. read a book you didn't like?
5. saw a horror film?
6. smoked a cigarette?
7. played a new game or sport?
8. ate a hamburger?

READING

2 a Read the web postings.
Are any of them true for you?

File   Edit   View   Favorites   Tools   Help

◀ Back ▾   ▶   ✖   🔄   🏠   🔍 Search   ⭐ Favorites   🌐 Media   ⏱   ✉ ▾   🖨   ▭

Address   http://www.discussionboard.com

Happy to say, I've never …

Do you ever feel you're a little bit different from the crowd? What things are you happy you've never done? To post your comment, click here.

I've never had a mobile phone. Why do people these days make phone calls while driving their cars or shopping in the supermarket? When I leave my house, I'm happy to get away from my phone for a few hours!
Frances

I've never read a Harry Potter book or seen any of the films.
Jill

I've never played golf. Why pay money to hit a ball around a large area of land that was once beautiful countryside?
Simon

I've never liked The Beatles. I don't understand people who do.
Maxim

I've never worked for a company with good management. I've never believed managers when they say "people are the most important thing in our company".
Shilpa

I've never smoked, or eaten a McDonald's hamburger.
Marina

I've never wanted to stop smoking.
Thorsten

I've never been to a gym. I've never understood people who climb mountains or do extreme sports!
Denise

I've never said "never"!
Pamela

---

b Compare your answers.

GRAMMAR

Present perfect
verbs

3 In the article, Frances says *I've never had a mobile phone*. Is she talking about:

1 the past? 2 the present? 3 her whole life up to now?

4 Complete the sentences with 've (have) or 's (has). 🔴 3.38 Listen to check. ℗

> **present perfect (*have/has* + past participle)**
>
> 1 I _____ never **played** golf.
> 2 You _____ never **been** to my flat.
> 3 He _____ never **eaten** a hamburger.
> 4 We _____ never **had** a garden.
> 5 They _____ never **worked** in an office before.

5 a Find the past participles of these verbs in the article.

Regular (-ed)	Irregular	
1 play *played*	7 go *been*	11 eat _____
2 like _____	8 have _____	12 understand _____
3 work _____	9 read _____	13 do _____
4 believe _____	10 see _____	14 say _____
5 smoke _____		
6 want _____		

b What are the past participles of these verbs? Look at *Irregular verbs* on p160 to check.

ride take drink fly drive meet be

6 Make sentences with the present perfect.

1 I / never / do / any extreme sports.
2 I / never / understand / maths.
3 We / never / have / a TV at home.
4 My brother / never / smoke.
5 My parents / never / go / to the USA.
6 I / never / be / interested in football.
7 My mother / never / like / cooking.
8 Jo / never / work / in an office before.

WRITING

7 a Write six sentences with never about yourself or people you know, three true and three false.

b Listen to each other's sentences. Which do you think are true? Which are false?

I've always wanted to ...

I've always wanted to swim with dolphins.

I've always wanted to go to Egypt.

LISTENING

1 🔴 3.39 Listen to Andrei and Anne talk about things they've always wanted to do. Match the speakers to the pictures.

2 a 🔴 3.39 Listen again. Why do they want to do these things?

b Read the script on p157 to check.

SPEAKING

3 a Think of some things you've always wanted to do.

b Tell each other about the things. Ask questions to find out more.

I've always wanted to ride an elephant. Why?

Great places

13.2 goals
- talk about experiences ♻
- talk about places you've been to

VOCABULARY
Sights

Vocabulary reference
Sights, p147

> The Winter Palace in St Petersburg is very famous.

1 Which of these things can you see in the town or city where you are now?

> a castle   city walls   a fountain   a museum   a palace   ruins   a sculpture
> a statue   a tomb   a waterfall   caves   gardens   a skyscraper

2 Talk in groups.

1 Can you think of famous examples of the sights in 1?
2 What kind of sights do you like going to see?

READING

3 What do you know about these places? Have you been to any of them?

Salto Angel, Venezuela

Park Güell, Barcelona

Taj Mahal, Agra

4 a Work in groups of three. A, read about Salto Angel below. B, read about Güell Park on p123. C, read about the Taj Mahal on p127. Find out what these numbers mean.

- **Salto Angel:** 979, 1933, 1937
- **Güell Park:** 60, 1900–1914, 1923
- **Taj Mahal:** 1631, 20,000, 25 million

The people behind the places

Jimmie Angel

Salto Angel At 979 metres high, Salto Angel in Venezuela is the highest waterfall in the world. The local Pemon people have always known about the falls and call them Parekupa-Meru (meaning 'waterfall of the deepest place'), but it was a pilot from the USA, Jimmie Angel, who made them famous around the world. He flew over the falls in 1933 and then landed his plane on Aiyan-tepui, the mountain at the top of the falls, in 1937. Later, the falls took his name: Salto Angel in Spanish, Angel Falls in English. They're very difficult to get to, but you can see them from the air or from a boat on the Churun river.

b Tell each other about the people and places.

LISTENING

Prema   Monica

5 🔘 3.40 Listen to Monica and Prema talking about the places in the article. Who's been to Güell Park? the Taj Mahal? Angel Falls?

6 a 🔘 3.40 Listen again. Are these sentences true or false?

1 Monica grew up in Barcelona.
2 She thinks Güell Park is beautiful.
3 Prema would like to visit the Taj Mahal.
4 She had a two-week holiday in Venezuela.
5 She saw Angel Falls from a boat.
6 Monica doesn't like flying.

b Read the script on p157–158 to check.

7 Which of the places sounds the most interesting? Why?

Have you ever … ?

1 **a** You can use the present perfect to talk about your life up to now. Complete the sentences with been, seen and heard.

present perfect *has / have* + past participle
❓ 1 Have you **been** to Güell Park? ✅ Yes, I have.
2 Have you ever _____ the Taj Mahal? ❌ No, I haven't.
➕ 3 I've _____ to Angel Falls.
4 I've _____ it on television.
➖ 5 I haven't _____ there.
6 I've never _____ of it.
ever = at any time (in your life)

b 🔊 **3.41** Listen to check. ⓟ

2 **a** Complete the conversations with verbs in the present perfect.

1 **A** *Have you seen* (you see) the Forbidden City in Beijing?
  B No, but I _____ (hear) of it.

2 **A** _____ (you hear) of Petra in Jordan?
  B Yes, I _____. Everyone says it's beautiful.

3 **A** _____ (you eat) sushi?
  B No, I _____. What's it like?

4 **A** _____ (you read) *Anna Karenina*?
  B I _____ (not read) it, but I _____ (see) a film of it.

5 **A** _____ (you play) golf?
  B No. I _____ (see) it on TV, but I _____ (never try) it.

Grammar reference
and practice, p141

b Ask the questions in pairs and answer with your own ideas.

3 **a** Mark the words that link. Remember that consonants at the ends of words link to vowels at the start of words.

1 It's‿a very unusual place.

2 I've been there lots of times.

3 I've never heard of it. (x2)

4 I've seen it on television. (x2)

5 What's it like?

b 🔊 **3.42** Look at the script on p158 and listen to check. ⓟ Practise saying 1–5.

4 **a** Make a list of:

1 five famous cities around the world. *Shanghai, New York, …*
2 five cities in the country where you are now. *Riyadh, Jeddah, …*
3 five places in the town or city where you are now. *the castle, the Arts Theatre, …*

b In groups, find out who's been to the places on the list. Then use follow-up questions to find out more.

Have you been to …?

What's it like?

Would you like to …?

Have you seen …?

Is it …?

Have you heard of …?

Does it have …?

Get information and recommendations

13.3 goals
⊚ talk about experiences ♻
⊚ find out information about things

TASK LISTENING

1 You want to take a visitor to a nice restaurant. How do you choose the restaurant? Do you:

- go to a restaurant you know?
- try a new place you've heard about?
- look for places on the internet?
- ask friends about places they know?
- look in a local guide?
- do something else?

2 **3.43** Listen to Kieran asking three colleagues about restaurants.

1 Why does he want to go to a restaurant?
2 Does he choose the Italian, Indian or American restaurant?

TASK VOCABULARY

Getting information

3 a Can you remember what they said? Match 1–7 with a–g.

1 **Have you been to** that new Italian restaurant, Sicilia?
2 **You could ask** Prema.
3 **Have you tried** Sicilia, the Italian place?
4 **What was it like?**
5 It's really nice.
6 Take her to Akash.
7 You'll love it. Really.

a OK, **I'll think about it**. Thanks.
b No, I haven't, sorry.
c OK, **I'll try it**.
d OK, **I'll ask her**. Thanks.
e Akash? **I've never heard of it**.
f Yes, we went there two, three weeks ago.
g It was OK, but quite expensive.

b **3.43** Listen again to check.

4 In pairs, take turns to say sentences 1–7 and remember the answers.

TASK

5 a Choose one situation and think of things to ask about.

You're taking a visitor out for a meal. Think of some restaurants and cafés to ask other students about.

You're thinking about going on holiday somewhere different. Think of some places you've never been to.

You want to do a new sport or activity. Think of some sports and activities you've never tried.

You'd like to do an evening class and learn a new skill. Think of some things you'd like to try.

You'd like to take some interesting books on holiday with you. Think of some books you've heard of, but haven't read.

b Ask other people for information and recommendations.

6 Choose one of the recommendations. Explain why you chose it.

Have you been to that new Thai restaurant?

No, but have you tried ...?

Have you read *One Hundred Years of Solitude*?

Keyword *thing*

1 a Complete the sentences with thing or things.

1 What _____ are you happy you've never done? Unit 13
2 You don't always have time to do all the tourist _____ . Unit 13
3 This is the best _____ … paracetamol. Unit 12
4 The first _____ I saw was a huge spider on the wall. Unit 11
5 Where are the plates and _____? Unit 5

b In which sentences does thing(s) mean *object(s)*? In which sentences does it mean *activities*?

2 a Match 1–6 with a–f.

1 What's that over there?
2 Are you working late tonight, Chris?
3 Let's go. The next train's at 5.20.
4 You and your sister really get along well.
5 So, what are we doing today?
6 What do you do on Saturdays?

a Yes. I need to finish a few things before I go home.
b Yes, I guess we like similar things.
c That thing? It's a unicycle.
d Not much. Watch TV, read a book, things like that.
e Well, the first thing is, I need to get some money.
f OK, I'll just get my things and we can go.

b Cover a–f. Test each other. Take turns to say 1–6 and remember a–f.

3 Find someone in the class who:

1 always has a lot of things in their pockets.
2 has lots of things to do this weekend.
3 likes doing similar things to you.
4 likes cycling and running and things like that.
5 has a lot of things to do at work this month.
6 needs to buy a few things on the way home.

Across cultures Your experiences

1 a 🔊 **3.44** Listen to Jessica, David and Hyun talking about their experiences of other cultures. Match each person with a country and a topic.

Egypt Brazil Spain   food people music

b Talk together. What did they say about each topic? Listen again to check.

2 a Match 1–7 with a–g.

1 I was surprised that
2 It's something people do in Spain
3 It's more than just
4 I remember walking
5 I couldn't believe how
6 I got interested in Brazil
7 I've never been there, but

a because of the music.
b food.
c I've read a lot about it.
d on special occasions.
e I really enjoyed the food.
f friendly people were.
g to work for the first time.

b Read the script on p158 to check.

3 a Think of your experiences of other cultures. For example:

• listening to music or eating food from other countries
• meeting people from other countries
• reading books or watching films from other countries
• going to language classes
• seeing art or cultural exhibitions from other countries
• travelling to another country

b Talk about your experiences with another student.

13 EXPLORESpeaking

Goal
⊙ start and finish conversations in different situations

1 a 🔘 **3.45** Listen to three conversations. Match them with pictures A–C.

b Read conversations 1–3 to check.

2 a Put the highlighted expressions from the conversations into the right groups.

Starting a conversation	Finishing a conversation
How are things?	I'll talk to you later.

b 🔘 **3.46** Listen to check. 🅟

3 a How can you reply to the expressions in 2a? In groups, think of ideas.

> How are things?

> Fine, thanks.

> I'm great, thanks …

b Compare with the responses in the conversations.

4 a Cover the conversations. Make sentences with these words.

1 Can / talk?
2 Are / doing / anything now?
3 Excuse / got / moment?
4 haven't / seen / long time
5 Have / got / time / a cup of tea?
6 I'll talk / later
7 See / party
8 It / nice talking / you
9 I'll call / time
10 Thanks / help

b In pairs, take turns to say sentences 1–10 and reply.

5 Read the two situations.

> **1**
> It's Monday. You phone a friend to talk about your weekend.
> 1 Say hello and check your friend has time to talk.
> 2 Ask about your friend's weekend. Talk about your weekend.
> 3 Finish your conversation.

> **2**
> You work for a computer software company. You need to arrange a meeting with your colleague to plan next month's sales conference. Think about when you are free this week.
> 1 Say hello and check your colleague has time to talk.
> 2 Agree a day and time for the meeting.
> 3 Finish your conversation.

1

SU-MIN	Hello.
KURT	Hello, Su-Min. This is Kurt.
SU-MIN	Oh, hi, Kurt. How are things?
KURT	Fine, thanks. Listen, can you talk now?
SU-MIN	Well, actually, I'm going out in ten minutes. Is it important?
KURT	Erm, no, not really. Can I call you back later?
SU-MIN	Yeah, any time after eight is fine. I'll talk to you later, OK?
KURT	OK, thanks. Bye.

2

JULIA	Abdul … Excuse me, have you got a moment?
ABDUL	Yes, of course.
JULIA	Thanks. I wanted to ask you about the Maxwell account …
JULIA	… well, I shouldn't keep you, Abdul. Thanks for your help.
ABDUL	Any time.
JULIA	Thanks. See you at the meeting.
ABDUL	Yes, see you.

3

ANDREI	Pete! How are you? I haven't seen you for a long time.
PETE	I'm great, thanks.
ANDREI	Hey, are you doing anything now?
PETE	No, not really.
ANDREI	Have you got time for a coffee and a chat?
PETE	Sure, great idea …
ANDREI	… well, it was good talking to you, Pete.
PETE	Yeah, really nice.
ANDREI	Anyway… I'll text you some time.
PETE	Yeah, that would be nice. Take care.
ANDREI	You too. Bye.

6 Have two conversations in A/B pairs. A, start conversation 1. Then, B, start conversation 2.

> Hi, Masha, how are you?
> Have you got time for a chat?

13 Look again ♻

Review

VOCABULARY Sights

1 a Complete these words with vowels (a,e,i,o,u).

c_stl_
c_ty w_lls
f__nt__n
m_s__m
p_l_c_
r__ns
sc_lpt_r_
st_t__
t_mb
w_t_rf_ll

b Can you see these things in your country? Where? Are any of them famous sights?

c Do you recommend visiting them? Talk together.

GRAMMAR Present perfect

2 a Complete the questions with the past participles of these verbs.

buy do eat go meet play read see

1 Who's the most interesting person you've ever _____ ?
2 What's the worst film you've ever _____ ?
3 What the most expensive thing you've ever _____ ?
4 What's the most boring game you've ever _____ ?
5 What's the most exciting book you've ever _____ ?
6 What's the most difficult thing you've ever _____ ?
7 What's the most beautiful place you've ever _____ to?
8 What's the sweetest food you've ever _____ ?

b Ask and answer the questions together.

CAN YOU REMEMBER? Unit 12 – Health and advice

3 a Complete the conversation with these words.

got hear home I'm I've not should to you you

RUUD   Are _____ all right?
SALLY   No, _____ really. _____ a headache.
RUUD   Oh, _____ sorry _____ _____ that. Maybe _____ _____ go _____ .

b 🔊 3.47 Listen to check.

c Think of more expressions for health problems.

a stomach ache, a problem with my knee, ...

d Practise the conversation with different problems and advice. Take turns to start.

Extension

SPELLING AND SOUNDS wh-

4 a 🔊 3.48 Listen. How do we say wh in each word? Circle /w/ or /h/.

1 what /w/ /h/
2 who /w/ /h/
3 when /w/ /h/
4 which /w/ /h/
5 why /w/ /h/
6 white /w/ /h/
7 wheel /w/ /h/
8 whole /w/ /h/
9 whisper /w/ /h/
10 whose /w/ /h/

b Complete the rule. Then practise saying the words.

Say wh- as /h/ when it is before the letter _____ .

c 🔊 3.49 Spellcheck. Close your book. Listen to ten words and write them down.

d Check your spelling on p158.

NOTICE *both*, *neither*

5 a Read part of Kieran's conversation with Monica. Which highlighted word means *Sicilia and Browne's*? Which word means *not Sicilia and not Browne's*?

KIERAN   Have you been to Sicilia or Browne's?
MONICA   Yes, I have. Both of them.
KIERAN   Which one should we go to?
MONICA   Neither.

b Complete the conversations with both or neither.

1 MONICA   So were you on the river or on the mountain?
   PREMA   _____ . We were in a plane.
2 HYUN   Most of my CDs are samba and Brazilian jazz. I love _____ kinds of music ...

c Ask and answer questions about pairs of things. Try to use both or neither in your replies.

Have you tried ... ?
Do you like ... ?
Do you use ... ?

> Do you like tea or coffee?
> Neither.
> I prefer tea.

Self-assessment

Can you do these things in English? Circle a number on each line. 1 = I can't do this, 5 = I can do this well.

◎ talk about experiences	1 2 3 4 5
◎ say what you've never done and always wanted to do	1 2 3 4 5
◎ talk about places you've been to	1 2 3 4 5
◎ find out information about things	1 2 3 4 5
◎ start and finish conversations in different situations	1 2 3 4 5

• For Wordcards, reference and saving your work → e-Portfolio
• For more practice → Self-study Pack, Unit 13

14 Choices

Exercising your brain

READING

1 What do you think is good for your brain? What's bad for your brain?

I think sleeping's good for the brain.

2 Read the article about exercising the brain. Were your ideas the same?

Keep your brain in top condition

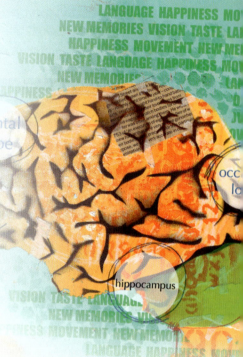

Your brain needs exercise in the same way as your body does. But using your brain doesn't need to be hard work. Have a look at these ideas.

1 Try writing backwards, or writing with your other hand. This makes new connections in your brain and helps you to get new ideas. The great thinker and artist Leonardo da Vinci often used mirror-writing.

2 Start using new parts of your brain. Take up new hobbies, like tennis, chess or dancing the tango.

3 Sleep. If you don't get enough sleep, it's harder for the brain to do some activities, like producing language and new ideas.

4 Chew gum. This exercises the hippocampus, a part of the brain that's important for making new memories.

5 Ask your brain to do old activities in new ways. For example, when you're on a train or bus, close your eyes and guess where you are by listening.

6 Don't eat too much junk food. Cholesterol is bad for both your heart and your brain.

7 Think young! Experiments have shown that when people start to believe they're old, they act old.

8 Play memory games. This keeps your brain young. Games like remembering long lists of words can take ten to fourteen years off the mental age of older people.

9 Learn a new language. This is one of the most difficult things your brain can do, so it's great exercise. It's good for your brain's frontal lobes, which usually get smaller with age.

10 Eat lots of fish. The omega 3 oils in fish like salmon and tuna are good for the brain.

11 Get enough exercise. The right amount of exercise can give people 30% less chance of developing Alzheimer's.

12 Relax. Too much stress is bad for the brain. The hippocampus is about 14% smaller in people who are always stressed.

3 Read again. Why is it a good idea to:

1 write backwards?
2 take up new hobbies?
3 get enough sleep?
4 chew gum?
5 think young?
6 play memory games?
7 learn a new language?
8 relax?

4 Have you tried any of the things in the article? Would you like to try any of them?

Lifestyle choices

VOCABULARY

too much,
enough,
not enough

1 a Complete sentences 1–4 with too much or enough. Then read the article to check.

> **too much, enough + noun**
> 1   If you don't get _____ sleep, it's harder for the brain to do some activities.
> 2   Don't eat _____ junk food.
> 3   Get _____ exercise.
> 4   _____ stress is bad for the brain.

b Match 1–3 with a–c.

1	enough	a	more than you need
2	not enough	b	what you need
3	too much	c	less than you need

2   🔴 **3.50** Listen to Sue and Dan. Who doesn't get much sleep? Who gets a lot?

3 a Can you remember what Sue and Dan said? Add too much, enough and not enough to the conversation.

SUE   Do you think you get _____ sleep?
DAN   No, not at the moment, because of the baby. I only slept about four hours last night.
SUE   Four hours? Poor you. That's _____ .
DAN   What about you?
SUE   I usually sleep for about nine hours, probably ten at the weekend. And I'm always tired.
DAN   Really? You know, I think that's probably _____ sleep.

b   🔴 **3.50** Listen again to check.

PRONUNCIATION

Review

4 a Mark the stress and weak forms in these sentences.

1   Do you think you get͜ enough sleep?
2   No, not at the moment, because of the baby.
3   That's not enough.
4   What about you?
5   And I'm always tired.

b Remember how we link consonants and vowels (get͜ enough). Mark the words that link.

c   🔴 **3.51** Look at the script on p159 and listen to check. ⓟ Practise saying 1–5.

SPEAKING

5 a Think about how much:

- sleep you get
- exercise you do
- fish you eat
- TV you watch
- work you do
- studying you do
- tea or coffee you drink

Is it too much, not enough, or enough?

b Compare your ideas in groups.

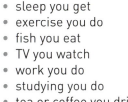

I get about five hours' sleep a night.

That's not enough!

Barry Cox

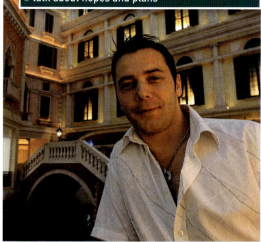

Barry Cox, an ex-supermarket worker from Liverpool in England, is now a popular singer in China. He sings in Cantonese.

LISTENING

1 Look at the picture and read about Barry Cox. Where's he from? What does he do?

2 a 🔊 **3.52** Listen to the first part of a radio interview with Barry Cox. Did Barry always want to become a singer? Is he happy with the choices he made?

b 🔊 **3.52** Listen again. What does Barry say about these things?

1 Spanish lessons
2 a Chinese supermarket
3 a singer from Hong Kong
4 a competition
5 being famous

3 Have you ever thought about changing your job or moving to another country?

VOCABULARY

Life changes

4 a What can you remember about Barry Cox? Put these sentences in the right order.

1 I **went to** a concert given by Leon Lai.
2 I decided to **move** abroad, to Hong Kong.
3 I **had** singing lessons.
4 I **took up** languages.
5 I **left** school at sixteen.
6 I **got** a job singing Canto-pop.

b Read the script on p159 to check.

c Make more expressions to describe life changes. Use the highlighted verbs in 4a and these words.

university (x2)   divorced   a car   a baby
dancing   home (x2)   school   married

went to university

5 a Write six sentences: three things you've done and three things you'd like to do.

I went to university in 1989. I'd like to move abroad one day.

b Compare your sentences with other students.

6 a What do you think Barry Cox wants to do in the future?

• stay in China   • continue singing   • move back to Liverpool
• do some travelling   • move to another country   • learn another language

b 🔊 **3.53** Listen to the second part of the interview to find out.

Hopes and plans for the future

GRAMMAR

be going to,
be hoping to,
would like to

1 Which sentence from Barry's interview is more certain? Which sentence is less certain?

1 I'm going to stay in China for another few years.
2 I'm hoping to continue with the singing.

2 a Complete the sentences in the table with these words.

I'm   are   He's   I'd   Would   Are

⊕	
1 _____ going to	
2 _____ hoping to	**stay** in China for another few years.
3 _____ like to	

❓		✓ ✗
4 **Is** he **going to** stay in China next year?		Yes, he **is**. No, he **isn't**.
5 _____ they **hoping to** move to another country?		Yes, they **are**. No, they **aren't**.
6 _____ you **like to** move back to Liverpool one day?		Yes, I **would**. No, I **wouldn't**.
7 What _____ you **going to** do this weekend?		

b 🔘 **3.54** Listen to check. **P**

3 Look at the game. Write questions with the words on the dark squares.

2 What are you going to do tomorrow?

FINISH

14 What / hoping / do / in the future?

13 Ask a question with *going to*.

12 Would / like / take up / a new hobby?

8 What / going / do / tonight?

9 Ask a question with *hoping to*.

10 Would / like / move / in the next ten years?

11 Start again.

7 Go to square 10.

6 What / going / do / this weekend?

5 Go back one space.

4 Would / like / learn / another language?

START

1 Go forward 2 spaces.

2 What / going / do / tomorrow?

3 Ask a question with *would like*.

Grammar reference and practice, p142

SPEAKING

4 Play the game in groups.

1 Take turns to throw a coin. For *heads*, move one space. For *tails*, move two spaces.
2 When you land on a square, ask the question or follow the instructions. The other players should ask questions to find out more.
3 If you land on the same square twice, ask another player the question.

14.3 Target activity

Plan a weekend break

TASK LISTENING

1 Look at the tourist information about La Mauricie on the website. Match pictures A–D with a place or activity on the website.

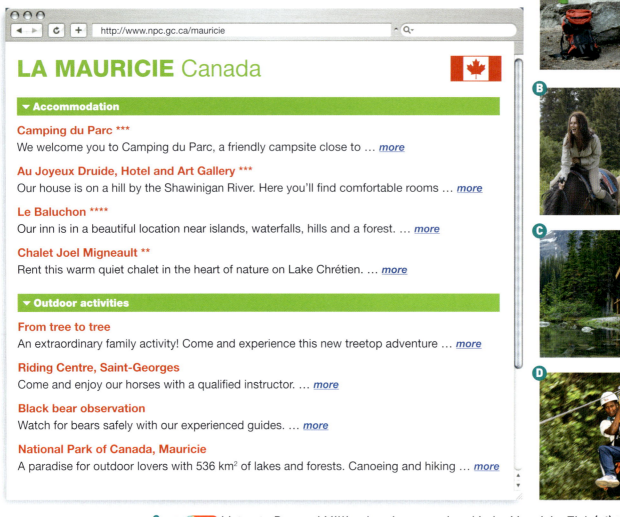

http://www.npc.gc.ca/mauricie

LA MAURICIE Canada

▼ Accommodation

Camping du Parc ***
We welcome you to Camping du Parc, a friendly campsite close to … *more*

Au Joyeux Druide, Hotel and Art Gallery ***
Our house is on a hill by the Shawinigan River. Here you'll find comfortable rooms … *more*

Le Baluchon ****
Our inn is in a beautiful location near islands, waterfalls, hills and a forest. … *more*

Chalet Joel Migneault **
Rent this warm quiet chalet in the heart of nature on Lake Chrétien. … *more*

▼ Outdoor activities

From tree to tree
An extraordinary family activity! Come and experience this new treetop adventure … *more*

Riding Centre, Saint-Georges
Come and enjoy our horses with a qualified instructor. … *more*

Black bear observation
Watch for bears safely with our experienced guides. … *more*

National Park of Canada, Mauricie
A paradise for outdoor lovers with 536 km^2 of lakes and forests. Canoeing and hiking … *more*

2 a ⏻ **3.55** Listen to Dan and Millie planning a weekend in La Mauricie. Tick (✓) the things they talk about on the website.

b ⏻ **3.55** Listen again. Where are they going to:

1 stay? 2 go on Saturday? 3 go on Sunday?

TASK VOCABULARY

Planning

3 a Can you remember Dan and Millie's conversation? Complete the sentences with these words.

expensive   Saturday   nice   accommodation   uncomfortable

Introducing / changing topic	Opinions	Agreeing / disagreeing
What are we going to do about _____ ? What are we going to do on _____ ?	I think it's too _____ . This campsite looks _____ to me.	Yeah, OK. Fine. But camping is really _____ .

b ⏻ **3.56** Listen to check. ℗

TASK

4 Work alone. You're going to La Mauricie for a weekend with some friends. Look on p130 and think about:

1 where to stay   2 what to do on Saturday   3 what to do on Sunday

5 Talk in groups and plan what to do.

6 Explain your ideas to other groups. Did you choose the same or different things?

Keyword *really*

really = very

1 a Look at these sentences from previous units. In which sentences can you change really to very?

> 1 But camping is really uncomfortable. **Unit 14**
> 2 I really like working with numbers. **Unit 7**
> 3 I'm really busy at work. **Unit 3**
> 4 I really miss the sun. **Unit 2**
> 5 I'm really interested in architecture. **Unit 2**
> 6 I really want that coat. It's cold here! **Unit 2**

b Complete the rules with very and really.

You can use _____ with adjectives, but not verbs.
You can use _____ with both adjectives and verbs.

2 a Add really to these questions.

1 Who do you admire?
2 What do you do if you're bored?
3 Do you know a good place to buy gifts?
4 What do you enjoy doing in the evenings?

b Ask and answer the questions.

really = truly

3 We also use really to say or ask if something is true. Match 1–3 with a–c.

1 He says he's a good driver
2 Do you really make
3 People believe jogging's good for you
a all your own clothes?
b but really it's bad for your back and knees.
c but really he's not.

4 a Complete these sentences with your own ideas.

1 A lot of people think ... but really ...
2 Everyone says ... but really ...
3 I often think ... but really ...
4 I sometimes say ... but really ...
5 My friend believes ... but really ...

b Compare your sentences with a partner.

> Everyone says English food's awful, but really it's quite nice.

Independent learning How can you learn languages?

a film with subtitles

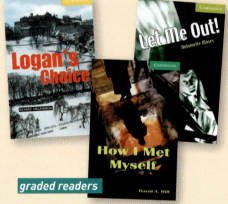

graded readers

a language exchange

1 **3.57** Listen to Greg from the UK and Paula from Argentina talk about how they learn languages. Circle the things they talk about.

having lessons	reading newspapers or magazines	a discussion group
making friends with local people	reading books	a language exchange
watching films with subtitles	reading graded texts	practising every day

2 a **3.57** Listen to Greg and Paula again. Which methods worked for them? Which methods didn't work? What do they want to try?

b Read the script on p159 to check.

3 Talk about:

• which methods you've tried for learning English.
• which methods you'd like to try.

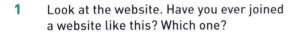

Tom   Marek   Jessie

FindOldFriends.com

You can get in touch with old friends on FindOldFriends.com. It's simple. Sign up with us, search for your friends online, then contact them by email.

File Edit View Insert Format Tools Message Help

Hi Marek

I was so pleased when I saw your name on the site! After school, I did a French degree at Liverpool University. After that, I didn't know what to do so I decided to travel. I spent a year in China teaching English, then I moved to the States. Now I'm living and working in LA, managing an internet business. I live alone with my lovely cat, George. In a few years' time, I'd like to get married and have kids, but I haven't found the right woman. Do you remember Jessie Morgan? I always liked her. She was so ambitious at school. I'd love to know what she's doing now. What's your news? It would be great to hear from you.

Tom

1 Look at the website. Have you ever joined a website like this? Which one?

2 Read the emails. Where did Tom, Marek and Jessie become friends? Where are they now?

3 Read again and find out two things:
1. Tom and Marek did in the past.
2. about their lives now.
3. they'd like to do or are planning to do in the future.

4 a *Time expressions* Cover the emails. Complete the sentences from Tom's email with these time expressions.

Now   After (x2)   In a few years' time   then

> ^{1}_____ school, I did a French degree at Liverpool University. ^{2}_____ that, I didn't know what to do. I spent a year in China teaching English, ^{3}_____ I moved to the States. ^{4}_____ I'm living and working in LA ... ^{5}_____, I'd like to get married and have kids.

b Read the email to check.

c Find and <u>underline</u> similar time expressions in Marek's email.

5 a Think of an old friend you last saw at school. Write notes about your life since you saw your friend.

> • left school in 1995   • went to art college

b Tell another student about your life. Decide what time expressions to use.

> After school, I went to art college. Three years later, I ...

Delete   Reply   Reply All   Forward   Print

Hi

It's good to hear from you, Tom. After university I decided to go back to Poland and spend some time with my family in Poznan. After a few months, I got a job and moved into a small flat of my own. Ten years later, I've got a great job and a wonderful wife. And you'll never guess who I'm married to – Jessie! We didn't see each other for years after university, but then we got in touch online. She came to see me and we got married last year. We're having a baby next summer and then we're going to move into a bigger place. She's an architect and is doing very well. If you'd like to visit Poland, give us a call. By the way, have you heard from Debbie? Jessie wants to get in touch with her.

Marek

6 a Write an email to your old friend. Write about:
- your life since you left school.
- your life now.
- what you'd like to do in the future.

b Exchange emails with a partner. Do you understand everything in the email? Talk about your emails together.

14 Look again ♻

Review

GRAMMAR Hopes and plans for the future

1 a 🔊 **3.58** Listen to Khalid talk about his hopes and plans. Tick (✓) the topics he mentions.

studying   children   work   sport
travel   marriage   children

b 🔊 **3.58** Listen again. What are his hopes and plans?

He's going to … He's hoping to … He'd like to …

c Talk in pairs. What are your hopes and plans?

d What do you think are typical hopes and plans for a 20 year-old, a 40 year-old and a 60 year-old?

VOCABULARY Planning

2 a Complete the conversation with these words.

enough   too   about   going   OK   looks

JESSIE	So, what are we ¹_____ to do about Marek's birthday?
TOMASZ	Well, we could arrange a big lunch in a restaurant. It could be a surprise.
JESSIE	Yeah, ²_____. Marek would like that. Where?
TOMASZ	Look at this restaurant guide. This place ³_____ good to me.
JESSIE	Hmmm. I think it's ⁴_____ expensive. What about Khan's?
TOMASZ	Yes, that's a good idea. And what are we going to do ⁵_____ invitations?
JESSIE	Well, I haven't got ⁶_____ time to phone everyone …

b Plan a party for someone in the class. Decide what event, what to do and where to go.

c Explain your ideas to the person. Do they like the plan?

CAN YOU REMEMBER? Unit 13 – Present perfect

3 a Complete the sentences with your own ideas.

1 When I was younger I didn't like _____, but now I do.
2 I've never liked _____.
3 When I was younger I liked _____, but now I don't.
4 I've always liked _____.

b Talk about your ideas. Are they the same or different?

> When I was younger I didn't like tomatoes, but now I do.

> I've never liked coffee.

Extension

SPELLING AND SOUNDS Silent consonants

4 a 🔊 **3.59** Read and listen to these words. Notice that the consonants in red are silent.

cou**l**d   **k**now   **w**rite   clim**b**   lis**t**en

b Work in pairs. Say these words and cross out the silent consonant in each.

talk half would	knee knew	wrong wrist
tomb plumber	two	sign autumn

c 🔊 **3.60** Listen to check. Practise saying the words.

d Spellcheck. 🔊 **3.61** Listen to six words from previous units and write them down.

e Check your spelling on p159.

NOTICE Gerunds

5 a You can use **-ing** to make nouns from verbs. These are called **gerunds**. You can use gerunds:

as a subject	**Using** your brain doesn't need to be hard work.
as an object	Leonardo da Vinci often used **mirror-writing**.
after prepositions	The hippocampus … is important **for making** new memories.

Find five more gerunds in the article on p114.

b Complete the conversations with the right words.

1 eat, eating
   A I don't _eat_ meat at all, only vegetables and things like that.
   B Why? Is _____ meat bad for you?

2 smoke, smoking
   A _____ is extremely bad for you.
   B Well, I only _____ three cigarettes a day.

3 swim, swimming
   A A lot of people say that _____ is the best exercise.
   B Maybe, but I can't _____.

Self-assessment

Can you do these things in English? Circle a number on each line. 1 = I can't do this, 5 = I can do this well.

◉ give opinions	1 2 3 4 5
◉ talk about hopes and plans	1 2 3 4 5
◉ make decisions	1 2 3 4 5
◉ write a profile for a networking website	1 2 3 4 5

• For Wordcards, reference and saving your work → e-Portfolio
• For more practice → Self-study Pack, Unit 14

121

Activities

Intro unit, p9, What's your email address? 8a

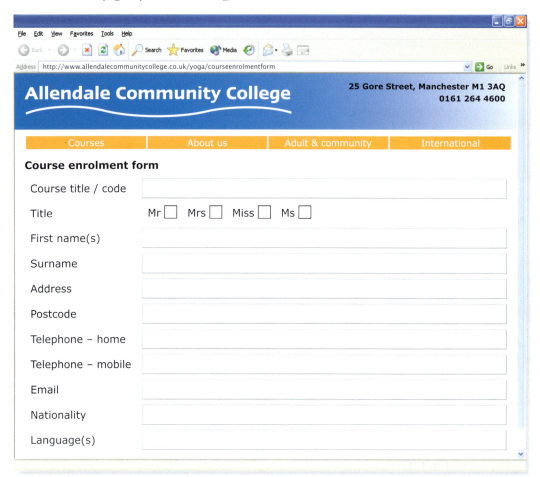

Allendale Community College

25 Gore Street, Manchester M1 3AQ
0161 264 4600

| Courses | About us | Adult & community | International |

Course enrolment form

Course title / code

Title   Mr ☐   Mrs ☐   Miss ☐   Ms ☐

First name(s)

Surname

Address

Postcode

Telephone – home

Telephone – mobile

Email

Nationality

Language(s)

Unit 2, p25, Look again 3b

1 When was the first football World Cup?
b 1930, in Uruguay.

2 What is the capital of Poland?
c Warsaw. Krakow was the capital from 1038 to 1596.

3 How long was the First World War?
a 4 years, from 1914 to 1918.

4 What are the official languages of Canada?
b English and French.

5 Where were the first Olympic Games?
b in Greece, over 2800 years ago.

Unit 11, p91, Getting a flight 5a (Student A)

You work at the airline check-in desk.
Your name is _____.

Remember that you need to:
- check the passenger's passport.
- give the passenger a boarding pass.
- tell the passenger which gate to go to, and what time they're boarding.

Look at the script on p156 for language you can use.
Use the information on the 'Departures' board on p90.
Remember that boarding time is normally 40 minutes before departure time.

Unit 3, p32, Explore speaking 5a (Student B)

CONVERSATION 1
Student A wants to talk to Paula but she isn't at home. Take a message.

CONVERSATION 2
Your name: Martin (or Martine) Duplessis
Your phone number: 205 2245 9108
You want to talk to Léon.
Your message: go to a football game on March 21st?

Unit 13, p108, Great places 4a (Student B)

Antoni Gaudi

Güell Park At the end of the nineteenth century, businessman Eusebi Güell bought a large hill in Barcelona, Spain. The land had no water and not many trees, but Güell asked Antoni Gaudi, an artist and architect, to design and build a small 'city' with 60 luxury houses and a park. From 1900 to 1914, Gaudi created one of the best-known and most unusual parks in Europe, with strange-shaped buildings and colourful sculptures which rise up from the earth. However, only two houses were built and, because Gaudi's style was not fashionable at the time, nobody wanted to buy them. Güell died in 1918 and in 1923 his family gave the park to the city.

Unit 10, p85, Arrangements 3a (Student B)

Monday
9am-3pm: meeting with East Asia sales team, Singapore
Flight: Singapore 17.10 > Perth 22.30

Tuesday
5.30 take Jamie to football practice

Wednesday
10.30 - meet XPress sales manager, my office
1.15 - talk to Ed + Jeanette (conference call)

Thursday
1.15 shopping with Mia - present for Gillian

Friday
business lunch, Sueli Olivera, Fairmont Hotel, 12.30
6pm Gillian's party (Royston Cafe)

Saturday

Sunday

Unit 5, p46, Target activity 5b-c (Student B)

Oxmantown Road, Dublin 7, North Dublin City

- one person, no sharing
- television
- no phone or internet
- central heating included
- washing machine
- no dishwasher
- no smoking
- no parking
- visits after 8 pm

Unit 5, p49, Look again 2d

The spare room

Unit 5, p47, Across cultures 4a

Personal space quiz

1. You're on a crowded bus. Do you:
   a) talk to people?   b) look out of the window?   c) read?

2. You go into a crowded café. There's only one seat at a table with people you don't know. Do you:
   a) sit down?   b) ask the people if you can sit down?   c) go to another café?

3. You're manager of a big team of workers. Do you want:
   a) a desk in an open office with your team?   b) a desk in an office with other managers?
   c) your own office with a door?

4. You're in a park, reading a book. Somebody you don't know sits near you. Do you:
   a) move to a different place?   b) do nothing because it's not a problem?
   c) do nothing, but feel uncomfortable?

5. You're talking to someone you just met at a party. Do you stand:
   a) 2 metres away?   b) 1 metre away?   c) 50 cm away?

Unit 7, p58, Work-life balance 1b

SO WHAT DO YOU DO ALL DAY?

Dagmara Makowska, 32, theatre manager in Bytom, Poland

🕐 **Work** *10 hours*

I work for a cultural centre, where I plan and organise theatre projects. Officially I work from nine to seven, but I often stay longer, especially when we're working on a big project. I sometimes work at weekends too.

🕐 **Travel** *2½ hours*

I live in Zabrze and work in Bytom, so I spend about two and a half hours on the bus every day. It's a lot of time, but I read a lot.

🕐 **Hobbies** *1–2 hours*

I like learning other languages. At the moment I'm trying to improve my English and Spanish. I go to Spanish classes once a week and I'm thinking about having private lessons too. I also watch English TV and read English books and newspapers.

🕐 **Me** *3½ hours*

'Me time' is really important to me, but I get back from work quite late most days, so I don't spend a lot of time with my family. I go to the cinema or theatre and meet friends when I can. But sometimes I do extra work, like writing theatre reviews, so I lose my free time.

🕐 **Sleep** *6 hours*

I like going to bed late but I need to get up at six in the morning to get to work, so I'm always tired. Sometimes I sleep more at the weekends, but then I have less free time!

Answer the questions. What does Dagmara do:

1. every day?
2. once a week?
3. on the bus?
4. in the evenings?

Unit 7, p61, Talking about now, 3a (Student A)

Unit 8, p67, Friends 2a

How we met

ED SMITH ON VIKRAM SETH

My dad was Vikram's English teacher at Tonbridge School in the 1980s, but the first time I met Vikram was in 1994, just after *A Suitable Boy* came out. He visited Tonbridge to give a reading and stayed the night with our family. I was sixteen and we didn't talk much. He spent most of the time talking to my father.

Six years later, in 2000, we met again in Australia. He was in Perth for work and I was there playing cricket. I rang his hotel and said, "Vikram, it's Edward Smith, Jonathan Smith's son." We met up and spent the afternoon chatting, and had dinner that evening. We talked for hours about books and music. It was wonderful. I'd left university a couple of years before and I missed talking about ideas.

Vikram's a serious person, but he's also great company, intelligent, creative and sometimes very funny. We only see each other from time to time but reading Vikram's books, listening to him, getting to know him – it's all taught me a lot.

1 When did Ed meet Vikram? How old was Ed?
2 Why did Vikram come to Ed's home?
3 When and where did they meet for the second time?
4 How did they spend their time together?
5 What's Vikram like? *He's a serious person, but …*
6 Do they see each other often?

Unit 8, p69, He's got a beard 3-4a

Discuss and then check your answers on p129.

Unit 9, p78, Target activity 4a (Student A)

CONVERSATION 1
You're at the train ticket window in Central Station in Colville. You want to go to Riverton, a nearby town. Ask questions to find out travel details. Buy a ticket.

CONVERSATION 2
You work at the ticket window in a coach station in Albany City. Answer the customer's questions.

Coach ticket: price one way $25.60, day return $45.00, open return $52.75. Next one leaves in 15 minutes and takes 3 hours 45 minutes; change coaches once. Another one leaves in 30 minutes and takes 3 hours; it's direct. Coach number 613. It's outside, look for sign.

Unit 9, p80, Explore speaking 7a (Student A)

CONVERSATION 1
– You're an employee in a tourist information office. Answer the visitor's questions:
– The Carlton **Inn** is on **Fifth** Avenue. The best way to get there is bus 7. A ticket costs $2.10.

CONVERSATION 2
– You're at a ticket window in a train station.
– You want a single ticket for the 4.40 train to Newmarket Central Station. Ask how long the journey takes.
– Repeat the main points at the end.

Unit 10, p87, Independent learning 3b

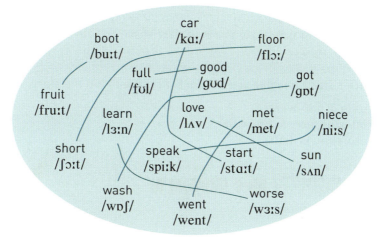

car /kɑː/
boot /buːt/
floor /flɔː/
full /fʊl/
good /gʊd/
got /gɒt/
fruit /fruːt/
learn /lɜːn/
love /lʌv/
met /met/
niece /niːs/
short /ʃɔːt/
speak /spiːk/
start /stɑːt/
sun /sʌn/
wash /wɒʃ/
went /went/
worse /wɜːs/

Unit 13, p108, Great places 4a (Student C)

Shah Jehan

Mumtaz Mahal

The Taj Mahal The Taj Mahal is the tomb of Mumtaz Mahal, the third and favourite wife of Shah Jehan, the Moghul emperor of India. When Mumtaz died in childbirth in 1631, the emperor decided to create a beautiful building in memory of his beloved wife, and it took 20,000 workers more than 20 years to complete. The Taj, in the city of Agra on the Yamuna river, is now one of the most famous places in the world: since 2000, it has had more than 25 million visitors. Today Mumtaz and her husband lie in the Taj together, but some people say that Shah Jehan wanted his own tomb to be in a second, black Taj, on the other side of the river.

Unit 11, p91, Getting a flight 5a (Student B)

You work for airport security.
Your name is _____ .

Remember that you have to:
- check the passenger's passport.
- X-ray all hand luggage.
- X-ray shoes.
- check for laptops.
- look in the passenger's bags.

Look at the script on p156 for language you can use.

Unit 11, p93, Telling a story 2a (Student B)

on holiday to France with some friends ➜ get bus and ferry to France ➜ have something to eat in ferry restaurant ➜ fall asleep ➜ wake up in ferry restaurant ➜ my friends not there ➜ ferry empty ➜ at Calais in France ➜ run to bus ➜ too late ➜ see bus driving off ferry … ?

Think of a good ending for Jack's story. Imagine you are Jack. Prepare to tell the story. Think about:

- the past simple of the verbs (e.g. go > went).
- where to use the (get the bus; the ferry to France).
- where to use storytelling expressions (Later, …).

Unit 5, p46, Target activity 5b-c (Student A)

Hazelwood, Dublin 9, North Dublin City

- share with four other students (but own bathroom)
- television, phone, internet
- central heating not included
- washing machine
- dishwasher
- near bus stop to city centre
- parking
- no smoking
- visits 9am – 1pm, weekends only

Unit 7, p61, Talking about now 3a (Student B)

Unit 8, p69, He's got a beard 3-4a

Answers
1   1970s, Northern Europe
2   Han Dynasty in ancient China, about 2250 years ago
3   1980s punk fashion, originally UK but popular in other countries
4   early twenty-first century, Nigeria
5   2010, international fashion

Unit 9, p78, Target activity 4a (Student B)

CONVERSATION 1
You work at the train ticket window in Central Station in Colville. Answer the customer's questions.

Train ticket: price one way $11.00, day return $19.00, open return $25.00.
Next one leaves in 15 minutes and takes 1 hour 10 minutes; change trains once.
Another one leaves in one hour and takes 45 minutes; it's direct. Go to platform 5.

CONVERSATION 2
You're in Albany City at the coach station. You want to go to another city, Kenover, by coach. Ask questions to find out travel details. Buy a ticket.

Unit 9, p80, Explore speaking 7a (Student B)

CONVERSATION 1
– You're in a new city. You're talking to an employee in a tourist information office.
– Ask for the best way to get to Carlton Hotel on Fourth Avenue. Ask how much a ticket costs.
– Check the information at the end.

CONVERSATION 2
– You're selling tickets at a train station. Answer the customer's questions:
– The train leaves at **4.50** and goes to Newmarket **North** Station. The journey takes 45 minutes.

Activities

Unit 11, p91, Getting a flight 5a (Student C)

You're the passenger.
Your name is _____.

Where are you going? Choose a destination from the 'Departures' board on p90. _____
How many pieces of hand luggage do you have? _____
Do you have a laptop in your hand luggage? _____

Look at the scripts on p156 for language you can use.
You need to go to check-in first, then go through security.

Unit 14, p118, Target activity 4

http://www.npc.gc.ca/mauricie

LA MAURICIE Canada

▼ Accommodation

Camping du Parc ***
We welcome you to Camping Du Parc, a friendly campsite close to La Mauricie National Park in Quebec, Canada. We offer a quiet site under the trees, a sky full of stars and a good campfire.
On site: a nice little beach, playgrounds, a safe cycling path. Nearby: some golf clubs, many fishing spots, in the heart of La Mauricie.

Au Joyeux Druide, Hotel and Art Gallery ***
Our house is on a hill by the Shawinigan River. Here you'll find comfortable rooms, a games room, and good home-grown food. We're also a gallery of modern art.
3573, Rue Bellevue, Shawinigan (Québec)

Le Baluchon ****
Our inn is in a beautiful location near islands, waterfalls, hills and a forest. We offer you comfort, a healthy break and excellent food.
3550, Chemin des Trembles, Saint-Paulin (Québec)

Chalet Joel Migneault **
Rent this warm quiet chalet in the heart of nature on Lake Chrétien. On site: hiking, mountain biking, volleyball, swimming, canoeing, kayaking and much more.
496, rue des Peupliers, Saint-Gerard-des-Laurentides (Québec)

▼ Outdoor activities

From tree to tree
An extraordinary family activity! Come and experience this new treetop adventure, unique in Mauricie. Climb trees and cross rope bridges on our specially designed course.
Open: May to October, reservations preferable.
Admission: children: from $16; adults: $25.95; special rates for families and groups.

Riding Centre, Saint-Georges
Come and enjoy our horses with a qualified instructor. Ride alone, in a group or as a family. Ponies available for children. Riding lessons for children and adults.
Open: all year
Rates: adults: $10 / hour; children: $5 / hour; special family and group rates.

Black bear observation
Watch for bears safely with our experienced guides. Learn what to do if you see a bear in the forest! Over 95% of people see bears.
Open: June to September, at sunset.
Rates: adults: $20; students: $10; special family and group rates.

National Park of Canada, Mauricie
A paradise for outdoor lovers with 536 km^2 of lakes and forests. Canoeing and hiking in summer and cross-country skiing in winter are the main activities.
Open: May 12 to October 15, 7 a.m. to 10 p.m.
Admission: $3.50 to $7 per person.

Grammar reference and practice

Intro
SUBJECT PRONOUNS AND POSSESSIVE ADJECTIVES

MEANING

Use possessive adjectives to say something belongs to you. Use possessive adjectives for names, addresses and phone numbers.

FORM

Subject pronouns	Possessive adjectives
I'm Anna.	My name's Anna.
Are you Maria? Are you Maria and Stefan?	What's your name? What are your names?
He's a student.	This is his phone number.
She's from Korea.	What's her address?
It's a beautiful cat.	What's its name?
We're from Italy.	Our home town is Milan.
They're from Norway.	What are their names?

Possessive adjectives always go before a noun:
What's her address? What's address her?

PRONUNCIATION

I	/aɪ/	my	/maɪ/
you	/juː/	your	/jɔː/
he	/hiː/	his	/hɪz/
she	/ʃiː/	her	/hɜː/
it	/ɪt/	its	/ɪts/
we	/wiː/	our	/aʊə/
they	/ðeɪ/	their	/ðeə/

You can say these words in a different way when they don't have stress:

you	/jə/	your	/jə/
he	/i/	his	/ɪz/
		her	/hə/, /ə/

PRACTICE

Complete the sentences with the words in the box.

> your   my   his   she   their   our   you   her

1 "What's _your_ name?"
    "I'm Anna. Nice to meet you."
2 They're from Japan but _____ children were born in Europe.
3 What languages do _____ speak, and what's your first language?
4 Her name's Astrid and _____'s from Mexico.
5 _____ name's Sameh and he's from Egypt.
6 We only speak English but _____ children speak three languages.
7 "What's your phone number?"
    "Well, _____ mobile number is 07786-330074."
8 _____ name is Fay and she's from Australia.

can FOR ABILITY

MEANING

I **can** swim. I **can't** swim.

FORM

> ➕ I **can** speak three languages.
> ➖ He **can't** remember her mobile number.
> ❓ **Can** you remember her surname?
> ✔ Yes, I **can**.
> ✖ No, I **can't**.

After *can*, use an **infinitive**: *I can speak three languages.*

PRONUNCIATION

In positive sentences and questions, you don't usually stress can. You say /kən/.
She can speak four languages. Can you speak English?

In negative sentences, you usually stress **can't**. You say /kɑːnt/ or /kɑːn/.
They can't remember her name.

In short answers, you stress **can** and **can't**. You say /kæn/ and /kɑːnt/.
Yes, I can. No, I can't.

PRACTICE

Make sentences and questions.

1 Can / Mike / Portuguese / speak ?
    Can Mike speak Portuguese?
2 Can / your / postcode / remember / you ?
3 can't / I / remember / name / your .
4 Can / 'hello' / in six languages / say / you ?
5 can / speak / four / I / languages .
6 can't / I / name / his / spell .
7 can / Arabic / She / and French / speak .
8 can't / email / I / remember / address / his .

1

POSSESSIVE *'s* and *s'*

MEANING

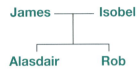

James —— Isobel
|
Alasdair   Rob

A noun with possessive *'s* has the same meaning as a possessive adjective (her, his, their ...):
James is Isobel's husband. Alasdair is her son.
Isobel is Alasdair's mother. Rob is his brother.
James is Alasdair and Rob's father. Isobel is their mother.

FORM

Singular
Isobel + 's = Isobel's husband
my friend + 's = my friend's name
Alasdair and Rob + 's = Alasdair and Rob's family

Plural (introduced in Unit 3, p28)
Do not add another s:
parents + ' = my parents' house

The noun with possessive *'s* goes before the other noun:
James is Isobel's husband.
~~*James is husband Isobel's.*~~

PRONUNCIATION

You usually say *'s* or *s'* as /s/ or /z/:
Jeff's /s/   *Matt's* /s/   *Rob's* /z/   *Isobel's* /z/   *my parents'* /s/

When a noun ends in -s, -z, -x, -sh or -ch, you say /ɪz/:
James's /ˈdʒeɪmzɪz/   *Alex's* /ˈælɪksɪz/

PRACTICE

1 ***Singular.* Add *'s* to the correct word in each sentence.**

1 Are you Rob's brother?
2 This is Sally, my brother girlfriend.
3 Are you Lucia English teacher?
4 My friend boss is really nice.
5 Maria Teresa family is from Madrid.
6 What's that man name?
7 Is that your sister bag?
8 My cat name is Alfie.

2 ***Plural.* Circle the correct word.**

1 This is my parents / parents' new car.
2 His parent's / parents live in Kyoto.
3 Hi. Are you Charles / Charles's father?
4 Natasha and Anna are my sisters / sisters'.
5 Her grandparents / grandparents' flat isn't very big.
6 What are your colleagues / colleagues' names?

be PRESENT: *am, is, are*

MEANING

Use the present tense of be (am, is, are) to talk about:
who: *I'm Rob. He's a student. They're my friends.*
what: *It's my bag. They're my books.*
where: *My bag's in my car. The books are on the table.*
how old: *I'm thirty.* ~~*I have thirty.*~~
times and dates: *It's 8.30. It's 1 March 2010.*
the weather: *It's hot. It's sunny.*
You can use am, is, are to talk about things which are true now, or always true:
James is in his office. It's 8.30. (true now)
Paris is in France. Rob and Alasdair are brothers. (always true)

FORM

➕	➖
I'm Rob.	I'm not Rob.
You're late.	You aren't late.
He's a teacher.	He isn't a student.
She's a doctor.	She isn't a journalist.
It's my bag.	It isn't my bag.
We're friends.	We aren't brothers.
They're Spanish.	They aren't Brazilian.

❓	✔ / ✘
Am I late?	Yes, I am. / No, I'm not.
Are you from Spain?	Yes, you are. / No, you aren't.
Is he a teacher?	Yes, he is. / No, he isn't.
Is she a doctor?	Yes, she is. / No, she isn't.
Is it your bag?	Yes, it is. / No, it isn't.
Are we late?	Yes, we are. / No, we aren't.
Are they here?	Yes, they are. / No, they aren't.

Contractions:
➕ I'm = I am   you're = you are   he's, she's = he is, she is
   it's = it is   we're, they're = we are, they are
➖ isn't = is not   aren't = are not

You can also contract are not and is not like this:
You are not late. → *You're not late.*
It isn't my bag. → *It's not my bag.*

PRONUNCIATION

You don't usually stress am, is, are in positive sentences or questions:
I'm a student. Are you a teacher?

But you usually stress am, is, are in negative sentences and short answers:
She isn't a teacher. Yes, I am. No, they aren't.

You stress not in sentences with I'm not, he's not, etc:
I'm not Rob. No, I'm not.

PRACTICE

Complete the conversations.

1 "Where *are* you from?" "I _____ from Korea."
2 "Vigo _____ in Portugal." "No, it _____ . It _____ in Spain."
3 "_____ you Rob's friend?" "No, I _____ . I _____ his boss."
4 "How old _____ your children?"
   "Our son _____ twelve and our daughter _____ eight."
5 "_____ you interested in yoga?" "Yes, we _____ ."
6 "_____ this your coffee?" "No. Maybe it _____ Jo's."
7 "Sorry, _____ I late?" "Yes, you _____ . Forty-five minutes!"
8 "Excuse me, where _____ the cinema?"
   "Sorry, we _____ from around here."

be PAST: *was, were*

MEANING

Use the past tense of be (was, were) to talk about things in the past:

When I was 19, I was a student.
In 1998, Leslie and I were colleagues.
Bec was in Delhi yesterday.

FORM

✚	➖
I **was** a journalist.	I **wasn't** an engineer.
You **were** late.	You **weren't** late.
He **was** a lawyer.	He **wasn't** a nurse.
She **was** a sales rep.	She **wasn't** a teacher.
It **was** an interesting job.	It **wasn't** an easy job.
We **were** friends.	We **weren't** friends.
They **were** students.	They **weren't** teachers.

❓	✔/✘
Was I late?	Yes, I **was**. / No, I **wasn't**.
Were you late?	Yes, you **were**. / No, you **weren't**.
Was he a doctor?	Yes, he **was**. / No, he **wasn't**.
Was she a lawyer?	Yes, she **was**. / No, she **wasn't**.
Was it a good job?	Yes, it **was**. / No, it **wasn't**.
Were we friends?	Yes, we **were**. / No, we **weren't**.
Were they here?	Yes, they **were**. / No, they **weren't**.

Contractions:
➖ wasn't = was not   weren't = were not

PRONUNCIATION

You don't usually stress was and were in positive sentences or questions:

I was a nurse. Were you a doctor?
Say *was* /wəz/ and *were* /wə/.

You usually stress was, wasn't, were and weren't in negative sentences and short answers:

It wasn't an easy job. They weren't friends. Yes, she was.
No, we weren't.
Say *was* /wɑz/, *were* /wɜ:/, *wasn't* /wɒznt/ and *weren't* /wɜ:nt/.

PRACTICE

Add **was, wasn't, were** and **weren't** to the correct places in the sentences.

        was
1 After university I ∧ an accountant for ten years.

2 Excuse me, you at Stamford University in 2005?

3 "How do you know Carl?"

   "We colleagues in the same office for a couple of years."

4 "Mario and Lucia at the party last night?"

   "No, they're on holiday."

5 I in Athens last Friday. It's a really interesting city.

6 "Where Mr Gomez at ten o'clock this morning?"

   "I don't know."

7 "How your exam?" "OK. It very difficult."

8 Alex and Paul at the same school but they in the same class.

2
a, an, some

MEANING

Use a / an with singular nouns. It means 'one'.
Can I have a cup of coffee, please? (= one cup of coffee)
Would you like an orange? (= one orange)

You often use some with plural nouns. You use it when it is not important to say how much or how many.
Can I have some oranges, please?
Can I have some books, please?

For some with uncountable nouns, see Unit 6, p137.

FORM

Use a, an and some before nouns.

Use a before words that start with a consonant (b, c, d, ...).
Can I have a newspaper, please?

Use an before words that start with a vowel sound (a, e, i, o, u).
Can I have an apple, please?

Use an when u- is /ʌ/: an umbrella
Use a when u- is /ju:/: a university

PRONUNCIATION

You don't usually stress a, an or some:

I'm a teacher. /ə/
Would you like a drink? /ə/
Can I have an apple? /ən/
Can I have some newspapers, please? /səm/

You usually stress some at the start of a sentence:
Some people don't like this newspaper. /sʌm/

PRACTICE

Add **a, an** or **some** to the sentences.

                 a
1 I live in Seoul. It's ∧ great city.

2 I really want new boots.

3 Would you like cup of coffee after your dinner?

4 I want to get good job.

5 My flat has spare room.

6 My home town has good clubs.

7 I want to go to café for lunch.

8 I'm architect.

9 Could you bring biscuits?

10 It's old computer but I like it.

133

PRESENT SIMPLE – POSITIVE

MEANING

Use the present simple to talk about things that are always true, or happen all the time, or happen regularly.
I have two children.
I play football on Saturdays.

FORM

Present simple verbs following **he**, **she** and **it** end in **-s**.

Most verbs	Verbs ending in consonant +y
I **work** in an office. You **work** here. He/she **works** there. We **work** at home. They **work** for a big company.	I **study** French. You **study** a lot. He/she **studies** every day. We **study** on Fridays. They **study** medicine.
Verbs ending in -s, -z, -ch, -sh or -x	**Irregular verbs**
I **miss** you. You **miss** me. He **misses** his wife. We **miss** you. They **miss** us. catch > catches watch > watches	I **have** a cat. You **have** three sisters. She **has** a new car. We **have** a big family. They **have** a brother. go > goes do > does

PRONUNCIATION

You usually say **-s** as /s/ or /z/.
works /wɜːks/   *speaks* /spiːks/   *plays* /pleɪz/   *studies* /'studiz/

You usually say **-es** as /ɪz/.
misses /'mɪsɪz/   *watches* /'wɒtʃɪz/

You say **goes** /gəʊz/ and **does** /dʌz/.

PRACTICE

Complete the sentences with the correct form of the verb in brackets.

1 When we're away from home I *miss* (miss) my parents. My wife _____ (miss) our flat.
2 My mum and dad _____ (speak) three languages. I only _____ (speak) one.
3 I _____ (have) two children and my sister _____ (have) five.
4 In the summer we usually _____ (stay) with our friends in Portugal. They sometimes _____ (stay) with us too.
5 My friends _____ (live) in the same town as me but my sister and her husband _____ (live) abroad.
6 I _____ (study) Japanese, but my friend Simon _____ (study) English.
7 My brother _____ (want) to travel in Europe. My friends _____ (want) to travel in South America.
8 My mum _____ (cook) dinner at the weekend. We all _____ (cook) during the week.

PRESENT SIMPLE – NEGATIVE

FORM

⊖	Contractions:
I **don't live** here. You **don't live** here. He / she **doesn't live** here. We **don't live** here. They **don't live** here.	⊖ do not = **don't** does not = **doesn't**

PRONUNCIATION

You usually stress **don't** or **doesn't** in negative sentences.
I don't work on Saturdays.
He doesn't live here.

PRACTICE

Complete the sentences with **don't** or **doesn't**.

1 They *don't* work here. They're here for the meeting.
2 Where's the café? Sorry, I _____ know. I'm new too.
3 Roberto _____ live in Lisbon. He lives in Oporto.
4 I'm sorry, I _____ eat seafood. It makes me ill.
5 Can you help us? We _____ know where to go.
6 My sister's at home a lot. She _____ have a job.

PRESENT SIMPLE – QUESTIONS

FORM

Add **do** or **does** to make a present simple question.

❓	✔ / ✘	
Do I work?	Yes, I **do**.	No, I **don't**.
Do you work?	Yes, you **do**.	No, you **don't**.
Does he/she work?	Yes, he/she **does**.	No, he/she **doesn't**.
Do we work?	Yes, we **do**.	No, we **don't**.
Do they work?	Yes, they **do**.	No, they **don't**.

PRONUNCIATION

You don't usually stress **do** or **does** in questions.
What do you do?

You usually stress **do**, **does**, **don't** and **doesn't** in short answers.
Yes, I do.   *No, she doesn't.*

PRACTICE

Put the words in order to make questions.

1 you / in / this neighbourhood / Do / work ?
   Do you work in this neighbourhood?
2 you / Do / near here / live ?
3 does / Where / live / your brother ?
4 What / do / play / sports / you ?
5 you / in the evening / watch TV / Do / always ?
6 she / go on holiday / Where / does / usually ?

SUBJECT AND OBJECT PRONOUNS

MEANING

You can use pronouns to talk about people, things and activities.

My grandchildren are great. I love them so much.

Where's Susan? Is she here?

I like watching TV. It's fun.

FORM

subject pronouns	object pronouns
I	me
you	you
he	him
she	her
it	it
we	us
they	them

Subject pronouns usually go before the **verb** in a sentence.
I like watching TV.

Object pronouns go after **verbs** and **prepositions**.
I love them.
I like talking to my husband and watching TV with him.

PRONUNCIATION

I	/aɪ/	me	/miː/
you	/juː/	you	/juː/
he	/hiː/	him	/hɪm/
she	/ʃiː/	her	/hɜː/
it	/ɪt/	it	/ɪt/
we	/wiː/	us	/ʌs/
they	/ðeɪ/	them	/ðem/

You can say these words in a different way when they don't have stress:
you /ju/, /jə/   him /ɪm/   her /hə/, /ə/
us /əs/   them /ðəm/, /əm/

PRACTICE

Circle the correct word.

1 He / him likes fishing in the sea with his friends.

2 Is she / her busy now?

3 Bob can meet we / us at 5.00 tomorrow evening.

4 She / her is a really nice person.

5 I like talking to he / her.

6 We / us play football at the weekend.

7 My cat doesn't like my boyfriend but she loves I / me.

8 Are they / them friends or colleagues?

9 Money doesn't make you / we happy.

10 I don't read newspapers. I don't like they / them.

4
SINGULAR AND PLURAL NOUNS

MEANING

Use plurals to talk about more than one.
I have a car. My friend has two cars.

FORM

	singular (one)	plural (two +)
Add *-s* to most nouns.	thing shop	thing**s** shop**s**
Add *-es* to nouns ending *-sh, -ch, -ss, -x, -z,* or *-s.*	dish boss	dish**es** boss**es**
For nouns ending in consonant + *y: y̶ > -ies*.	company city	compan**ies** cit**ies**
irregular plurals	person man woman child	people /ˈpiːpəl/ men /men/ women /ˈwɪmɪn/ children /ˈtʃɪldrən/

PRONUNCIATION

Say plurals in the same way as these present simple verbs:
works, watches, studies. See p134.

shops /ʃɒps/   books /bʊks/   things /θɪŋz/   cities /ˈsɪtiz/
dishes /ˈdɪʃɪz/   bosses /ˈbɒsɪz/

PRACTICE

Complete the sentences with the plurals of these words.

country   city   school   newspaper   sister   email
woman   party   friend

1 How many _countries_ are there in South America?

2 I send _____ to my boyfriend every day.

3 I have three _____ and one brother.

4 I don't like big _____. I prefer small towns.

5 When do you usually meet your _____?

6 I don't read _____. I don't like bad news.

7 Ask the _____ over there. They work in this shop.

8 All the _____ in my town have good teachers.

9 I like dancing, but I hate going to _____.

PAST SIMPLE

MEANING

1972   when I was five   for three years   NOW

Use the past simple to talk about events that are in the past and finished.
Pavel made the Stereobelt in 1972.
My family moved from Nigeria to Scotland when I was five.
I lived in France for three years.

FORM

I, you, he, she, it, we and they all have the same past simple form.

➕	I **went** to the cinema last night. We **moved** to Scotland.
➖	I **didn't go** to the cinema last night. ~~didn't went~~ We **didn't move** to Scotland. ~~didn't moved~~
❓	**Did** you **go** to the cinema last night? **Did** you **move** to Scotland?
✔	Yes, I **did**.
✘	No, I **didn't**.

Some past simple verbs are regular and end in **ed**.
move > moved   listen > listened   like > liked

Some past simple verbs are irregular.
go > went   make > made   buy > bought   have > had

See **Irregular verbs** on p160.

PRONUNCIATION

You usually say **ed** as /d/ or /t/.
moved /muːvd/   *listened* /lɪsənd/   *studies* /stʌdid/
liked /laɪkt/   *worked* /wɜːkt/

With a few verbs, you say **ed** as /ɪd/.
wanted /wɒntɪd/   *started* /stɑːtɪd/   *ended* /endɪd/
The infinitive of these verbs ends with a /t/ or a /d/:
want > wanted, start > started, end > ended

Don't say **ed** as /ed/.

PRACTICE

Complete the conversations with did or didn't.

1 "_____ you have a nice weekend?"
  "Well, no, I _____. It was terrible."
2 "When _____ you buy that mobile phone?"
  "I _____ buy it. My sister gave it to me."
3 "_____ you see your family last weekend?"
  "Yes, I _____. We had a great time."
4 "How much _____ your laptop cost?"
  "I _____ pay a lot – about $150. I bought it from a friend."
5 "Who _____ you see at the party?"
  "I _____ go. I stayed at home."
6 "_____ you like the film?"
  "Well, the story was OK but I _____ like the actors."
7 "_____ you call the hotel?"
  "Yes, I _____, and I got directions from them."
8 "_____ you go out last weekend?"
  "No, I _____. I _____ have time. I was really busy."

THERE IS / THERE ARE

MEANING

You can use *there is / are* to say that things or people exist, often in a certain place:
In my home town, there's a university and there are a lot of parks.
In my class, there's an architect and there are two doctors.

You usually give more information about the things or people:
There's a bus stop near my flat. (= where)
There's a train at eight o'clock this evening. (= when)
There are nine students in my class. (= how many)

You don't use *it's* or *they're* with this meaning:
~~It's a bus stop near my flat.~~
~~They're a lot of parks in Istanbul.~~

FORM

You use *there is* with singular nouns and *there are* with plural nouns. In the negative form, *there's no ...* and *there are no ...* are much more common that *there isn't* and *there aren't*.

	Singular	Plural	
➕	There's a bus stop near my flat.	There are two banks in Main Street.	
	There's There are	a lot of shops in my neighbourhood.	
➖	There's no bus stop. There isn't a bus stop.	There are no banks. There aren't any banks.	
❓	Is there a bus stop near here?	Are there any banks near here?	How many banks are there?
✔ / ✘	Yes, there is. No, there isn't.	Yes, there are. No, there aren't.	There's one. There are two. There aren't any.

Contractions:
there's = there is
You can use *there's* and *there are* with *a couple of* and *a lot of* if the noun is plural.

PRONUNCIATION

You don't usually stress *there*, *is* or *are*:
There's a bus stop near my flat. There are no banks. Is there a bus stop near here?

But you usually stress *is* and *are* in negatives (*isn't* and *aren't*), and short answers:
There isn't a bus stop. There aren't any bus stops.
Yes, there is. No, there isn't. Yes, there are. No, there aren't.

PRACTICE

Complete the conversations with is, 's, are, isn't, aren't.

1 "Excuse me, _____ there a bus stop near here?"
  "Yes, there _____ one at the end of the street, about five minutes' walk."
2 "_____ there any good cafés near your flat?"
  "Yes, there _____ two or three. There _____ a very nice one on the corner. We could go there."
3 "_____ there any books in that cupboard?"
  "No, there _____. There _____ only an old newspaper."
4 "_____ there a photocopier in your office?"
  "No, sorry, there _____ ."

6
COUNTABLE AND UNCOUNTABLE NOUNS

MEANING and FORM

Countable nouns can be singular and plural. Use **a** or **an** with singular countable nouns.

Uncountable nouns don't have a plural. You can't use **a** or **an** with uncountable nouns.

a book   some books

some pasta
(~~some pastas~~ ✗ ~~a pasta~~ ✗)

Many nouns can be countable and uncountable.

three potatoes   some potato   a chicken   some chicken

Countable	Uncountable
How many lettuces would you like?	**How much** lettuce would you like?
I'd like **a** lettuce. / **one** lettuce.	–
I'd like **six** carrots / **some** carrots.	Have **some** lettuce in your sandwich.
I don't eat **a lot of** carrots.	I'd like **a lot of** lettuce.

PRONUNCIATION

You usually stress question words, numbers and **lot**.

How many potatoes would you like?

I ate **two** apples for breakfast.

I don't want a **lot** of rice.

PRACTICE

1   Complete the sentences with **a**, **an**, **some**, **much** or **many**.

1   I eat _____ orange every day.
2   Would you like _____ pasta?
3   Can I have _____ apple?
4   I had _____ toast for breakfast this morning.
5   I'd like _____ biscuits.
6   Can I have _____ banana?
7   How _____ meat do you eat?
8   How _____ eggs would you like?

2   Circle the correct word.

1   How much / many cheese do you usually buy every week?
2   How much / many eggs would you like?
3   How much / many coffees did you drink yesterday?
4   How much / many fruit do you usually eat every day?
5   How much / many onions did you buy?
6   How much / many chocolate do you eat?

7
PRESENT PROGRESSIVE

MEANING

Use the present progressive to talk about present activities: things happening now or around now.
I can't talk now. I'm planning my seminar. (now)
They're working quite hard these days. (around now)

The present progressive is sometimes called the present continuous.

FORM

be + verb + -ing
➕   I**'m going** to a meeting now. She**'s** / He**'s planning** a seminar. You**'re** / We**'re** / They**'re working** quite hard these days.
➖   I**'m not feeling** well. She / He **isn't working** at the moment. He**'s not working** ... You / We / They **aren't writing** a report. You**'re not writing** ...
❓   **Am** I **working** late tonight? Where **are** we / they / you **going**? **Are** you **studying** law? **Is** he **working** hard? **Are** they **designing** a website?

You can also contract **are not** and **is not** like this:
He's not working at the moment.
They're not having a sale this week.
No, he's not. / No, they're not.

PRONUNCIATION

You don't usually stress **am**, **is**, **are** in positive sentences or questions.

They are working quite hard.

How is he feeling?

But you usually stress **am**, **is**, **are** in negative sentences and short answers.

They aren't writing a report.

Yes, he is.   *No, he isn't.*

You stress **not** in these sentences.

They're not writing a report.   *No, he's not.*

PRACTICE

Complete the sentences with present progressive verbs.

1   "I'm a student." "Really? What / you / study?"
    What are you studying?
2   "I / go / out now. Bye." "Bye. Have a nice time."
3   "Kevin, what / you / do ?"
    "I / talk / to someone on the phone."
4   "Is this a good time, Mary?"
    "Sorry, no. I / make / dinner."
5   "Can I use the computer?"
    "Sorry, but I / use / it at the moment."
6   "He / not / work / at the moment. He / do / a course in marketing."

8

Have got

MEANING

Use **have got** to talk about possessions (things you own), families and appearance.
I've got a silver Toyota.
She's got three children. They've all got blue eyes.

You don't use **have got** with adjectives, ages or activities.
I'm hungry. I've got hungry.
She's 29 tomorrow. She's got 29 tomorrow.
I always have lunch in the café next to work. I always have got …

FORM

I, you, we, they	He, she, it
➕ I've got long, brown hair.	➕ He's got three bikes.
➖ We haven't got any children.	➖ The flat hasn't got a balcony.
❓ Have they got a car?	❓ Has she got a computer?
✅ Yes, they have.	✅ Yes, she has.
❌ No, they haven't.	❌ No, she hasn't.

Contractions:
I've got = I have got   He's got = He has got
haven't = have not   hasn't = has not

Have and **have got** are both common in British English. **Have** is more common in American English and between international users of English.
Does she have long hair?
(British, American, international English)
Has she got long hair? (British English)

You don't use **have got** to talk about the past.
I had fair hair when I was a child. I had got fair hair…

PRONUNCIATION

You usually contract **have got** in conversation.
He's got long hair.   They've got a car.

You stress **got** in positive sentences and questions.
He's got three bikes.   Has she got a computer?
You stress **have** and **got** in negative sentences and short answers.
The flat hasn't got a balcony.   Yes, it has. / No, it hasn't.

PRACTICE

1 Complete the sentences with the correct form of **have got**. Use contractions where you can.

1 He *'s got* long brown hair and he's very tall.
2 They _____ three children and a couple of cats.
3 My flat hasn't got a garden, but it _____ a big balcony.
4 _____ you _____ a bike? We could cycle there.
5 Sorry, I can't read that. I _____ my glasses with me.
6 We _____ a car so we're going by train.

2 Circle the correct expressions. Sometimes both expressions are correct.

1 My cousin has / My cousin's got a small flat in the centre of town.
2 We usually have / We've usually got dinner at six.
3 Does she have / Has she got green eyes like her brother?
4 I'd like to have / have got a shower before we go.
5 When I was a teenager I had / I've got really long hair.

9

COMPARATIVES AND SUPERLATIVES

MEANING

Comparatives
The train is more expensive than the coach.
The train is cheaper than the plane.

Superlatives
The coach is the cheapest way to get to Edinburgh.
The plane is the most expensive.

You use **the** with superlatives because there can be only one 'best' or 'easiest'.

FORM

Comparatives	Spelling rule	Example
one-syllable adjectives	+ *-er* + *-r* if adjective ends in *-e*	longer safer
one syllable, ending in one short vowel + one consonant	double the last consonant + *-er*	bigger
two-syllable adjectives	more + adjective	more careful
two syllables, ending in -y	*y* > + *-ier*	easier
three syllables or more	more + adjective	more dangerous more interesting
irregular adjectives	good bad far	better worse further

Superlatives	Spelling rule	Example
one-syllable adjectives	+ *-est* + *-st* if adjective ends in *-e*	the longest the safest
one syllable, ending in one short vowel + one consonant	double the last consonant + *-est*	the biggest
two-syllable adjectives	most + adjective	the most careful
two syllables, ending in -y	*y* > + *-iest*	the easiest
three syllables or more	most + adjective	the most dangerous the most interesting
irregular adjectives	good bad far	the best the worst the furthest

(continued on p139)

(continued from p138)

PRONUNCIATION

You usually stress more, most and adjectives.
You say –er as /ə/, and –est as /ɪst/.
You don't usually stress than or the. We say them with /ə/.

The train is more expensive than the bus.
You can get the train but it's cheaper to get the bus.
I'm the tallest in my family.
It's the best way to get there.

But when the is in front of a word starting with a vowel, you pronounce it as /ðiː/.
the earliest /ðiːˈjɜːliːɪst/, the oldest /ðiːˈjəʊldɪst/

PRACTICE

1 Complete the sentences with the comparative form of the adjectives in brackets.

1 Buses in this city are a lot _____ than the underground. (slow)

2 Our new car is much _____ than our old one. (nice)

3 I think that cycling is _____ than driving. (dangerous)

4 Central Market's interesting but it's _____ than Riverside Market. (crowded)

5 Walking's _____ for your health than driving. (good)

6 You can get the bus or a taxi to the station but it's a lot _____ to get a taxi. (expensive)

7 We could go to the cinema but I think the concert looks _____. (interesting)

8 I like walking into town but it's _____ to drive. (quick)

9 The small shops near me are nice but the supermarket's _____. (cheap)

2 Comparative or superlative? Circle the correct answer in each sentence.

1 I think Rio de Janiero's the most beautiful / more beautiful city in the world.

2 An open return is the most expensive / more expensive than a day return.

3 I love Italian, Chinese and Japanese food but I think Japanese food is the healthiest / healthier.

4 I think driving's the safest / safer than riding a motorbike.

5 This is the biggest / bigger park in my town.

6 I'm the tallest / taller than my brother.

7 In fact, I'm the tallest / taller person in my family.

8 I bought a new computer but it's the worst / worse than my old one.

10
PRESENT PROGRESSIVE – FUTURE ARRANGEMENTS

MEANING

You can use the present progressive to talk about future arrangements, often with a future time phrase.
I'm meeting Jon for coffee this evening.
We're flying to Germany tomorrow.

FORM

See PRESENT PROGRESSIVE, p137.

PRONUNCIATION

See PRESENT PROGRESSIVE, p137.

PRACTICE

1 Complete each sentence with the correct verb in the present progressive.

| see   go (x2)   have (x2)   give   get (x2)   meet   work |

1 She _____ us at 6.30 tomorrow night in front of Bellini's Restaurant.

2 We _____ to Frankfurt for a conference next month.

3 Sorry I can't come. I _____ late tonight.

4 I think he _____ a taxi to the airport tomorrow morning.

5 I _____ a film with some friends tonight.

6 Professor Hunt _____ a lecture on Matisse this afternoon.

7 We _____ a meeting on Thursday afternoon so don't forget to come.

8 I _____ to the hairdresser's this Saturday.

9 They _____ the 10.30 coach to Seattle.

10 I _____ a party on Friday. Can you come?

2 **a** Put the words in order to make questions.

1 after / are / this class / going / Where / you ?

2 are / getting up / tomorrow / What time / you ?

3 Are / friends / seeing / tonight / you ?

4 are / birthday / How / next / spending / you / your ?

5 are / at / doing / the weekend / What / you ?

6 Are / having / a holiday / in / six months / the next / you ?

7 you / next week / doing / are / What ?

8 soon / you / for food / Are / going / shopping ?

b Ask and answer the questions.

11
ARTICLES

MEANING

Use a/an (indefinite article) when you talk about a person or thing for the first time.
Is there a post office on this street?

Use the (definite article) when the listener knows *which* person or thing you are talking about. For example:
- The listener knows because you talked about it before.
  We've got two cars, a Fiat and a Honda. We use the Fiat to get around the city.
- They know because it's clear from the situation.
  Can you close the door, please?
- They know because there's only one (in the world, or in our situation).
  The sun is really bright today.
  This is why you usually use the with ordinal numbers and superlatives, because there is only one *first* or *best*.
  The first floor   The best cafe   The last time

You don't use an article when you talk about things in general. This is sometimes called zero article.
I don't like coffee. the coffee
Bananas are my favourite fruit. The bananas ...

FORM

You can use a/an before singular countable nouns.
She's got a boy and a girl.

You can use the before:
- singular countable nouns.
  She's got a boy and girl. The boy's thirteen and the girl's ten.
- plural countable nouns.
  The shops are closed today.
- uncountable nouns.
  Have you got the luggage?

You don't use the with possessives.
This is my uncle. the my uncle

You can use zero article before:
- plural countable nouns: *I don't like snakes.*
- uncountable nouns: *I love chocolate.*

PRONUNCIATION

You don't usually stress articles. You say a /ə/ and an /ən/.

You usually say the /ðə/. But when a vowel sound follows the, you pronounce it /ðiː/:
the alphabet   the easiest way   the umbrella

PRACTICE

Add the, a or (–) to these sentences.

1 Look at moon. It's beautiful.
2 Would you like drink?
3 I've got sister and brother. My brother lives in São Paulo and my sister lives in Brasilia. (x2)
4 I love animals.
5 Excuse me, when's next train to Istanbul?
6 This is announcement for all passengers flying to Kuala Lumpur.
7 My brother has got fantastic flat near sea. (x2)
8 Cars are more expensive than motorbikes.
9 Do you prefer tea or coffee?
10 Is there bank near here?

12
GIVING ADVICE WITH *if*

MEANING

You can use if sentences to give advice.
If you get stomach ache, try some black toast.

FORM

If + present simple,	imperative
If you get stomach ache,	try some black toast.
If you have a temperature,	don't go to work.

If + present simple,	should + infinitive
If this doesn't work,	you should go to a dentist.
If you have a cold,	you shouldn't go to work.

You can change the order. When the *If* part of the sentence is first, put a comma (,) between the two parts.
If you get stomach ache, try some black toast.
Try some black toast if you get stomach ache.

If you have a cold, you shouldn't go to work.
You shouldn't go to work if you have a cold.

PRONUNCIATION

You usually stress *if*, *don't* and *shouldn't*.
If you have a temperature, don't go to work.
If you have a cold, you shouldn't go to work.

You don't usually stress *should*.
If these remedies don't work for you, you should go to a dentist.

PRACTICE

1 Match sentence beginnings 1–8 with the endings.

1 If your TV doesn't work,
2 You should exercise more
3 Don't forget to take an umbrella
4 If you want a new job,
5 Check a dictionary
6 If you feel stressed,
7 If you want to see him,
8 You shouldn't go to the gym

a) check the adverts in the newspaper.
b) give him a call.
c) if you have backache.
d) call the repairman.
e) you should go for a walk and try to relax.
f) if you want to be fitter.
g) if it rains.
h) if you want to know the meaning of a word.

2 Add the words in brackets to the sentences. Add capital letters and punctuation.

1 Go and see the dentist ∧ you have toothache. (if)
                            if
2 you want some fruit go to the shop (if, you should)
3 don't eat food with lots of salt you want to be healthy (if)
4 eat a lot late at night you want to sleep well (if, you shouldn't)
5 you go out forget your keys (if, don't)
6 go to bed early you feel tired (if, you should)
7 take these tablets you have a headache (if)
8 check the internet you want travel information (if, you should)

13
PRESENT PERFECT

MEANING

Use the present perfect to talk about experiences up to now, from the past to the present.

I went to France in 2004. I went to China in 2007. I went to India in 2009.

I've been to France, China and India.

NOW

Don't use the present perfect with finished times in the past. Use the past simple.
~~I've been to France in 1990.~~ I went to France in 1990.
~~I've seen Frank yesterday.~~ I saw Frank yesterday.

You can use **ever** in questions. **Ever** means 'at any time in your life'.
Have you ever been to France?

FORM

Make the present perfect with **have** / **has** + past participle.

I, you, we, they	he, she, it
➕ **I've seen** all the James Bond films.	➕ **She's visited** more than twenty countries.
➖ **We haven't met** Frank. **We've** never **met** Frank.	➖ **He hasn't been** to Japan. **He's** never **been** to Japan.
❓ **Have they been** to Spain? ✔ Yes, **they have**. ✖ No, **they haven't**.	❓ **Has she met** Frank? ✔ Yes, **she has**. ✖ No, **she hasn't**.

Contractions:
➕ I've = I have   you've = you have
we've = we have   they've = they have
he's = he has   she's = she has   it's = it has
➖ haven't = have not   hasn't = has not

Most past participles are regular and end in –ed. They're the same as the past simple.
like > liked   smoke > smoked   visit > visited

Some past participles are irregular, but the same as the past simple.
buy > bought   have > had   meet > met

Some past participles are irregular and different from the past simple. They often end with *n*.
eat > ate > eaten   do > did > done   see > saw > seen

Go has two past participles, **been** and **gone**.
He's been to India. (= he went to India and he came back)
He's gone to India. (= he went to India and he's in India now)

For past participles, see **Irregular verbs** on p160.

PRONUNCIATION

You usually stress the past participle. You don't usually stress **have** / **has** in positive sentences and questions.
I've seen all the James Bond films.
Has he met Frank?

But you stress **have** / **has** in negative sentences and short answers.
We haven't met Frank's wife.
Yes, they have. No, she hasn't.

You usually say **been** as /bɪn/.

PRACTICE

1 **a** Make questions with the present perfect.

1 you / go to India?   *Have you been to India?*
2 you / meet someone famous?
3 you / have a holiday abroad?
4 you / swim in the sea?
5 you / read a book more than once?
6 you / learn a foreign language apart from English?
7 your country / win the football world cup?
8 you / ride a motorbike?
9 you / do karate or judo?
10 you / be on a ship?

b Ask and answer the questions in pairs.

2 (Circle) the correct verb in the present perfect or the past simple.

1 Have you seen / Did you see Stefan at the party last night?
2 She's been / She went to Paris six times and now she wants to go again!
3 I've left / I left university about five years ago.
4 Where have you been / were you last night?
5 The first modern Olympics have been / were in Greece in 1896.
6 The modern Olympics have been / were in Greece twice.
7 My brother's a journalist. He's visited / He visited a lot of countries.
8 My great-grandfather was a journalist. He's visited / He visited a lot of countries in the 1890s.
9 I never / have never smoked.
10 I started / have started school when I was five.

14
FUTURE – *be going to, be hoping to, would like to*

MEANING

You can use **be going to** when you talk about future plans.
I'm going to start a new course soon. I paid for the first month yesterday.

You can use **be hoping to** when you talk about hopes for the future. It is less certain than *be going to*.
I'm hoping to go to university next year. I've got an interview next week.

You can use **would like to** when you talk about what you want in the future.
I'd like to go to Japan one day.

FORM

be going to, be hoping to + infinitive

I'm **going to start** university next year.
I'm **hoping to move** abroad one day.

I'm **not going to start** university next year.

❓
Are you going to start university next year?
✅ Yes, I **am**. ❌ No, I'm **not**.
Is he hoping to start his new job next week?
✅ Yes, he **is**. ❌ No, he **isn't**.
What **are you going to do** next weekend?

would like to + infinitive

I'd **like to start** university in September.

I **wouldn't like to work** abroad.

❓
Would you like to go to university one day?
✅ Yes, I **would**. ❌ No, I **wouldn't**.
What **would you like to** do with your life?

PRONUNCIATION

You can say **going to** as /ɡəʊntə/ or /ɡəʊɪŋtuː/.
In fast speech, people often say /ɡənə/.

In positive sentences and questions, you don't usually stress the auxiliary verb (**be** or **would**).
I'm hoping to move abroad next year.
Are you going to move abroad next year?
I'd like to start university in September.

In negative sentences and short answers, you usually stress the auxiliary verb (**be** and **would**).
We aren't going to have a holiday this year.
I wouldn't like to go to university.
Yes, I am. No, I wouldn't.

PRACTICE

1 Complete the sentences with **be going to** and the correct verb.

| ~~do~~ | finish | go | stay | change | ask | visit | make |

1 "Did they clean the car?"
  "No, but they *'re going to do* it this afternoon."
2 "Have you ever been to India?"
  "No, but I _____ next year."
3 "How's your new job?"
  "I don't like it. I _____ jobs again soon."
4 "Did she finish the report?"
  "No, she _____ it tomorrow."
5 "Is dinner ready?"
  "No. I _____ it now."
6 "Can Sam come to the park later?"
  "No. He _____ at home and study."
7 "Did you ask Jessie to come to the party?"
  "No. I _____ her tonight."
8 "What are your plans for the summer?"
  "Oh, we _____ relatives in New Zealand."

2 a Put the words in the right order to make questions.

1 which / country / would / you / visit / most like to?
2 most like to / which / person / would / you / meet?
3 do / what / are / you / next summer / going to?
4 learn / you / hoping to / are / one day / another language?
5 like to / would / another country / you / live or work / in / one day ?
6 are / what / you / hoping to / in the next five or ten years / do?
7 are / you / what / do / at work or school / in the near future / going to?
8 would / what / buy / like to / soon / you ?

b Ask and answer the questions.

Vocabulary reference

5 Places

an airport

a bank

a bridge

a bus stop

a castle

a hospital

a market

a museum

a school

a theatre

a college /
a university

a train station

a factory

a farm

a motorway

a petrol station

a canal

a beach

hills

mountains

a field

a forest

an island

a river

a lake

a park

the sea

a desert

Homes

upstairs
a window
a balcony
a garden
a door
downstairs

a block of flats / an apartment block
a flat / an apartment
the fifth floor
the first floor
the ground floor

an armchair

a bookcase

curtains

a rug

a picture

a lamp

a dishwasher

a bin

a desk
a study / an office

the ceiling
chairs
a table
the floor
a dining room

6 Food

meat

 chicken

 lamb

 beef

 sausages

seafood

 fish

 salmon

 prawns

 shellfish

carbohydrates

 rice

 pasta

 noodles

 couscous

 bread

 pastries

 a cake

 biscuits

vegetables

 broccoli

 peas

 potatoes

 carrots

 lentils

 olives

 lettuce

 mixed salad

 onions

beans

corn

courgettes

 peppers

an aubergine

squashes

mushrooms

fruit

 watermelon

 a melon

 a banana

 an apple

 an orange

 a lemon

 a pineapple

 a plum

 cherries

 a kiwi fruit

 berries

 a mango

dairy products

 cheese

butter

 yoghurt

 cream

other

 oil

salt

 pepper

 eggs

 nuts

 chocolate

 sweets

 chips

 toast

 a sandwich

herbs

 spices

7 Jobs

an accountant · an architect · a builder · a cook / chef

a doctor · an engineer · an IT technician · a journalist

a lawyer · a marketing assistant · a musician · a nurse

an office manager · a plumber · a shop assistant · a teacher

a waiter · a police officer · a driver · a sales rep

Study subjects

Arts, Humanities, Social Sciences

Architecture · Art · Drama · History

Languages · Economics · Music · Literature

Sciences

Biology · Chemistry · Geography · Mathematics*

Professional

Accounting · Education · Journalism · Law

Marketing · Medicine · Engineering · Management

Mathematics: in British English, people often say *maths*, and in American English *math*.

8 Family

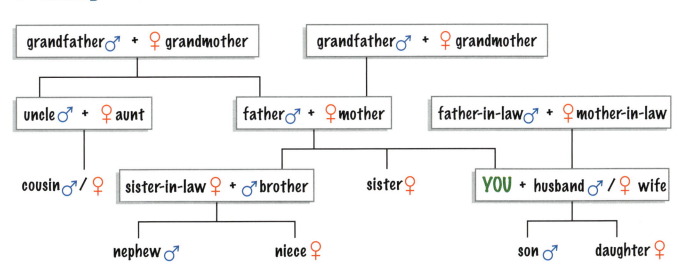

grandfather♂ + ♀ grandmother   grandfather♂ + ♀ grandmother

uncle♂ + ♀ aunt   father♂ + ♀ mother   father-in-law♂ + ♀ mother-in-law

cousin♂ / ♀   sister-in-law♀ + ♂ brother   sister♀   YOU + husband♂ / ♀ wife

nephew♂   niece♀   son♂   daughter♀

6 Independent learning 3a

book¹ /bʊk/ *noun*
1 a set of pages with writing on them fastened together in a cover: *I've just read a really good book.*
2 a set of pages fastened together in a cover and used for writing on: *an address book*
book² /bʊk/ *verb*
to arrange to use or do something at a time in the future: *I've booked a hotel room.* ◦ *We've booked a trip to Spain for next month.*

match¹ /mætʃ/ *noun* (*plural* **matches**)
1 a sports competition in which two people or teams compete against each other: *a football match*
2 a thin, wooden stick which makes fire when you rub one end of it against a rough surface: *a box of matches*
match² /mætʃ/ *verb*
If two things match, they are the same colour or type: *I can't find anything to match my green shirt.* ◦ *Your socks don't match.*

8 Independent learning 4a

necklace /'nekləs/ *noun*
a piece of jewellery that you wear around your neck: *a pearl necklace*

exhibition /ˌeksɪ'bɪʃᵊn/ *noun*
when things such as paintings are shown to the public: *There's a new **exhibition of** sculpture on at the city gallery.*

traditional /trə'dɪʃᵊnᵊl/ *adj*
following the customs or ways of behaving that have continued in a group of people for a long time: *traditional farming methods*

image /'ɪmɪdʒ/ *noun*
1 the way that other people think someone or something is: *They want to improve the **public image of** the police.*
2 a picture, especially on film or television or in a mirror: *television images of starving children*
3 a picture in your mind: *I have an **image of** the way I want the garden to look.*

fashionable /'fæʃᵊnəbl/ *adj*
popular at a particular time: *fashionable clothes*

8 Personality

adventurous /əd'ventʃᵊrəs/ *adj*
liking to try new or difficult things: *I'm going to be more adventurous with my cooking.*

creative /kri'eɪtɪv/ *adj*
good at thinking of new ideas and making interesting things: *Her book is full of creative ways to decorate your home.*

funny /'fʌni/ *adj* **1** making you smile or laugh: *a funny story*
2 strange or unusual and not what you expect: *This chicken tastes a bit funny.*

hard-working /hɑːd'wɜːkɪŋ/ *adj*
doing a job seriously and with a lot of effort: *She's a very hard-working student.*

independent /ˌɪndɪ'pendənt/ *adj*
not wanting or needing anyone else to help you: *She's a very independent four-year-old.*

intelligent /ɪn'telɪdʒᵊnt/ *adj*
able to learn and understand things easily: *She is a highly intelligent young woman.*

outgoing /aʊt'gəʊɪŋ/ *adj* Someone who is outgoing is friendly, talks a lot, and enjoys meeting people.

serious /'sɪəriəs/ *adj*
A serious person is quiet and does not laugh often: *a serious child*

From *Cambridge Essential English Dictionary*

12 The body

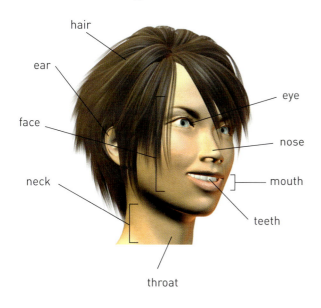

hair
ear
eye
face
nose
neck
mouth
teeth
throat

head
shoulder
stomach
arm
elbow
back
wrist
hand
thumb
leg
finger
knee

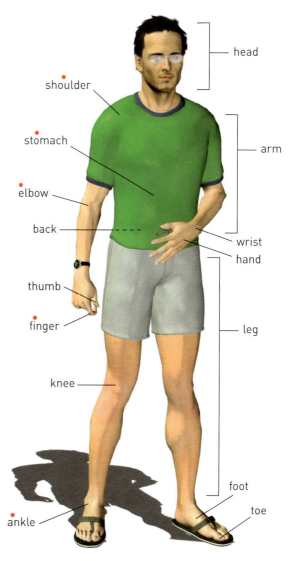

heart
skin
muscle
foot
toe
ankle
bone

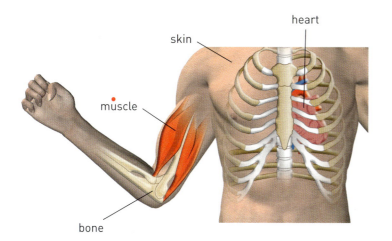

13 Sights

a castle city walls a fountain a palace ruins a sculpture

a statue a tomb a waterfall caves gardens a skyscraper

1.1

1 ASTRID Hello, I'm Astrid. I'm from Mexico. I speak Spanish, English, French and a little German.

2 ANDREW Hello, my name's Andrew and I'm from Wales and I can speak some French, some Japanese and some Hungarian.

3 ANNA Hi, my name's Anna. I'm from the United States, from San Francisco, and I speak French and Arabic.

4 SAMEH My name is Sameh and I am from Egypt. My home town is Cairo and I speak Arabic and English.

5 ANRI Hi, my name is Anri. I'm from Japan. I speak English and Japanese.

6 CLAUDIA Hi, my name is Claudia. I'm from Austria. My home town is Graz. It's quite small. I speak German of course, erm, a bit of French, erm, Russian and English.

1.2

COUNTRIES:

the United States   Mexico   Wales
Austria   Egypt   Japan

LANGUAGES:

French   Arabic   Spanish   English
German   Japanese   Hungarian
Russian

1.3

TOM Hello, Allendale Community College.

AGATA Er, hello, I'd like to join your yoga course.

T The beginners' course?

A Yes.

T Yes, that's fine. What's your name, please?

A It's Agata Karolak.

T Agata ...

A Karolak.

T How do you spell that?

A It's K–A–R–O–L–A–K.

T L-A-K. Right. OK ... What's your address?

A 152 Bentley Road, Manchester.

T 152 ... And the postcode?

A Yes, it's M20 6RU.

T M20 6RU. And what's your phone number?

A My home number? It's 0161 228 3434 ...

T 0161 228 ...

A ... 3434.

T ... 3434. Thanks. And your mobile number?

A Oh, erm, sorry, I can't remember it at the moment ...

T That's OK. Do you have an email address?

A Yes, it's ak97@kmail.com.

T ak97?

A Yes.

T Right. Where are you from?

A Er, Poland.

T And, er, what languages do you speak?

A Well, English, er, Polish of course, and a bit of German.

T OK ... How would you like to pay?

1.4

1
Twenty-five Gore Street
A hundred and thirteen Station Road
Eighty-four First Avenue

2
M one, three A Q
T five S, three X two
C A, nine oh five oh one

3
oh one six one, two six four, four six double oh
seven eight oh, four five two, double one, double one
oh double two, two five eight, six four, nine one

1.5

1 WWW dot BBC dot co dot UK
2 Rob Silva at airnet dot BR
3 M Suzuki at spaceblue dot JP
4 sport dot indiatimes dot com
5 WWW dot cambridge dot org

1.6

1 Tom can't spell Agata's surname.
2 Agata can't remember her mobile number.
3 She can remember her email address.
4 She can speak three languages.

1.7

1
ROB Maria Teresa! Er, this is Sally, my girlfriend.

SALLY Hi!

R Sally, this is Maria Teresa, my Spanish teacher.

MAITE Hi Sally, nice to meet you.

S Yes, it's good to meet you too.

2
ROB Mum, dad, meet Krishnan. He's a colleague from work.

JAMES, ISOBEL Hello!

R Er, Krishnan, this is my mother, Isobel ...

KRISHNAN Hi.

R ... and my father, James.

K Hi, pleased to meet you.

1.8

ONE SYLLABLE:

wife, son, boss, friend

TWO SYLLABLES:

father, mother, husband, daughter, brother, sister, boyfriend, girlfriend, teacher, student, colleague

1.9

JAMES Hello, I'm James.

MAITE Hi, I'm Maria Teresa.

J Nice to meet you. And this is Isobel, my wife.

ISOBEL Sorry, what's your name again?

M It's Maria Teresa. But please call me Maite.

I Hello, Maite. Are you one of Rob's colleagues?

M No, I'm not. I'm his Spanish teacher. And you?

J Oh, we're Rob's parents.

1.10

1 Hi, I'm Sally.   2 You're Krishnan.
3 This is James. He's my husband.
4 We're Rob's parents.   5 They're Rob's friends.   6 I'm not his sister. I'm his girlfriend.   7 Sally isn't Rob's colleague.   8 Rob and Krishnan aren't brothers.

1.11

1 Are you Rob's father? Yes, I am. No, I'm not.   2 Is Krishnan your colleague? Yes, he is. No, he isn't.   3 Are they your parents? Yes, they are. No, they aren't.

1.12

easy – difficult
interesting – boring
well paid – badly paid
different every day – the same every day
great – terrible

1.13

1 He was an office manager.   2 They were at home.   3 She wasn't at the party.   4 They weren't in the office.
5 Was it interesting?   6 Yes, it was.
7 Were they at the party?   8 No, they weren't.

1.14

SALLY When I was at university in 2007, I was an assistant in a clothes shop. The shop was near the university so a lot of our customers were students. One of the other assistants was a student too, but the others weren't. The job was OK, but it wasn't well paid. It was a good first job, but it wasn't a job for life for me.

1.15

MICHEL OK, this is about my friend, Roberto. He's Brazilian and is about fifty-five years old and he's very friendly ... I think he knows everybody! We were colleagues but not in the same office. He was in Rio in Brazil and I was in Brussels. He was director of a shipping company. Now he's a mathematics teacher and he teaches children in Rio. We're still good friends ... by email of course.

DONNA OK, this is about Adam. He's twenty-six, like me, and he's Canadian. We were best friends at school and we were also neighbours. In fact, we were always together. Later we were at college together, but I was a business student and he was in the media department. Now he's a TV presenter and I'm an assistant office manager. And ... he's my husband!

1.16

1 We were classmates at school.
2 We were at university together.
3 We were in the same office.
4 We were neighbours in Melbourne.
5 She was my teacher.

1.17

SEUNG-WAN In Korea, when two male friends meet, they usually just shake hands or just say hello. When two female friends meet, they hug but they don't kiss usually. When male and female friends meet, they also just say hello.

1.18

PAUL In England, er, when two male friends meet, they usually just say, "Hi, how are you?" When two female friends meet, they usually kiss. When male and female friends meet, they usually kiss.

1.20

1 u–n–i–v–e–r–s–i–t–y
2 s–h–o–p a–s–s–i–s–t–a–n–t
3 g–i–r–l–f–r–i–e–n–d
4 d–a–u–g–h–t–e–r
5 n–e–i–g–h–b–o–u–r–s
6 j–o–u–r–n–a–l–i–s–t

1.21

CARLY I'm from Canada but I live and work in Japan. When I'm in Japan, away from home, I really miss the snow in winter, erm, and my brother, Scott.

PAULA When I'm not at home, erm, I really miss the sun, I miss my friends, and especially I miss my dog.

KHALID When I'm away from home, I really miss my mother and my sister. I also miss the food. Sudanese food is really nice.

ANGHARAD When I'm away from home, I really miss my family, my rabbits and the food.

1.22

SCOTT OK, so would you like anything from home?

CARLY Can you get some newspapers? *The Globe and Mail* and the *Financial Post* are fine.

S Yeah, OK. Would you like some magazines as well?

C No, thanks. And, let's see ... can you bring my boots? The black ones? They're in my room.

S But you can buy boots in Japan.

C Yeah, but I like those boots ... please?

S Well, all right. Is that all?

C Yeah, that's all, thanks. Oh, wait a minute. Could you bring my winter coat? The long brown one?

S Carly, no! It's really heavy.

C But I really want that coat. It's cold here!

S Yeah, but my suitcase is full.

C You can bring another suitcase.

S I don't have one ... and my flight's this afternoon.

C Well, put it in a box or a rucksack or ...

S A rucksack? Well, OK then ... can I use your old rucksack? It's here.

C Of course. Thanks a lot, Scott.

1.23

1 a cup of coffee
2 some books
3 a glass of apple juice
4 an apple
5 some magazines
6 a sandwich
7 a newspaper
8 an orange
9 some oranges
10 some clothes

1.24

TWO SYLLABLES:
coffee, apple, sandwich, orange
THREE SYLLABLES:
magazines, newspaper, oranges

1.25

1 I speak English and French. 2 Erkan speaks English, too. 3 I live in a small house. 4 My mother lives in the same street. 5 We have a nice living room. 6 It has lots of nice cafés and clubs. 7 Friends often stay with me. 8 He stays with me.

1.26

ERKAN Hello, you must be Koji. Nice to meet you.

KOJI Hi, Erkan. Nice to meet you, too.

E Yeah, come in.

K Thanks for meeting me.

E It's a pleasure. Would you like something to drink? A cup of coffee?

K Erm, just a glass of water, please.

E Are you hungry? Do you want something to eat?

K No, I'm fine, thank you. The hotel food is very good.

E Great. So, tell me, what would you like to do? Are you interested in seeing some sights?

K Yes, I am. I'm really interested in architecture. I'd love to see the Blue Mosque actually.

E Yeah, no problem. And would you like to take a boat trip on the Bosphorus?

K Oh yeah, please. I like boat trips.

E OK. You can see most of the important buildings in Istanbul from the boat.

K That sounds great.

E What else would you like to do?

K Well, I'd like to eat some real Turkish food later.

E No problem. We can go to a restaurant this evening. You can try some Turkish *meze*.

K Mm, great! Thank you.

1.27

1 Would you like something to drink? Erm, just a glass of water, please.
2 Do you want something to eat? No, I'm fine, thank you. The hotel food is very good.
3 Are you interested in seeing some sights? Yes, I am. I'm really interested in architecture.
4 And would you like to take a boat trip on the Bosphorus? Oh yeah, please. I like boat trips.
5 What else would you like to do? Well, I'd like to eat some real Turkish food later.

1.29

wa<u>n</u>t <u>S</u>weden <u>l</u>ots <u>pl</u>ease ho<u>s</u>t <u>Sp</u>ain <u>gr</u>eat <u>gu</u>est

1.30

swim host student guest please help speak travel great lots

1.31

1 talking to my husband
2 watching something good on TV
3 going fishing
4 taking photos
5 playing the drums
6 listening to jazz
7 going to parties
8 seeing my grandchildren
9 reading a good book
10 learning new things
11 meeting new people
12 dancing the tango

1.32

1 I don't like bad news.
2 You don't read newspapers.
3 We don't go out a lot.
4 They don't watch TV.
5 My dad doesn't like my music.
6 She doesn't like my boyfriend.
7 Money doesn't make you happy.

1.33

MOIRA In my free time, I like reading a lot. I read books and newspapers but not magazines, and I don't watch TV. I really enjoy books about people – real people. And I like cooking so I read cookbooks, of course. And at the weekend, my friends come to my flat and I make dinner for them, usually Italian or Chinese or Thai food. I don't go to restaurants. I enjoy my own food.

SAM Well, I love being outside. I'm a real outdoor person, so in my free time, I go for walks in the park or go jogging or I drive to the sea and walk there. I like playing tennis, too, but I don't go to a gym. I play on an outside tennis court. On Friday evening, I go shopping for food. I don't shop at weekends. Weekends are for having fun.

🎧 1.34

1

INTERVIEWER So, Min, what do you think about New Year?

MIN Well, we have two New Years, one on January the first, and *Seollal*, in January or February. That's a three-day holiday.

I Oh really? What does *Seollal* mean?

M Ah, well, it's our traditional New Year. *Seollal* is an important holiday for us. I love it.

I What do you usually do?

M Er, my family and I sometimes go to the sea, in Gangneung. You can stay up and see the first sunrise of the New Year. But, usually, I go to my parents' house, and my brother and his family often come too. It's a family time.

I And do the children do anything special?

M Yes, erm, they dress up in special clothes and we all play family games, like *yunnori*. It's like chess.

I Do you eat a special meal?

M Er, what do we eat? Well, we usually have soup with rice cakes in the morning.

I And do you go out at all?

M Yes, sometimes. In the afternoon or evening, we always see friends. They come to us or we go to their homes and play more games. It's very nice.

2

INTERVIEWER So, Paul, do you like New Year?

PAUL Do I like New Year? Er no, not really, no, I don't.

I Oh. Why not?

P I don't know ... for me, New Year's just a normal day, it's not special.

I So, what do you usually do, then?

P I stay at home and read or, you know, watch a film.

I And what time do you go to bed?

P Erm, I usually stay up late, have a beer, watch the fireworks at midnight from the window. I guess I go to bed at one or two.

I So what does your wife do? Does she stay at home with you?

P No, she loves New Year. Well, she loves parties. She usually goes out with friends from work.

I Does she ask you to go with her?

P No, no, but it's OK. She has a good time, I have a good time. And that's it really.

I Right.

🎧 1.35

1 always, sometimes, never, often
2 enjoy 3 usually 4 important
5 afternoon 6 traditional

🎧 1.36

1 Do the children do anything special?
2 Yes, they do. No, they don't.
3 What do you usually do?

4 What do we eat?
5 Does she stay at home with you?
6 Yes, she does. No, she doesn't.
7 What does your wife do?
8 What does *Seollal* mean?

🎧 1.37

1 Do you like birthdays?
2 What do you do in the morning?
3 Do you go to work?
4 What kind of food do you eat?
5 Do you see friends?
6 Do you go out at night?
7 Does your husband like birthdays?
8 What does your family do?

🎧 1.38

1

ROCIO Hi, Blake. Are you free on Saturday evening?

BLAKE Saturday evening? Erm ... yes, I am.

R Oh, good. Do you want to come to my place for dinner?

B Yes, please. That sounds great.

R Is seven o'clock OK for you?

B Yes, seven's good.

R OK, then, see you on Saturday.

B Thanks, Rocio. See you then.

2

LÉON Are you interested in football, Roberto?

ROBERTO Yes, of course.

L OK, well, I have two tickets to the Chelsea-Real Madrid game on October 24th. Would you like to come with me?

R October 24th? Oh no, I'm sorry. I can't. I have a seminar that weekend.

L OK, well, maybe next time.

R Yes. Sorry, Léon.

🎧 1.39

RUTH In Britain, it's OK to talk about your health and your problems with your friends and your family. Er, I don't usually talk about money with my work colleagues or new people. I don't talk about religion or politics with people that I don't know, for example, er, somebody I meet at a party. I never ask people how old they are if I meet them for the first time.

🎧 1.40

AMINA Because religion and politics are very important in Arab culture, you would discuss them with everyone including new people you just meet at a party. But health problems and money problems are usually very personal and so you would not discuss them.

🎧 1.42

1 Can I talk to Blake, please?
2 Sorry, he isn't here at the moment.
3 Can I take a message?
4 Sorry, can you slow down a bit, please?
5 Sorry, can you say that again?
6 I see. Right. OK.

🎧 1.44

1 which 2 shopping 3 children
4 match 5 chocolate 6 watching
7 relationship 8 fishing

🎧 1.45

REGULAR

1 used   4 wanted
2 worked   5 listened
3 liked   6 loved

IRREGULAR

7 made   11 bought
8 went   12 met
9 cost   13 said
10 had   14 sold

🎧 1.46

SANG-MI My first mobile phone. Hmm. I think it was in 1998. I didn't use it a lot. I can't remember my first text message – maybe six or seven years ago? I'm not very good with technology. The first time I used a computer was at school. That was about twenty-five years ago. I think I bought my first CD in 1993 – it was Cesaria Evora, my favourite singer. I got an MP3 player last year and that's the first time I bought music online. My boyfriend gave me a digital camera in 2003, but it wasn't very easy to use. I have a good one now and I use it all the time.

🎧 1.47

1 keys 2 address book 3 toothbrush
4 passport 5 comb 6 mobile
7 map and directions 8 tickets
9 pen 10 sunglasses 11 money
12 driving licence

🎧 1.48

MICK Here's your ticket.

SANG-MI Thanks, Mick. Did you call Mr Donovan's office?

M Yeah, I did. His assistant will meet you at the airport in Seattle tomorrow evening and take you out for a meal.

S Oh right. And did you get some US dollars for me?

M Yes, the money's in the packet with the tickets.

S Oh, great, thanks. What time's the meeting with Mr Donovan on Friday?

M I'm not sure, sorry. But he sent these directions to the office.

S OK. Thanks a lot, Mick. I'll see you next Thursday.

M Bye. Good luck with Mr Donovan.

🎧 1.49

SANG-MI Hello, Mr Donovan. It's very nice to meet you.

MR DONOVAN And you too, Mrs Bourn. How was your flight?

S It was very good, thank you. Very comfortable.

D And did you find the office OK?

S Yes, thanks. Your directions were very good.

D What did you think of the restaurant? It's one of my favourite places.

S It was great, thank you. We had a lovely meal.

D Good, good. So, no problems, then?

S No, everything's fine.

D Good, then let's have a coffee and get started.

🔴 **1.50**

SANG-MI Hi Tom, it's me.

TOM Hi Sang-mi. Is everything OK?

S Yeah, fine. But I forgot my sunglasses and my toothbrush. (Ah!) So, how are you?

T Fine. Did you have a good journey?

S No, I didn't. You know I hate flying.

T So, what did you do last night?

S I went out for dinner with some of Mr Donovan's colleagues.

T Did you have a good time?

S Well, they were very nice but I didn't really like the restaurant.

T Oh dear. And what about the meeting with Mr Donovan?

S Well, I couldn't find the office. I didn't understand his directions at all. But the meeting went well. I have a new client!

T That's great, Sang-mi.

🔴 **1.52**

What did you do last night?
I went out for dinner.
Did you have a good time?
Well, I didn't like the restaurant.
Did you have a good journey?
Yes, I did.
No, I didn't.

🔴 **1.53**

ONYINYE I remember when my family moved from Nigeria to Scotland. That was an important event. I was, erm, five years old so I was very young and it's a very different country because Nigeria is very hot and sunny – in Africa – and, uh, Scotland is very cold and, uh …

CHIE Wet?

O … wet, yes. And in, in Europe. And the country itself is very different. My memories of Nigeria – I was only five so I don't have too many – but a lot of red sand, and the trees were different, erm, the houses were different. Everything was different. But, erm, when I moved to Scotland, at first it was like a big holiday because we were moving and it was very exciting, until the first winter, and I saw snow for the first time which was a shock. And, uh, it was a big thing. We all went outside and we built a snowman and we had lots of fun, but it made us all realise that it wasn't a holiday any more.

🔴 **1.54**

ANDREW I first went swimming six years ago, when I was twenty-eight. Erm, I was on a boat in Indonesia with some friends. Everyone wanted to go in the water but I never learned to swim at school. I said, 'I can't swim, I hate the water', but then my friend Jack pushed me into the sea. It was terrible! But after a minute I relaxed and started swimming. It was very strange … but now I love swimming.

🔴 **1.56**

1 they 2 month 3 this 4 thanks
5 weather 6 three 7 brother
8 birthday

🔴 **2.1**

Province of San Luis: mountains
Buenos Aires: a market
Paceville: the sea, a beach
London: a bridge, a river

🔴 **2.2**

boring – exciting
safe – dangerous
noisy – quiet
expensive – cheap
ugly – beautiful
polluted – clean

🔴 **2.3**

In the kitchen: (a) a cooker (b) plates (c) a shelf (d) a cupboard (e) cutlery (f) a drawer (g) a fridge (h) a toaster (i) pots and pans
In the living room: (j) a computer (k) a plant (l) a sofa
In the bathroom: (m) a washing machine (n) towels (o) a bath
In the bedroom: (p) a wardrobe (q) bedclothes

🔴 **2.4**

CAROLE I live in a small flat with, er, four rooms. There's a living room, a kitchen, a bathroom of course, a bedroom, but my favourite room in my flat is my kitchen. I have my breakfast in the kitchen, I have my dinner in the kitchen, I read in the kitchen, I think I do almost everything in the kitchen! Erm, I enjoy cooking, I love cooking for other people so, yeah, that's why the kitchen's my favourite room.

🔴 **2.5**

1

CAROLE OK, shall we start in here?

ESTRELLA OK.

C Er, well, it's very simple really. Erm, you can see the cooker, but there's no microwave, I'm afraid …

E No problem. Where are the plates and things?

C Right, plates and mugs and stuff are up here on the shelf …

E Oh yes.

C … cutlery's here, and pots and pans are down here at the bottom.

E OK. Where's the washing machine?

C Ah, that's not in here, it's in the bathroom.

E Right.

C There are a couple of yoghurts in the fridge, just help yourself.

E OK.

C Right, where next?

2

CAROLE OK, you can sleep in here of course, the bed's quite comfortable.

ESTRELLA OK.

C Those bedclothes are for you …

E Great.

C … and there are some extra bedclothes and clean towels in the wardrobe if you need them.

E Right.

C And please use the wardrobe on the left. It's empty.

E OK, thanks.

3

CAROLE OK, er, if you want to watch something, there are a lot of DVDs here … and a lot more in the drawer here.

ESTRELLA Alright.

C Erm, there's a computer but it doesn't have internet at the moment unfortunately.

E That's OK, I'll manage.

C Now, the big plant in the corner … could you water it three or four times a week?

E Sure.

4

CAROLE OK, any questions?

ESTRELLA Erm, are there any shops near here where I can buy food?

C There are no shops near here, no … you'll have to walk into the centre. It's ten minutes.

E That's not a problem. Is there an internet café?

C Er, yes, there is. There's a small one next to the bus stop. It's called Café Contact, I think.

E Oh right, I know it. Erm, can you show me the bathroom?

C Sure. The shower's pretty easy to use. You just …

🔴 **2.6**

1 There are a couple of radios in the house. One's in Cheryl's room.

2 There are a lot of eggs in the fridge, so please use them.

3 There's a microwave in the kitchen. It's a bit old but it's OK.

4 There are a lot of plates in this cupboard – on the top shelf.

5 There's a couple of towels in the wardrobe. They're for you.

6 There's no computer in the flat but there's an internet café on the corner.

7 **A** Are there any pens in that drawer?
  B No, there aren't.

8 **A** Is there a washing machine in here?
  B Yes, there is.

2.7

CONNOR Hello?

ALICJA Hi, my name's Alicja. I'm interested in the room you have to let.

C Oh yes. Would you like to come and see it?

A Yes, I think so. Can I ask a few questions first?

C Sure.

A Does the room have its own bathroom and kitchen?

C Well, it has a bathroom with a shower, but you'll share the kitchen with two other women. They're very nice!

A OK. Is there a washing machine?

C Yes, it's in the kitchen, and there's a dishwasher. Everything's new.

A Great. And is it near a bus stop for the city centre?

C Yes, it's five minutes from the bus stop. Or you can walk there in about forty, forty-five minutes.

A That's great. Is heating included in the rent?

C Yes, it's a hundred euros a week for everything, except the telephone. When do you need the room?

A Well, now really.

C That's no problem.

A So can I see the room this evening?

C Yes, any time after six.

A How about six thirty?

C That's fine. Now, do you know where it is?

A Er, not exactly.

C OK, well, if you're coming from the city centre, you can get the number forty-three bus ...

2.8

ESTRELLA A couple of years ago, I lived in this flat in Barcelona. It was on the third floor of an old house, big, really beautiful.

MIKE That's great.

E Yes, well, it was beautiful but it was also very old, and in my bedroom there was this really big crack in the ceiling.

M Right.

E It didn't look very nice of course but I didn't really think it was dangerous.

M OK.

E Anyway, everything was fine and after a couple of years I left the flat and a friend of mine went to live there.

M Right.

2.9

ESTRELLA Anyway, everything was fine and after a couple of years I left the flat and a friend of mine went to live there.

MIKE Right.

E And then, about a month later, it was quite early in the morning I think, she was in the kitchen, cooking, when she heard this amazing 'crash!' and the whole flat shook.

M Really? It was the bedroom, yeah?

E Yeah, the bedroom ceiling fell down. On the bed.

M That's terrible. Was she OK?

E Yes, she was fine. She was in the kitchen.

M So what did she do?

E I can't really remember, I was so shocked when she told me! But I know she moved out of the flat.

M And that was your bedroom!

E Yes.

M It's a good thing you moved out when you did.

E Yeah, that's what I thought. Anyway, when I ...

2.10

1 OK. | Right. | Yeah.
2 Really?
3 That's great. | That's wonderful.
4 That's terrible. | Oh no! | That's awful.

2.14

1 wife   2 page   3 wrote   4 have
5 life   6 live   7 plane   8 safe
9 postcode   10 decide

2.15

ANDREW Do you like shopping?

DORIEN I absolutely hate going shopping.

A Oh me too. I hate shopping too, you know the only shopping I like is on the internet.

D Oh.

A You know.

D When they deliver it at home.

A Yeah anything like that, I just hate shopping. I don't understand why people love shopping.

D I don't. I normally do it after work, quick you know?

A Yeah.

D So you don't have to go into town on a Saturday.

A Oh yeah. How about food? Do you, I mean, obviously you have to buy food?

D I go once a week to the supermarket and then I buy my shopping for the whole week.

A It's a very very good idea. Yeah, me too.

2.16

A a music shop
B a shoe shop
C a newsagent
D a bookshop
E a pharmacy
F a sports shop
G a computer shop
H a clothes shop
I the toilets
J a cash machine / an ATM
K the entrance / the exit
L an escalator
M information
N a lift
O the stairs

2.17

1

SHOP ASSISTANT Are you OK? Do you need some help?

JON Well, I'd like a new tennis racket. But I don't know what to get.

SA Well, all of these are good, but I like this one.

J Hm. It feels great ... Yes, OK, I'll take this one.

SA OK, great.

J And, erm, I need some tennis balls too.

SA How many would you like? They're in packets of three.

J Oh, er, I'll have six, please, two packets.

SA Fine. Is that everything?

J Yes, I think so. How much is that?

SA Right, it's thirty-five fifty, please.

J OK, er, thirty, five and er, fifty.

SA Thanks.

J Thanks for your help. Bye.

SA Bye.

2

JON Hi. I'm looking for the new book by Paulo Coelho.

SHOP ASSISTANT Paulo who?

J Coelho. C-O-E-L-H-O.

SA I'll check. No, sorry, it's not in at the moment. It should be in next week, on Tuesday.

J Tuesday? OK, thanks ... erm, and do you have any street maps? Of Melbourne?

SA Yes, they're over there, on that wall.

J Oh, right. Er, how much is this one?

SA It's five ninety-nine.

J OK, I'll have it, thanks.

3

JON Could I try these shoes on, please?

SHOP ASSISTANT Yes, sure.

J ... They feel a bit big. Do you have them in a size 10?

SA Yes, just a moment. I'll have a look for you ... There you are.

J Oh, thanks very much ... Oh, these are better.

SA Are you sure?

J Yeah, yeah, they're fine. How much are they?

SA They're seventy-nine ninety-five.

J OK. I'll have them.

SA And would you like anything else?

J No, that's fine, thanks.

2.18

1 How much is this one?

2 How many would you like?

3 Do you have any street maps?

4 Would you like anything else?

2.19

1 How many tomatoes would you like?
2 How much milk do you have in your tea?
3 Would you like some rice?
4 I'd like an apple, please.

5 I buy a lot of bread every week.
6 Can you buy some bananas?
7 I'd like some lettuce in my sandwich.
8 I need six tomatoes.

2.20

INDRA   Excuse me, er, do you speak English?
ASSISTANT   Yes, of course. What would you like?
I   Mm, I'm not sure. What's that one?
A   It's fish with potatoes. Or there's chicken with rice.
I   I'll have the fish, thanks.
A   Here you are.
I   Thanks. Does it come with anything?
A   You can have vegetables, or salad, over there.
I   Vegetables … yes, could I have some of those carrots, please? Thank you. Sorry, where are the drinks?
A   You can order hot drinks here, or there are cold drinks in the fridge.
I   Oh right. Can I have a tea, please?
A   Yes, of course. Here you are.
I   Thanks … How much is that?
A   Nine euros, please.
I   Thanks.

2.22

1 about   2 four   3 noun   4 you
5 house   6 out   7 ground   8 count

2.23

1 I have a part-time job.
2 I'm a chef.
3 I work in a bakery.
4 I'm doing a full-time course in catering.
5 I'm studying history at Berlin University.
6 I look after my children.
7 I'm self-employed.

2.25

DORIEN   Erm, I spend 35 hours a week at work, and, erm, I spend about 15 hours a week on the river rowing, and I sleep about seven and a half, eight hours a night – I need my sleep – erm, and because I don't have any family here, they don't take up any time. Erm, and the rest of the time I spend with my mates.
INTERVIEWER   Aha. Are you happy about that?
D   I am actually. I would like to work a bit less, but who doesn't?
I   I see.

2.26

1
DEAN   Hello.
CARLA   Hi, Dean. This is Carla. Listen, can you talk now? I'm planning my seminar and I want your advice.
D   Sorry, Carla, but I'm in the middle of dinner. Can I call you later?
C   Yes, no problem. Talk to you later.
D   OK, bye.

2
DEAN   Hello.
MIA   Hello, sir, I'm calling from Clear View Windows. We're having a special sale this week …
D   Sorry, but I'm not interested.
M   OK. Thank you.

3
DEAN   Good morning. Dean Browne speaking.
LUISA   Hello, Dean. This is Luisa Riego from Madrid.
D   Hi Luisa. Look, I'm sorry but I'm working on the report for our conference. Could I call you back in half an hour?
L   Yes, of course, Dean. Goodbye.

4
SAM   Hi, Dad, I need some help with my homework.
DEAN   Well, actually, Sam, I'm quite busy right now. Can we talk when I get home?
S   Yeah, OK. See you later.
D   OK, bye.

5
GLYN   Dean, this is Glyn. Is this a good time?
DEAN   Yes, of course. I'm just watching the news. How are you?
G   I'm good, thanks. So, what are you doing these days?
D   Oh, you know, I'm working hard as usual … not much free time. And you?
G   Well, I'm doing a marketing course in the evenings after work, so it's a bit busy. It's good though …

2.28

I'm planning my seminar.
Dean's working on a report.
He isn't watching the news.
They aren't working at the moment.
A   Are you feeling OK?
B   Yes, I am.
A   Is he working hard?
B   No, he isn't.
What are you doing these days?
What are they studying?

2.29

LIAM   So, Dmitri, what do you do?
DMITRI   Er, I'm a fashion designer.
L   Ah, so you make clothes, yeah?
D   Well, erm, I design clothes and I make them but, er, I don't really like making them. Designing clothes is much more interesting!
L   So who do you work for?
D   I'm self-employed.
L   So you work … where?
D   I work at home. I have a small workshop in my flat.
L   Ah! How is it being self-employed? I mean, can you get enough work?
D   Er, well, yeah, at the moment I'm working on two projects. I'm designing costumes for a theatre company, for a play called *Stuff Happens*.

L   Oh, right.
D   And I'm also doing some work for a restaurant – not fashion design but interior design – so I'm choosing the colours and, erm, furniture and, er, pictures and stuff like that.
L   Ah, that sounds interesting.
D   Yeah, it's something new for me but I'm enjoying it. But what about you? What do you do?
L   Well, I'm a student at Trinity College, Dublin. I'm doing a Master's degree in business administration.
D   And do you go to classes every day, or … ?
L   No. Sometimes I have meetings with my tutor … but I'm working on my dissertation right now so I'm usually in the library or at home.

2.30

ANNABEL   Where I work, it's quite informal. Everyone wears casual clothes, usually, but when we have meetings with clients, er, we wear smart clothes. Er, I have ten people working for me and we're a great team. We make decisions together. Everyone can say what they think in meetings and things. That's one reason why I like it here, actually. It's important to work as a team.

GEOFF   It's quite formal where I work so all the men wear a suit and tie. Most of the senior managers are men but there are a few women now. Erm, and the company president has a lot of control and makes all the important decisions – but he also looks after his employees quite well. Uh, for example, if we've got a problem, we can go and ask him for help … I think it's good to have a strong leader.

2.32

1 A   How many hours do you work?
  B   Oh, about eight hours. I leave the office at about 5.30.
2 A   How long do you sleep?
  B   I don't know exactly. Probably six or seven hours a night.
3 A   How much time do you spend at home?
  B   I don't know. Maybe about 13 hours a day, and most of that is sleeping.
4 A   How much time do you spend with family or friends?
  B   I'm not sure. Probably about five hours a week with friends.
5 A   How much time do you spend on public transport?
  B   About two or three hours. The buses are slow.

2.34

office   course   because   conference
city   call   client   place   can   centre

2.35

MALE: brother, father, dad, grandfather, nephew, son, uncle.
FEMALE: aunt, daughter, grandmother, mother, mum, niece, sister.
BOTH: child, children, cousin, parents, twins.

2.36

PART A

ONYINYE People say I have a large family but I don't think I have. There are seven people in my family. I have four sisters, so five girls, and then my mum and my dad. But most of my family live in Nigeria. And, erm, my uncle and aunt, for example, they have nine children or eight children. So my family with five children is not really a large family!

CHIE Oh not really, no.

O But, erm, here people say that five girls is a large family.

C Yes.

O Yeah.

PART B

ONYINYE I'm lucky because I live with my sister, so I see, I see her a lot of the time.

CHIE That's nice.

O And I see my parents quite often as well but, erm, they don't live in the neighbourhood but they live in another part of England.

PART C

ONYINYE The member of my family that I'm closest to is my sister. And it's funny because I'm thirty years old and she's twenty years old but, erm, our mum says we're like twins, just born ten years apart. We look very similar and, er, we have similar style, we like similar things, so that's why I'm the closest to her.

2.37

most of my family   a lot of the time
another part of England
a member of my family

2.39

1 Have you got glasses?
2 Yes, I have. / No, I haven't.
3 They've got pale skin.
4 I haven't got a lot of jewellery.
5 Has she got a tan?
6 Yes, she has. / No, she hasn't.
7 She's got a *bindi*.
8 He hasn't got a beard or moustache.

2.40

LESLEY Well, one person I really admire is my neighbour Sybil. Er, she's Scottish and she's in her eighties so she doesn't go out much now, er, but she's very outgoing and loves talking – in fact, er, she sometimes talks too much but that's OK. We don't see each other a lot ... we have coffee together maybe once or twice a month. We get on really well, I guess because we're interested in the same things, like books and food.

Er, she lives alone. Her husband died a few years ago. She's got a daughter who lives in another city and the daughter keeps asking her to go and live with her but Sybil says no every time. She's very independent and I think she loves her own flat and her own, you know, quiet life.

Anyway, once, when I was at her flat, I noticed a silver cup and a photo of her in an old-style sports car. I found out that when she was younger, she was very adventurous and even got into car racing! Her uncle was a rally driver and he trained her for the Ladies Hillclimb Championship race. For this race, they had to drive their cars up a mountain road to the top as fast as possible, and she actually won the race! She was beautiful then ... and she still is now ... very slim, always in perfect clothes. Er, her hair's silver but she's got bright blue eyes. It's hard to imagine she's over eighty, but she is. I think she's great.

2.41

1
We don't see each other a lot.
We get in touch maybe twice a year.
We spend a lot of time together.
2
We get on really well.
We can talk about everything together.
We're very close.
We don't know each other very well.
3
We're interested in the same things.
We like different things.

2.42

One is /θ/ in *thanks*.
Two is /ð/ in *brother*.
Three is /ʃ/ in *short*.
Four is /ʒ/ in *usually*.
Five is /tʃ/ in *children*.
Six is /dʒ/ in *jewellery*.
Seven is /ŋ/ in *outgoing*.
Eight is /j/ in *yellow*.

2.43

alphabet   because   next   office   together

2.46

1 each   2 niece   3 jeans   4 agree
5 team   6 free   7 believe   8 teacher
9 green   10 reading

2.47

1 get the underground
2 get the bus
3 get the train
4 cycle
5 ride a motorbike
6 get a taxi
7 drive
8 walk

2.48

MEERA Morning, Vijay.
VIJAY Good morning!
M Sleep well?
V Yes, thanks. Ah, tea ...
M So what are we doing today?
V Well, could we go and have a look round the city? It's so interesting to see a new place.
M Sure, good idea.
V Actually, the first thing is I need to get some money. Is there a cash machine near here?
M No, but there are a couple next to Halwasiya market, in Hazratganj.
V Erm, where's that? In the centre?
M It's the main shopping area, yes.
V All right. And another thing ... are there any bookshops here? English bookshops?
M Ha! Are you bored?
V No, of course not but you know I like reading and I didn't bring any books because they're so heavy.
M OK. The best bookshop is Universal Booksellers. That's in Hazratganj too.
V Great. Do you know when it's open?
M I think it opens at ten or ten-thirty and closes around eight-thirty.
V OK, so what's the best way to get there? Can we walk?
M Well, we could but it's hot and quite crowded.
V How long does it take?
M About twenty minutes.
V Hm. Is there a bus?
M Not from here, no. It's better to get a taxi ... or we could get an auto.
V An auto?
M I mean an auto-rickshaw.
V OK, good idea. Where's the nearest rickshaw stop?
M There isn't a stop. We just have to walk until we see an auto and then stop it.
V OK.

2.49

1
A Where's the nearest bus stop?
B It's on Station Road.
A What's the best way to get there?
B Oh, you can walk.
A How far is it?
B About half a kilometre.

2
A Is there a bank near here?
B Not really. The nearest one is next to the train station.
A Is there a bus?
B It's better to get the metro.
A How long does it take?
B About fifteen minutes.

3

A Er, where can I buy some shoes?
B The best shoe shop is Porter's.
A Is it far?
B No. It's a ten-minute walk.
A What time does it open?
B It opens at nine-thirty.

🔴 **2.50**

quick, quicker, the quickest
safe, safer, the safest
long, longer, the longest
careful, more careful, the most careful
crowded, more crowded, the most crowded
dangerous, more dangerous, the most dangerous
easy, easier, the easiest
good, better, the best
bad, worse, the worst
far, further, the furthest

🔴 **2.51**

ASSISTANT Can I help you?
VIJAY Yes, I want to go to Basingstoke today. How much does a return ticket cost?
A A day return or an open return?
V Erm, what's the difference?
A Well, the open return's more expensive, but you can come back any time. With a day return, you come back today.
V Right ... how much does an open return ticket cost?
A To Basingstoke? It's £15.45.
V And what time does the next coach leave?
A It leaves at 4.15, in fifteen minutes.
V Is it direct?
A No. You need to change coaches once, so it's quite slow ... but the 4.30 coach is direct.
V Oh, that's good. How long does it take to Basingstoke?
A The direct coach? About an hour and a half.
V All right. I'd like an open return ticket on the direct coach, please.
A Thank you ... here's your ticket and change.
V Thanks. Er, which coach do I get? The number?
A Number 342.
V OK, and where do I get it?
A Just outside those doors. You'll see the sign.
V OK, thanks a lot.

🔴 **2.52**

MARIKE One of the best things about Amsterdam is we don't have a big car culture. In fact, the government here thinks about public transport and bicycles first, and cars second. I think that's different from many other countries. People say Amsterdam's a centre of bicycle culture and, erm, that's true. I mean, we have about 400 kilometres of bike lanes. And also, we have bike traffic lights. They look the same as traffic lights but they, erm, they have the shape of a bicycle. Do other countries have those? I don't know. Anyway, some streets don't have bike lanes but you can cycle on them and cars will go around you or follow you. As I said, we're really bicycle-friendly.

HASAN In Dubai, everyone I know uses a car. They're cheap because they're tax free and petrol's not too expensive ... well, actually, prices are going up. We also use taxis a lot but it's harder to find a taxi than before. There aren't enough these days. There are some buses, too, but it's easier and people really love their cars. They're air-conditioned, quiet and private ... Of course the roads in Dubai are very crowded, but we have a new metro now so maybe that will change things. But if you want to go to the desert or mountains or to, say, Abu Dhabi, the car's the best way. We have great roads.

🔴 **2.53**

VIJAY Hello?
SARA Vijay, hi. It's Sara.
V Oh, hi. How are you?
S Great. What about you?
V Yeah, good.
S Listen, do you want to meet up soon?
V Yeah, when? This week?
S Yeah! Thursday? Or Friday?
V Well, Thursday's a problem but I'm free on Friday.
S OK, Friday. Why don't we go out for dinner?
V OK.
S Do you know a good place?

🔴 **2.55**

1 SARA Was that Campie Street? P for Peter?
2 VIJAY No, Cambie Street. B for Bob.
3 V Sorry, not the Palace Theatre. I mean the Royal Theatre.
4 S Sorry, is that 393 or 353?
5 V Well, it's not next to the theatre, exactly. It's near it.

🔴 **2.56**

1 sweeter 2 shortest 3 funny
4 getting 5 meeting 6 swimming
7 moving 8 sitting 9 planned
10 driver

🔴 **3.2**

MIA Some of these films look quite interesting.
JON Yeah. Why don't we go and see one some time this week?
M Yeah, OK. Would you like to see *Family Law*? I heard it's really good.
J Hm, I don't know. It sounds a bit boring. We could see *The Others*.
M Well, I don't usually like horror films, but that one sounds good.

🔴 **3.3**

KIMIKO Hi Jon.
JON Hi! Kimi, what happened?
K I was stuck in traffic and then I got a phone call from my boss. I told you it was a difficult day.
J Yeah, you did. Well, we're walking to Delmonico's now for a pizza. Can you join us?
K Thanks, Jon, but I feel really tired. I think I'll stay at home.
J Are you sure?
K Yeah, sorry.
J OK. Well, erm, how about on Friday?
K Sorry but I'm flying to Singapore this Friday.
J You're not going for work, I hope.
K Yep, for a sales meeting.
J So when are you back?
K Er, it's only a short trip. I'm coming back on Monday night. I'll call you for a chat tomorrow, OK?
J OK, well, have a good evening.
K Thanks, Jon, and enjoy your pizza. And say hi to Mia.
J Will do. Bye now.
K Bye.

🔴 **3.5**

a coffee break | a yoga class |
a guitar lesson | a tennis match |
a cinema programme

🔴 **3.6**

REETA Listen, erm, I have no plans for this weekend so would you like to come over to my place and watch a film?
JANE Well, yeah, that sounds great. Which day?
R Er, how about Saturday night?
MATTHEW Sorry, I'm going out on Saturday. What about Sunday?
R Fine with me. Jane?
J Yeah, that sounds good.
R OK, then why don't you come over at 6.00 and we can have pizza first.
M Great.
R Great. So, do you want to bring a film? Or I can rent something ...
M Erm, how about *The Bourne Supremacy*?
J What's it like?
M Well, it's an action film, I guess. It's about an American spy who loses his memory.
J Oh, right. Who's in it?
R Matt Damon.
M Yeah, that's the one.
J Hm, I don't really like action films.
R OK. Then let's watch ... erm ... *Pan's Labyrinth*.
J *Pan's Labyrinth*? Sounds unusual. What's it about?

R It's about a young girl and it's set in Spain ... in the 1940s, I think. It's really good.

M Hm.

R Matthew's not sure.

M No ...

J I've got an idea. I read about this film called *Yeelen* ...

R *Yeelen*?

J Yeah, it's from Mali, I think. It's about this young man with magical powers.

M That sounds interesting.

J Yeah, I'd really like to see it.

R OK, I'll try to get it. How do you spell the title?

3.7

1 A You look stressed. Is there a problem?
   B Yes, there is! Do you know anything about computers?

2 A Can I see the room this evening?
   B Sure. How about six thirty?

3 A Do you know that Dave's getting married?
   B Yes, I heard about that.

4 A Don't forget the party on Friday.
   B What party? No one told me about that.

5 A Hello, can I help you?
   B Yes, please. I have a question about my ticket.

6 A How was your day?
   B It was terrible! I don't want to talk about it.

7 A So, do you want to buy these jeans?
   B Hmm. I don't know. I'll think about it.

3.8

1 Yuri Gagarin went into space in 1961.
2 An adult elephant has 24 teeth.
3 The first modern Olympics were in 1896.
4 Mount Everest is 8,848 metres high.
5 There are 11 people in a cricket team.
6 The Great Wall of China is about 6,500 kilometres long.
7 It takes 8 minutes and 18 seconds for light to travel from the sun to the earth.
8 People started writing about 5,000 years ago in Mesopotamia.

3.9

1 is /æ/ in *black*.   7 is /ɒ/ in *lot*.
2 is /ɑː/ in *park*.   8 is /ɔː/ in *sport*.
3 is /e/ in *help*.   9 is /ʌ/ in *but*.
4 is /ɜː/ in *first*.   10 is /ʊ/ in *good*.
5 is /ɪ/ in *six*.   11 is /uː/ in *food*.
6 is /iː/ in *meet*.   12 is /ə/ in *sister*.

3.10

1 horror   2 morning   3 comedy
4 beautiful   5 mother   6 moustache

3.11

SUZI So Michelle, do you have any plans for tomorrow?

MICHELLE Hm, not really. Why don't we go to Heidelberg?

S That sounds good. We could do some shopping.

M Hm, I don't know. Let's visit the castle.

S All right. But I need to buy a coat.

3.13

1 good   2 page   3 message
4 great   5 dangerous   6 religion
7 girl   8 arrangements   9 together
10 colleague   11 engineer   12 Egypt

3.14

BELINDA Good morning.

CHECK-IN ASSISTANT Good morning, madam. Tokyo?

B That's right.

C Can I see your passport, please?

B Here you are.

C That's fine. Do you have any hand luggage?

B Just this bag.

C Did you pack your bag yourself?

B Yes, I did.

C Are you carrying anything for anyone else?

B No.

C Right, thank you. Here's your boarding pass. Boarding is at 11.55 from gate 20.

B Thanks.

C Enjoy your flight.

3.15

1 Can I see your passport, please?
2 Do you have any hand luggage?
3 Did you pack your bag yourself?
4 Are you carrying anything for anyone else?
5 Boarding is at 11.55 from gate 20.

3.16

OFFICER 1 Keys?

BELINDA I've put them in my bag.

O1 OK. Is there a laptop in here?

B No.

O1 And your shoes, please.

B Oh, OK.

OFFICER 2 Come forward, please.

B Oh, I'm so sorry.

O2 Keys? Wallet?

B Uh, they're in my bag.

O2 Mobile?

B That too.

O2 Are you wearing a belt?

B Oh yes, sorry.

O2 That's fine, thank you.

B Thanks.

...

OFFICER 3 Could you open your bag, please?

B OK.

O3 That's fine. Enjoy your trip.

B Thanks.

3.18

1 When was the last time you saw a spider?
2 Do you like pasta?
3 Is there an art gallery near here?
4 Can you open the door, please?

5 Have you got a pen I can use?
6 What's the name of the person next to you?
7 Do you like cats?
8 What's the easiest language to learn?

3.19

1 **To start a story:**
   It was two in the morning.
   I was with some friends.
   Well, this was a few weeks ago.

2 **To link a story:**
   Later, ... and then, ...
   After that, ...

3 **To end a story:**
   It was really strange.
   I had a great time.
   In the end, ...

3.20

HOLLY Well, I was in my car in the Rocky Mountains in Canada and I was on a highway with lots of beautiful mountains and trees nearby. It was a sunny day and everything was perfect. Suddenly I saw a family of bears – a mother bear and two cubs – near the side of the road. I love bears! So I stopped the car, got out and started taking photos. I wasn't very close to the bears but the cubs got frightened and the mother looked angry. She started walking towards me. I ran back to the car but I couldn't open the door and the keys were inside. I was really frightened. The mother bear came closer. Suddenly a big tour bus drove up and stopped. The bears ran into the trees. The driver shouted at me, 'Never, never get out of your car when you see bears! They're not pets, they're dangerous!' He and a passenger opened the car door for me and I thanked them and left. That was a real lesson for me.

JACK Well, this was a couple of years ago. I went on holiday to France with some friends. We got the bus and the ferry to France and had something to eat in the ferry restaurant. Then I fell asleep. Later, I woke up in the ferry restaurant but my friends weren't there. The ferry was empty! We were at Calais in France. I ran to the bus but I was too late. I saw the bus driving off the ferry. So I walked off the ferry and phoned my friends. They were all on the bus. We arranged to meet in Paris later that day so I got a train to Paris. It was a terrible journey, but in the end it was OK because I met a really nice Frenchman, Charles, on the train. We're still friends today.

3.21

SAM I was in London at the time and wanted to go to Dublin in Ireland to see my friend, Margaret. This was last year ... and I had to get up really early to catch the plane. The flight was at five in the morning or something. So I got up in the dark and drove to the airport, only to see that my flight was cancelled. There wasn't another flight that day or night, so I booked a seat for early the next morning. I spent all day and all night at the airport. It was so boring! At around midnight I tried to sleep on some free seats but it was really uncomfortable so in the end I stopped trying. I was really tired and in a very bad mood by the next morning. The plane finally took off at nine o'clock but then an hour later they said the plane couldn't land in Dublin and we had to go to Cork, in the south of Ireland! Anyway, I met a lot of really nice people during the journey. We stayed in a lovely five-star hotel in Cork, paid for by the airline, and we had a lot of fun that night. My friend came to get me in her car the next day and it was fine. It was a terrible journey but I also had a really great time.

3.22

1 He drove to the airport.
2 The flight was cancelled.
3 He booked a seat on another flight.
4 He spent all night at the airport.
5 The airport was uncomfortable.
6 He caught the plane to Dublin.
7 The plane took off at nine o'clock.
8 It had to go to Cork in the south of Ireland.
9 He stayed in a five-star hotel.
10 He had a great time there.

3.25

/ŋ/ skiing long running thing
/ŋg/ longer stronger youngest

3.26

1 longer 2 flying 3 youngest
4 thing 5 skiing 6 long

3.27

1 Your head weighs about 5.5 kilos.
2 The stomach can hold 4 litres of food.
3 You use 12 muscles to smile. You use about 70 muscles to speak.
4 Our eyes never grow. Our nose and ears never stop growing.
5 The body loses more than half a kilo of skin every year.
6 Over 50% of the bones in your body are in your hands and feet.
7 The smallest bone is in your ear. It's the size of a grain of rice.
8 Your thumb is the same length as your nose.
9 Children have 20 first teeth. Adults have 32 teeth.
10 Your heart beats about 100,000 times every day.

3.28

A I've got a pain in my back.
B I've got a sore throat.
C I've got a temperature.
D I've got a problem with my knee.
E I've got a headache.
F I feel sick.
G I've got a cold.
H I feel tired.

3.29

PHARMACIST Hello. Do you need any help?
MARC Yes. Er, I need something for … well, I guess for pain.
P OK, what are your symptoms?
M I've got a pain in my back and I've also got a headache, but that's all.
P How long have you had the symptoms?
M The back pain started last night and I've had the headache for about an hour.
P OK. There are a few things you can try. Are you allergic to anything?
M Just dairy products.
P Are you taking any other medicine?
M No, not at the moment.

3.30

PHARMACIST OK, and do you prefer taking medicine in a drink or tablets?
MARC Tablets, please.
P This is the best thing … paracetamol. It's for all aches and pains. So it has everything you need.
M All right.
P Don't take any other painkillers with paracetamol, nothing. You mustn't take anything else.
M Yes, OK.
P And if they don't work in a day or two, you should go to the doctor.
M All right. Thank you.

3.33

If you get stomach ache, try this remedy.
If you try the salt water remedy, don't use really hot water.
If you get a temperature, use an onion.
If they don't work for you, you should go to a dentist.

3.34

ANGHARAD If I have a cold, I usually take medicine like aspirin or I put my head over a hot bowl with hot water and inhale the steam.
AMINA Really? My mother and my grandmother do that, but I think, I don't really do that. When I've got a cold, I either go to the doctor, or I just try and ignore it, and just get on with my normal work.
RUTH My grandmother told me that if you drink hot honey and lemon juice, it's the best cure for a cold, but I'm not sure if that's true. I prefer paracetamol.
NATHALIE Yes, me too. That's … my mother always tells me to drink black tea with honey too, and to eat soup because you're not very hungry when you have a cold.
AMINA Hmm. My mum always makes chicken soup when I've got a cold. It's the best thing.

3.35

YUKIO OK, collocations are words that go together. You see them and hear them everywhere, the same expressions again and again. Like, in English, we say *watch TV* and *spend money*, for example, but, erm, when I first started learning English, I said *see TV* and *use money*. And the reason was that in Japanese, our collocations are *see TV* and *use money* – so I just translated them and thought they were OK … but they weren't. So I think it's important to learn collocations, you know, words that go together … and not just single words. It helps you speak more naturally.

3.37

1 Saturday 2 way 3 waiting
4 explain 5 play 6 saying
7 emails 8 holiday

3.38

I've never played golf.
You've never been to my flat.
He's never eaten a hamburger.
We've never had a garden.
They've never worked in an office before.

3.39

ANDREI Well, I've always wanted to go to Egypt …
ANNE OK.
ANDREI … to see the, er, pyramids. I've, I've read so many books about them and I just want to see them in real life. I've never been there. I just want to go inside a pyramid.
ANNE Why do you like the pyramids?
ANDREI I don't know, when I was a child I thought they were great and you read stories about them and you imagine what they're like. I've always wanted to go, yeah.
ANNE Maybe you will, one day.
ANDREI Maybe one day, yeah. What about you?
ANNE Erm, I've always wanted to swim with dolphins.
ANDREI Dolphins?
ANNE Dolphins. Er, many, many years ago I went on holiday to Scotland and I went on a boat trip …
ANDREI OK.
ANNE … and we saw some dolphins and they were swimming next to the boat and it was absolutely fantastic.
ANDREI Dolphins in Scotland?
ANNE Yes. Unfortunately I couldn't jump in the water but because of that I've always wanted to swim with dolphins. Somewhere warm would be best.

3.40

PREMA Monica, have you been to, er, Güell Park?
MONICA Güell Park.
P Güell.
M Yes, of course. It's a very … unusual place.

P But you're not from Barcelona?

M No, I grew up in Pamplona … but I've been to Barcelona lots of times. I have family there.

P Right. Anyway, I've never heard of this park. It sounds beautiful.

M Well, I don't think it's beautiful exactly.

P No?

M No, I don't really like Gaudi's style, this kind of art … but, er, it's a special place, for sure. You should see it if you get a chance.

P Right. Have you ever seen the Taj Mahal?

M Well, I've seen it on television.

P OK.

M But no, I haven't been there. What about you?

P No.

M But you're from India, right?

P Yes but India's a big place.

M Hm, OK.

P You know, I've always wanted to go there but when you live in a place …

M … you don't always have time to do the tourist things.

P Right. But I've been here, to Angel Falls.

M So you've been to Venezuela?

P Yeah, I had a holiday there.

M Wow.

P Two weeks.

M So what's it like?

P Oh, it's wonderful. The weather was nice and sunny so we had a great view. You know, you can't always see the waterfall.

M Right. So were you on the river or on the mountain … ?

P Neither. We were in a plane.

M Well, it sounds great – but I think I'd prefer a boat.

P Yeah?

M Yeah, I don't like flying.

3.41

1 Have you been to Güell Park?
   Yes, I have.
2 Have you ever seen the Taj Mahal?
   No, I haven't.
3 I've been to Angel Falls.
4 I've seen it on television.
5 I haven't been there.
6 I've never heard of it.

3.42

1 It's a very unusual place.
2 I've been there lots of times.
3 I've never heard of it.
4 I've seen it on television.
5 What's it like?

3.43

1

KIERAN Graham, hi. A quick question.

GRAHAM Sure. What is it?

K Look, my wife's sister arrived here yesterday …

G Oh, right. From France?

K Yeah, and, er, we'd like to take her to a nice restaurant tonight.

G OK.

K Er, have you been to that new Italian restaurant, Sicilia?

G No, I haven't, sorry. You could ask Prema.

K OK, I'll ask her. Thanks.

2

KIERAN Hi, Prema?

PREMA Yeah, hi.

K Have you tried Sicilia, the Italian place?

P Yes, we went there two, three weeks ago.

K Right. What was it like?

P Erm … it was OK but quite expensive.

K Too expensive?

P Hm, yeah. I mean, the food's good, but there are better places.

K Right.

P Why do you ask?

K Oh, my sister-in-law's here and we'd like to take her out tonight.

P Well, let's see … uh, have you been to Browne's?

K Browne's? The English restaurant?

P No, it's American food. It's really nice.

K OK, I'll think about it. Thanks.

3

KIERAN Monica, can I ask you a question? About restaurants?

MONICA Of course.

K Er, we want to take a guest to dinner tonight. Have you been to Sicilia or Browne's?

M Yes, I have. Both of them.

K Which one should we go to?

M Neither.

K Neither! Why not?

M Sicilia just sells expensive pizzas, and the last time I went to Browne's, the food wasn't very good.

K Oh.

M Take her to Akash.

K Akash? I've never heard of it.

M It's a small restaurant, really nice people, not too expensive, wonderful Indian food. You'll love it. Really.

K OK, I'll try it. Where is it exactly?

M Well, you know the Royal Bank on Chester Street …

3.44

JESSICA I never really liked shellfish until I went to the north of Spain and some friends took me to a fish restaurant by the sea. They ordered a *zarzuela* which is a huge plate of shellfish. It was a great evening and I was surprised that I really enjoyed the food. After that, I often ate shellfish because it's something people do in Spain on special occasions. It's more than just food. It's like you're celebrating life when you sit down and have *zarzuela* or *paella*.

DAVID I lived in Egypt for a year and I remember walking to work for the first time. It was unbelievably hot and it was only 8 in the morning. As I walked down my street a man came up to me and said "Welcome to Egypt" with a huge smile on his face. I smiled back. It was a lovely moment. As I walked to work four or five more people smiled at me and said "Welcome to Egypt." I couldn't believe how friendly people were to complete strangers, so hospitable. In Britain, most people don't talk to strangers. Yeah, walking around in public in Egypt was completely different.

HYUN Well, I'm Korean but I've always loved Brazilian music. I've got a very big collection of CDs, maybe 250, that I bought in music shops in Seoul and also online. Most of my CDs are samba and Brazilian jazz. I love both kinds of music because they're very lively but also relaxing … and of course I got interested in Brazil because of the music. I've never been there but I've read a lot about it and I've met a few Brazilians in Seoul. They were really surprised and happy I knew about their music. My dream is to go there and hear the music in its own country one day.

3.46

Starting a conversation:
How are things? | Can you talk now? | Excuse me, have you got a moment? | I haven't seen you for a long time. | Are you doing anything now? | Have you got time for a coffee and a chat?

Finishing a conversation:
I'll talk to you later. | Thanks for your help. | See you at the meeting. | Well, it was good talking to you. | Anyway, I'll text you some time. | Take care.

3.47

RUUD Are you all right?

SALLY No, not really. I've got a headache.

RUUD Oh, I'm sorry to hear that. Maybe you should go home.

3.49

1 whose 2 whisper 3 when
4 whole 5 which 6 why 7 what
8 who 9 white 10 wheel

3.50

SUE Do you think you get enough sleep?

DAN No, not at the moment, because of the baby. I only slept about four hours last night.

S Four hours? Poor you. That's not enough.

D What about you?

S I usually sleep for about nine hours, probably ten at the weekend. And I'm always tired.

D   Really? You know, I think that's probably too much sleep. I'm sure it's not good if you get too much.

S   Yeah, you may be right. It's nice though!

3.51

1   Do you think you get enough sleep?

2   Not at the moment, because of the baby.

3   That's not enough.

4   What about you?

5   And I'm always tired.

3.52

INTERVIEWER   Right, in the studio we have Barry Cox, ex-supermarket worker from Liverpool in England, who is now a popular singer in Macau in China. Barry, did you always dream of becoming a singer?

BARRY   No, not really. But I knew I wanted to do something different, even when I was a teenager.

I   So, what took you to China?

B   Well, after I left school at 16 I took up languages. I started Spanish lessons, but then I changed my mind and decided to learn Chinese.

I   How did you learn it?

B   Well, I walked into my local chip shop and asked the Chinese owners for a meal and language lessons! The owner's nephew wanted English lessons, so we helped each other and became good friends. I met lots of Chinese people in Liverpool through him.

I   Did you go to lessons?

B   Not exactly! I spent years learning Cantonese with my new friends. I got a job in a Chinese supermarket as well.

I   So, when did you decide to become a singer?

B   Well, I went to a concert given by Leon Lai, a very popular singer in Hong Kong, and after that I knew exactly what I wanted to do. I entered a singing competition at Chinese New Year. I was awful but people liked me. So after that, I had singing lessons.

I   And when did you become successful in China?

B   Well, I decided to move abroad, to Hong Kong. After a few years' hard work, I got a job singing Canto-pop, which means popular love songs. I even won a competition. And now I'm singing at a great venue in Macau.

I   And you're known as Gok Pak-wing in China?

B   That's right. I'm pretty famous!

I   So, do you think you've made the right choices in your life?

B   Absolutely. I'm having a fantastic time in Macau. When you go back home,

you see all of your friends doing exactly the same as ten years ago. I do things and have done things that most people could only dream of doing.

3.53

INTERVIEWER   And what about the future? What are you going to do next? Are you going to stay in China?

BARRY   I'd like to stay in China for a while, yeah. I'm hoping to continue with the singing, yeah. I really love it. But I don't think I want to stay in China for the rest of my life.

I   Would you like to move back to Liverpool?

B   Well, no, I don't think so. I'm going to stay in China for another few years and see what happens with the singing. I'd like to move to another country one day and learn a new language. Japan could be interesting.

3.54

1   I'm going to stay in China for another few years.

2   He's hoping to stay in China for another few years.

3   I'd like to stay in China for another few years.

4   Is he going to stay in China next year? Yes, he is. No, he isn't.

5   Are they hoping to move to another country? Yes, they are. No, they aren't.

6   Would you like to move back to Liverpool one day? Yes, I would. No, I wouldn't.

7   What are you going to do this weekend?

3.55

DAN   OK, so what are we going to do about accommodation?

MILLIE   Well, let's have a look at the website.

D   Hm, this campsite looks nice to me. I think we should stay there.

M   Camping! I don't think so! I want to be comfortable.

D   Come on, the kids would love it.

M   But camping is really uncomfortable. And we need a kitchen, so what about this chalet on the lake?

D   Erm ... yeah, OK. It looks very nice. Let's try that.

M   And what about food?

D   Well, we can talk to someone about that when we get there.

M   Fine.

D   And what are we going to do on Saturday?

M   Let's go to the National Park.

D   Yeah, we can go hiking or canoeing!

M   I suppose so. I'd like to go hiking, I'm not so sure about the canoeing. What about Sunday?

D   We could go and watch the bears!

M   Er, yes, but it could take a long time before we see one. What about doing the tree-to-tree climbing thing?

D   Mmm. I think it's too expensive, it's 25 dollars each. Let's go horse riding.

M   Yes, that's a great idea. Everyone will love that. Right, we need to book some of these things then.

3.56

Introducing / changing topic:
What are we going to do about accommodation?
What are we going to do on Saturday?
Opinions:
I think it's too expensive.
This campsite looks nice to me.
Agreeing / disagreeing:
Yeah, OK.
Fine.
But camping is really uncomfortable.

3.57

GREG   OK, Paula, what things have you tried to learn a language?

PAULA   Erm, one thing that really worked for me was, erm, reading magazines and newspapers, erm, especially ads because you have the words and the images together and the sentences are very short so that was very useful.

G   Newspapers aren't too difficult?

P   Er, well maybe short articles, not the long ones. Erm, and, er, I've tried reading books, longer novels, but that didn't work, at the beginning at least.

G   Right.

P   What about you?

G   Yeah, I've, I've found newspapers too difficult, erm, when I've been learning Japanese but I've, erm, tried reading graded texts and that's helped.

P   What do you mean, 'graded texts'?

G   Erm, they're designed for people learning the language so they're made simpler.

P   OK, like shorter and ...

G   Yeah.

P   OK. Erm, I'm learning German now and what I'd like to try, erm, is to join some sort of, like, speaking ... like a discussion group. I've never done that. I think it could be really useful.

G   Yeah. I'd like to try a ... a language exchange, maybe with a Japanese student.

P   And meet and talk.

G   Yeah.

3.58

KHALID   I'm going to finish my studies by the end of next year and I will be looking for a job. In the near future, like in the next five or ten years, I hope to start my own business, find someone special and get married, maybe. Erm, one day, I would like to travel around the world.

3.61

1   walk   2   should   3   comb
4   thumb   5   often   6   designer

Vowels

Short vowels

/ə/	/æ/	/ʊ/	/ɒ/	/ɪ/	/i/	/e/	/ʌ/
teacher ago	married am	book could	on got	in swim	happy easy	wet any	cup under

Long vowels

/ɜː/	/ɑː/	/uː/	/ɔː/	/iː/
her shirt	arm car	blue too	or walk	eat meet

Diphthongs

/eə/	/ɪə/	/ʊə/	/ɔɪ/	/aɪ/	/eɪ/	/əʊ/	/aʊ/
chair where	near we're	tour	boy noisy	nine eye	eight day	go over	out brown

Consonants **voiced** **unvoiced**

/b/	/ð/	/v/	/dʒ/	/d/	/z/	/g/	/ʒ/
be bit	mother the	very live	job page	down red	magazine	girl bag	television
/p/	/θ/	/f/	/tʃ/	/t/	/s/	/k/	/ʃ/
park shop	think both	face laugh	chips teach	time white	see rice	cold look	shoe fish
/m/	/n/	/ŋ/	/l/	/r/	/w/	/j/	/h/
me name	now rain	thing drink	late hello	carry write	we white	you yes	hot hand

Irregular verbs

Infinitive	Past simple	Past participle
All forms are the same		
	cost	
	cut	
	put	
	set	

Past simple and past participle are the same

bring	brought
build	built
buy	bought
catch	caught
feel	felt
find	found
get	got
have	had
hear	heard
hold	held
keep	kept
learn	learned
leave	left
lose	lost
make	made
mean	meant
meet	met
pay	paid
read /riːd/	read /red/
say	said
sell	sold
send	sent
sit	sat
spend	spent
stand	stood
teach	taught
tell	told
think	thought
understand	understood
win	won

Infinitive	Past simple	Past participle
All forms are different		
be	was / were	been
begin	began	begun
break	broke	broken
can	could	been able to
choose	chose	chosen
do	did	done
drink	drank	drunk
drive	drove	driven
eat	ate	eaten
fall	fell	fallen
fly	flew	flown
forget	forgot	forgotten
give	gave	given
go	went	been / gone
know	knew	known
ride	rode	ridden
see	saw	seen
show	showed	shown
sing	sang	sung
speak	spoke	spoken
swim	swam	swum
take	took	taken
wear	wore	worn
write	wrote	written
Infinitive and past participle are the same		
become	became	become
come	came	come
run	ran	run